TALKING WITH MOTHERS

This book is about being a mother – a mother with a baby inside her and then outside her. It is about fears, fantasies and expectations. Among other things the author attempts to stimulate and support the natural reflectiveness of the pregnant woman.

Centring on almost weekly conversations with 'Barbara', this focus on one woman and her feelings conveys the continuity in the inner world of a woman through the phases of carrying, bringing into existence, nurturing and weaning a baby. The reader is thus able to share the suspense inherent in every pregnancy and in every woman's mind as she approaches labour and her first meeting with her baby.

Dana Breen introduces other women's reflections on their own experience to give more breadth, and judiciously adds research findings and psychoanalytic ideas to provide a way of thinking about motherhood. *Talking with Mothers* is a sustained reflection on women's mixed but powerful feelings of wanting – and yet not wanting – this irreversible change in their life, of anxiety about loss of their previous self and joy in their future as mothers.

DANA BIRKSTED-BREEN is a Training Psychoanalyst of the British Psycho-Analytical Society. She has a doctorate from Sussex University and is in private practice in London.

Also by Dana Breen

THE BIRTH OF A FIRST CHILD
Towards an Understanding of Femininity

TALKING
WITH
MOTHERS

DANA BREEN

With a new Preface

'an association in which the free development of each
is the condition of the free development of all'

Free Association Books / London / 1989

Published 1989 by
Free Association Books
26 Freegrove Road
London N7 9RQ

First published by Jill Norman Ltd 1981

British Library Cataloguing in Publication Data

Breen, Dana
  Talking with mothers.
  1. Motherhood. Interviews
  I. Title
  306.8'743

  ISBN 1–85343–074–9

Typeset by Inforum Ltd, Portsmouth

Printed and bound in Great Britain by
Bookcraft (Bath) Ltd.

This revised edition of
Talking with Mothers
by Dana Breen
was finished in March 1989.

The new material was commissioned and edited by Ann Scott
and produced by Martin Klopstock and Selina O'Grady for
Free Association Books.

It was printed on a Miller TP 41
on to 80 g/m² vol. 17.5
New Edition Cream Antique Wove

Contents

Acknowledgements

I am above all indebted to 'Barbara', who shared her feelings with me week after week for many months. I think I can say that we both enjoyed this experience, and I thank her for it. I am also grateful to the many other women who gave generously of their time and thoughts. I was moved by the uniqueness of their experience.

From our two children, Sasha and Noah, I have learnt a great deal: what it means to be a mother myself; to change my preconceived ideas of good mothering, which didn't seem to fit their needs or mine; and about uncertainty, compromise and joy.

Sheila Kitzinger and Susan Lipshitz both read the manuscript, and I should like to thank them for their encouragement and comments.

Preface (1989)

REPETITION and change are both characteristics of human existence. I have been interested in the normal life events which can facilitate change of a positive nature. In fact I believe that some moments in the life of a person necessitate change if they are to be lived, not just survived. These will be moments which can lead to psychological growth, or else to psychological disturbance.

This perspective led me in the late 60s to engage in researching the impact on women of becoming a mother. I argued that pregnancy is not an illness from which a woman recovers back to her old self (what I called the 'hurdle' model), but that the birth of a baby, as any major life event, offers an opportunity for a woman to work through psychological conflicts, to modify her perception of herself and others and integrate this new experience, so that she will not be the same after the birth of the baby as she was before (a developmental model). Indeed it is those women who are unable to integrate the experience and change with it who will run into serious difficulties in pregnancy, childbirth or postnatally.

The results confirmed this point of view and also brought up some unexpected findings. When I published the study* I was struck by just how eager women were to read about this topic. I realized that there was a need for a book which would go deeper into the actual experience of having a baby. This, coupled with my own personal experience of becoming a mother, gave impetus to my decision to embark on more research, this time of a less formal kind. The open-ended interviews I used made me aware of the fundamental importance of the setting of pregnancy, childbirth and early motherhood, something which I had not looked into in the original study. By 'setting' I am referring to

---

* Breen, D. (1975) *The Birth of a First Child*. Tavistock.

7

the emotional reaction and climate provided by other members of the family, but also very importantly to the setting of the birth and the role of the professionals involved at this time.

I found that the actual experience of childbirth (what happens, how it is lived, the sensitivity of the people involved) was of utmost importance in determining how a woman would feel about herself and her baby and hence in shaping that very important early relationship between mother and baby. I could see that the experience of childbirth would be important in facilitating or hindering the positive change I referred to earlier. On the whole I found that the less 'technological births', an environment which was supportive but non-intrusive, and the continuity of care (from few medical staff) were most helpful in promoting a sense of well-being, a positive relationship to the baby and a life experience which was enhancing. Non-technological births are of course not always possible, and the setting can help to make up for it in other ways.

Since the time of this research, which was completed in the late 70s, there has been a certain move, following consumer complaints, towards a more natural approach to childbirth, and certain obstetricians have created environments where a woman can give birth in a relaxed, unpressurized setting in the position of her choice and at her own pace. This, however, is still far from the norm, and recent newspaper articles decrying the increase in caesarean sections, for instance, seem to be a replica of articles I read ten or fifteen years ago.

Something which has developed in the last ten years is the support group of various kinds, antenatal groups, postnatal groups, yoga groups for pregnant women, etc. One of the things I hope to have shown in this book, as a sub-text, is how important it can be for a woman to share her feelings in a situation which is continuous and accepting.

Pregnancy is a time of psychological as well as physiological preparation. It is a time for reassessment of the past and for thoughts about the future, a time for thinking about one's place in the natural cycle of life and death. A certain amount of anxiety in pregnancy, as in any other major life event, is an indication – if it is not overwhelming – that this psychological work is taking place, that a woman is preparing herself by being receptive to the natural fears in the face of a situation which carries many unknowns. As Bel Mooney said in her review of the book: 'it does help to be prepared for not being prepared, to expect panic and bad temper, to be open about the dread of not being able to cope.'

Finally I want to say something about fathers. Although my research was about motherhood, it is true to say that many of the feelings and anxieties I describe are present for men too. One big difference is that the woman carries the baby inside her body, and this colours her experience. Whereas a woman may be concerned about what can come out of her body, a man may be concerned about whether his sexuality can result in something good. Specific to the man is that he has to deal with feelings about being at times in a passive role, with not being the centre of attention and with the painful feelings which are aroused around being excluded from an intimate mother and baby relationship. Men sometimes deal with this by withdrawing into a 'masculine' world. But for them too, if they are able to stay open to their feelings, the birth of a child can be an opportunity for psychological growth.

You sleeping I bend to cover.
Your eyelids work. I see
your dream, cloudy as a negative,
swimming underneath.
You blurt a cry. Your eyes
spring open, still filmed in dream.
Wider, they fix me —
death's head, sphinx, medusa.
You scream.
Tears lick my cheeks, my knees
droop at your fear.

Adrienne Rich

Introduction

THIS is not a manual or a reference book. It will not tell you why your ankles are swelling in the last three months of pregnancy, what to do when you feel labour pains, or how to deal with a crying baby. There are many such books already.

This book is about being a mother – a mother with a baby inside her and then outside her. It is about fears, fantasies and expectations: first about containing another being inside one's own body, then about being responsible for a tiny, helpless, often incomprehensible creature with a life of its own.

The changes a woman experiences during pregnancy can be of such magnitude, the experience so strong, the feelings so disturbing, that she becomes, sometimes for the first time in her life, preoccupied with making sense of her feelings. Pregnancy, especially a first pregnancy, is often experienced as a time of reclusion, a time apart from the continuing and unquestioning humdrum of daily existence. This book attempts among other things to stimulate, encourage, support and guide the natural reflectiveness of the pregnant woman.

After the birth the mother is plunged into relentlessly unending tasks, and unceasingly called upon to respond to her baby's demands. Now she may feel she has no time to herself, and no time to reflect upon herself. The attention she received while she was pregnant is now diverted to the baby and she can find herself very much alone with the no less momentous feelings stirred up by her involvement with this tiny, demanding being who is both a part of her and separate from her and who revives in her her own earliest experiences of being mothered. This book attempts also to contribute towards an understanding of the often puzzling and acute feelings women experience with their baby during this extremely exhausting but potentially enriching time.

Most books concentrate on one period only – pregnancy, or

childbirth, or a certain period after the birth; and in this latter case the focus is the baby (how he or she develops, and how to deal with him or her). Most books also tend to look at pregnancy as a hurdle which is to be surmounted in order to return to a pre-pregnant state. Although the wish to return to a 'pre-bulging', 'normal' state is a common experience in pregnancy, it expresses an anxiety about change. As with other important events in life, whether changes are subtle or dramatic, one is never quite the same afterwards, and this is what makes for growth. Also, most books confine themselves to the physical aspects while the psychological side often goes no further than, for instance, the statement that women's emotions tend to fluctuate during pregnancy because of alterations in the hormones. Pamphlets distributed at antenatal clinics convey the idea that women are taken over at this time by emotions which have nothing to do with their normal selves, and most women find such an attitude condescending – probably because of its gross simplification in the description of women as almost possessed by physical forces. For example: 'During the first three months of pregnancy it is not at all uncommon for women to feel quite miserable and depressed. This happens even in women who have been longing and waiting to become pregnant and is not usually related to psychological factors . . . the probable reason lies in the complex series of chemical changes that are taking place throughout the body and in particular in the placenta.'[1] To ascribe such feelings to the hormonal fluctuations only is to forget their meaning, and a woman's wish to make sense of what she feels rather than think of pregnancy as totally foreign to her, even if at times she does feel possessed by strange emotions.

Occasionally a book will be concerned with the experience of having a baby, but there is generally no sense of continuity, no portrayal of what the experience is like over the months for one individual woman. This only reproduces what unfortunately tends to happen to a woman at the antenatal and postnatal clinic, when, more often than not, she is treated like a machine whose different parts have to be checked by different 'specialists' along a conveyor belt and programmed to produce the goods at a specific time. Her physical self is inspected inside out, compared with a chart, discussed and set right. What seems to be lost is her *experience* of having a baby, the feelings intimately connected with all these events. Although there may be important landmarks along the way it is still only *one* process, experienced by *one* woman over a long period of time. An indication of compartmentalization is the very fact that there exists no one word to express the total experience of having a baby. We talk about 'conception', 'pregnancy', 'childbirth', 'postnatal period' and tend to think of these as separate entities, hurdles to be overcome or tests to be passed. This is using a scientific model, looking at the process as an outsider who splits up states which appear dissimilar and categorizes them: 'the pregnant woman', 'the labouring woman', 'the young mother'. To a woman having a baby such classification may be quite inappropriate.

I have chosen to follow in this book one woman and her feelings over the months in order to convey the inner world of a woman during the experiences of carrying, bringing into existence and nurturing a baby. The book centres on my almost weekly conversations with this woman, whom I shall call Barbara, through the latter months of her pregnancy and during the year after the birth of her baby. It is meant to be read as a whole, somewhat like a novel, and to communicate the suspense inherent in every pregnancy and in every woman's mind as she approaches labour, the first meeting with her baby, and the integration of this new person into her life. It follows psychological time, so that we find Barbara worrying about breast feeding when she is four months pregnant, or reflecting, long after the birth, on her reasons for getting pregnant. Themes appear again and again in her mind from a slightly different angle, with a new understanding, with more anxiety or with greater honesty. I have attempted to convey how preoccupations recur in constant or modified versions only to disappear as suddenly as they appeared.

Biological time sets objective landmarks, but psychological landmarks may be quite different. The feeling of separateness from the baby, for instance, can clearly emerge long before the birth – or on the contrary be absent for many months afterwards when a woman feels her baby to be an extension of herself, or even imagines that she still carries a baby inside her body.

Finally, this book is about what it feels like to be a mother, to live with the day to day insecurities, hopes and fears. That is why, in choosing to follow one woman through her daily existence, I have done as little editing as possible of my tape-recorded conversations with her. I never arrived with set questions. The questions, probings and comments emerged from these encounters. Some of the time I expressed my own values forcibly; much of the time I was silent and just listening.

At appropriate times in the flow of the themes I have introduced other women's reflections on their own experience to give more breadth, and I add research findings and psychoanalytic ideas to provide a way of thinking about such experiences. I do not aim to cover every possible situation. Nor do I aim to show Barbara as 'representative'. What I attempt is to recapture the flavour of one person living this momentous experience with her mixture of feelings, her free flow of ideas, her juxtaposition of banality with striking insight, and the fantasies which are hinted at through her words.

I hope those of my readers who are pregnant will find the book useful in making sense of their own experience, will be stimulated to reflect further on themselves, and will receive a sense of sharing, even if I do not always cover their own particular situations. Social and economic situations vary, circumstances leading to the pregnancy vary, but each woman's experience is unique and each woman's circumstances are unique.

CHAPTER ONE

I'm going to be awfully worried

BARBARA is twenty-five years old. Her situation is what one could call highly traditional. When she was twenty-one she married an old boy-friend she had been seeing on and off in her late teens. She became pregnant very quickly, not out of any deliberate decision to have a child, but more because they did not discuss and actively decide on contraceptive measures. The birth of this first child, a boy, put a considerable strain on the relationship. It was a very difficult birth for which Barbara was totally unprepared. She felt reluctant to have another child and began using the contraceptive pill.

Barbara's husband, Patrick, is a mechanic in a family enterprise. The couple live in a two-bedroom terraced house on the outskirts of Birmingham. Patrick helps little around the house and has a clear notion of what is a 'man's job' and a 'woman's job'. When upset, worried or angry he tends to withdraw rather than talk about his feelings. Barbara, by contrast, is interested in exploring her feelings and becomes irritated by his inability to do so.

Barbara has long fair hair and large blue eyes. She seems unassuming and at times reminds me of a doll, yet underneath this appearance I discovered a very sensitive, thoughtful and determined woman.

Giving birth to her first child, Peter, was a frightening experience for Barbara. She was unprepared for what was happening in her body and uninformed about the possible occurrences during labour. She was reluctant to go through it all again. When she did eventually become pregnant again, she sought information and support. I met her when I was planning to run a discussion group for pregnant women. The group never got off the ground but she agreed with interest to participate in my research project.

Barbara felt under great pressure from her husband to have a second child:

Barbara   I said to my husband I'm going to be terrible, I'm going to be awfully worried; but then – it was a good thing – all my friends got pregnant. Suddenly everyone was pregnant so I thought, Well, if they are all doing it, it can't be that bad the second time. That was it. Bingo, I didn't mind any more. Then after I'd accepted it and thought, Right I'm going to have another one, it suddenly became very important. I thought, Gracious, I must get pregnant quickly or else I shan't want to again – so that was it, I was pregnant within six weeks. But I still get worried about it, I'm still edgy about it.

Many couples, like Barbara and her husband, do not discuss the problem of contraception and do not imagine pregnancy as a real possibility and a normal result of intercourse. Contraceptives are thought to be unromantic; sex must not be talked about. A very high proportion of first pregnancies are unplanned.

When reliable contraception is used, having a baby becomes a decision: a decision some couples would rather not have to take; the contraceptive pill feels 'too safe' – too safe to let chance tilt the balance and make the decision for them.

Sometimes the method of contraception is changed as something of a half-conscious preparation for conception. Sarah, one of the women interviewed, switches from the pill to the cap in order to 'get rid of' the chemicals in her body, in order to purify and prepare her body for the inception* – the pill coming to represent all the destructive forces aimed at the baby. Another, Lesley, switches similarly as an intermediate step towards fertility; as a process in making up her mind, the increasing risk accompanying the increasing wish.

Whether within or outside marriage, the wish to get pregnant is never a simple one: many conscious as well as less conscious reasons come into play. In women impatient for a first pregnancy, the wish to find out about their body, about their ability to get pregnant, the wish to explore this mysterious, intriguing, often imagined side of themselves is an important aspect. Lesley

---

* Doctors now tend to recommend for medical reasons that women stop taking the pill a few months before conceiving.

always had a fear that she might be infertile, and the wish to find out precipitates her decision to get pregnant. Lynn never imagined having a baby and it simply does not occur to her to use contraceptives. Jean decides to have a baby because she is 'getting old', though on further inspection it turns out that she is also competing with a younger sister who has just become pregnant. Sheila desperately wants a baby from the man she knows she cannot marry, while Kate, by becoming pregnant, will put pressure on her parents to let her get married. In such cases there is often a fine dividing-line between 'decision' and 'accident'.

Even when planned, the decision to have a baby, and the conception, whether immediate or not, are followed by conscious or unconscious misgivings. The first few months are filled with such doubts, confusion, regrets, anxieties or disbelief. Abortions are considered with more or less conviction. Jean Hanford, in a paper on pregnancy,[2] suggests that symptoms such as nausea and vomiting are most frequent in the early months of pregnancy because mixed feelings are prevalent then. Nausea and vomiting are now thought by some to relate to conflicting feelings of both wanting and not wanting the baby, rather than, as had been thought previously, to pure rejection. (Indeed, women who have decided to have their baby adopted rarely exhibit such symptoms.) These mixed feelings of wanting and not wanting are probably very general, in our culture at least, where there are many practical and emotional drawbacks to having a baby.

Although I myself planned and wished to have a baby, the following dream, which I had a few days after conceiving my first child, depicts this ambivalence: 'There was a red bug inside the room I was in; an insect which looked like a winged human. It reminded me of the sort of picture one might find in a children's book. I was trying to get the insect out of the room. In fact it was really rather harmless. It stung and gave a red pimple but was not dangerous at all. I couldn't get it out of the room.' When I woke up, I was struck by this dream, which was in very vivid and definite colours. It was totally different from any dream I had ever had before. I felt certain that I was pregnant, although I had not yet missed a period, and certain that the dream was expressing my mixed feelings about the 'baby-insect' inside my body. The colours were strong and clearly delineated like those in an animated children's cartoon, expressing the fact that my pregnancy would mean going back into the past and re-experiencing childhood feelings and relationships.

This is probably the most important task facing a first-time mother – reappraising her relationship with her parents and integrating her 'old self' with her new one. For Abigail Lewis it meant accepting being a woman: 'The defiant tomboy that was me will be finally and irrevocably lost, but someone else will be born, though not so apparently as the baby is born. Or at least I hope so. I can't go on resenting. One must learn to change with changing circumstances.'[3]

In the third month of my second pregnancy I had the following dream: 'We were getting installed in a new house, and I suddenly realized that in the confusion we had got two tumble dryers, a large and a small one. I wondered if we really needed two and whether I should try to sell one of them, but finally I put them both in the kitchen, one on top of the other. On waking I linked the two tumble dryers with the two children; a rather humorous connection I thought, and quite realistically linked to the practical hard work. Although my second pregnancy was planned, it seems that in part of myself I felt it was somewhat of an accident, something which had happened 'in the confusion', and I wondered if I could backtrack.

The first three months of pregnancy are often the most difficult. There is nothing tangible to grasp, fantasy cannot be modified, or grounded in any reality. There are no antenatal check-ups to reassure the mother that everything is progressing normally. Even the usual pregnancy symptoms cannot be clutched at for reassurance. 'I find with my second pregnancy that I have no nausea or any of the changes I felt the first time, like sore and swollen breasts. It makes me wonder if everything is really all right, or if, maybe, the baby isn't developing normally' (Lesley, two months pregnant). At this time mixed feelings are at their height. The woman still looks like any other woman and it is hard for her to think of herself as pregnant. Part of her is still, in a way, not pregnant. Feelings of depression are frequent. One part of her is delighted by the pregnancy; another part does not want the baby. If she feels guilty about not wanting the baby she may get depressed. She is afraid that such thoughts and feelings will harm the baby. Lesley connects the two directly: 'I've had a few sleepless nights worrying about how the baby would be – healthy or not – but also feeling that I didn't really want to have it.'

Some women are not conscious of being pregnant for several months and ascribe their tiredness and nausea to an unknown illness. Other women take pleasure in the fact that no one else is aware of the pregnancy. 'I feel as if I've got a precious secret hidden in my centre – I experience it as a little cherry stone' (Lesley, one month pregnant).

One woman fears this precious treasure might fall out; she tenses all her muscles, particularly around the openings (mouth, anus); she fears that intercourse might hurt the little being, that telling other people might bring bad luck – the 'evil spirit' which will abort her. Another woman feels taken over by a 'parasite', invaded by a 'foreign body' which saps her energy. One woman fights the intruder by becoming unusually active whereas another sinks into passivity and into a sense of being ill.

Ann Faraday reports dreaming, a few days after she conceived her second child, that she was being pursued by wild animals: 'My body was in some way aware of the impending uprush of "animal nature" before my conscious mind even suspected it.'[4]

One woman tries to forget all about her body while another woman looks out for every sign of change; she protects her body, takes care of it, selects her nourishment meticulously, feels uneasy if anything touches or rests against her lower abdomen; she recalls everything her body underwent in the months before conception, however remote, and she fears it could make her a bad host for the baby. Is the being inside her body good or bad? Is *she* good or bad for *it*? These are the greatest worries. Lesley dreams that her naval gapes, forming a pouch. Inside there is rubbish. She wakes up anxious, wondering if the baby is normal.

Sometimes her anxiety is so great that a woman blocks off her feelings, cannot be introspective, wishes to protect herself and the baby from the intrusion of thoughts or feelings which could be harmful. She fears the baby can read her mind.

At other times anxiety is expressed but concentrated in one particular area, as if naming it and giving it specificity can help to

master it. This is the case with Barbara. Her anxieties centre upon
the delivery. She has been frightened by her first unpleasant
experience.

Barbara I don't know what happened the first time; I might
blame it on induction but maybe it wasn't that. They broke the
waters and then they put me on a drip. That started at ten in
the morning. By teatime that day I was having pretty good
contractions, and the hospital were pleased with the contractions. They were coming regularly and they were strong, but
they weren't having any effect; the cervix wasn't really opening and they didn't know why. I was pretty much in control
then; I wasn't comfortable but I wasn't upset. I went on all
night like that and they gave me a couple of pethidine injections, which I didn't really need, but the next morning they
said there still wasn't much improvement: the cervix was
hardly dilated at all, so they said they were going to give me an
epidural.* They would leave me on a drip. It was going to be
another day or so. The epidural was fine – I knew what it was
but I didn't know how it would feel, and the discomfort I had
been having disappeared altogether for the first period of it.
And then the contractions got gradually closer together so
they were coming pretty much for a delivery. The effect of the
epidural lasted an hour and forty minutes, but they are not
allowed to give you the drug again for a certain time, so all of a
sudden, instead of being prepared for the contractions, you're
in the middle of one; you've had an hour and forty minutes
with nothing and you've got to have twenty or forty minutes of
contractions which you're not prepared for since it hasn't
worked up to it; and it was just a nightmare from twelve
midday that day until eleven o'clock that night. At eleven they
said I was about three fingers dilated and they didn't think it
could go any longer; they called the surgeon and said they
were going to do a caesarean, and I didn't care – anything. And
an emergency came in, so they couldn't do it at eleven. About
one o'clock they took me down to the operating theatre and he
said he just thought that if he cut he could do a vacuum

* An anaesthetic which is injected into the spinal area and serves to anaesthetize
the lower body.

extraction and get him out that way. I said, 'You can do anything, I don't care what you do'; so that was it. So I didn't have to have a caesarean in the end; they did manage to get him out normally, it's just I had to have more stitches. The delivery didn't worry me at all, but knowing that it goes on for hours and hours . . . then I thought, I just wanted to die. I thought I was making a lot of fuss, but they said I didn't really make a noise or fuss about it – but, oh my goodness, it was dreadful. It's not a thing that I can look back on, and think, I can manage. I'm really frightened this time, and that's what frightened me about it. But they said afterwards they just didn't know why; there just didn't seem to be any reason; it's just one of those things where the cervix is pretty fibrous and just won't open up.

Dana Breen How overdue were you?

Barbara Twenty-one, no twenty-two, no I was twenty-two, I was twenty-one when I became pregnant with Peter.

Dana I meant how many days overdue were you?

Barbara Oh well, the baby . . . I wasn't sure about my dates, the baby was either due on 31 July or 6 August. I was sure it was the 6th but they took it as the 31st to be safe; they induced on the 4th, he actually arrived on the 6th. This time I keep telling them, 'Please don't induce, please leave me alone'; I'd be better trying to carry on trotting about the ward if I must be in hospital, or at home, than lying in bed thinking: Here it comes again.

Dana It seems crazy to induce when you don't even know if you're late.

Barbara My blood pressure was going up and I'd started to get some oedema so they said come in, but the next day it had gone down again, so it wasn't a crisis. I resent that now. I think: You should have left me alone, I'd have coped a lot better on my own; so this time I shall keep saying: Don't let's just have it, I'd rather start on my own and see how I get on.

Dana Were you actually in hospital for three days?

Barbara I went in at night on the 3rd, and the 4th they induced and I was in labour from ten in the morning on the 4th until he was delivered at half past one in the morning on the 6th.

Dana It's a long time.

Barbara It was a long time and . . . I probably got panicky in the end, because after a day I thought: Hey, this is enough. The first day wasn't dreadful pain or anything like that but what probably upset me was they kept saying 'Everything is fine except . . . the cervix isn't opening' – but I can't remember thinking: Oh my goodness it's all going wrong. I don't remember thinking that, but I could have done.

Her fear of repeating such an experience prompted Barbara to answer my newspaper advertisement about a group for pregnant women in the hope of getting some help or support, though she had no idea what form this could take.

To many women, and men, having a first child represents becoming an adult. The birth itself is often experienced as a test, an examination which the woman will either pass or fail. On this are pinned her feelings about her femininity. She fears she won't stand up to the test or even that she will make a fool of herself.

Barbara may have felt she was too young to have a child. When I ask how overdue the baby was she thinks I am asking about her age, as if this would explain why her cervix wasn't 'ripe', ready to engender. Later in this same interview she tells me about a dream she has had recently, a repeat of one she had when pregnant with Peter: 'I was in hospital and I'd had the baby and it was tiny, tiny, tiny little thing; they showed me and I thought: That can't be, it's a doll.' Barbara feels she can only be a child with a doll, not a woman with a baby. This helps us to understand why she couldn't stand up for herself in hospital and follow her own intuition.

Barbara I was depressed for a little while because I'd prepared for breast feeding. Friday morning when the first feed was due, they said to me they'd got to cot-nurse Peter and so they were going to give him a bottle, and I said OK. They keep them in a cot, they don't move them for twenty-four hours if they have forceps or vacuum extractions, they keep them quiet. You don't pick them up or anything.

Barbara was not sure she wanted to breast feed her first child. She felt guilty that she had not done so and we can assume that she had mainly felt she ought to, that it was the right thing to do, that, as women are often told, 'it is best for the baby'.

But it is also the case that first-time mothers often hand over the mothering role to the hospital staff. In fact maternity units at the moment are organized in such a way that mothers are expected to do just that: the infant is removed to the nursery at night and for parts of the day, and the mother is told when and what to give her baby, and what or what not to do with her or him. A strict routine is expected. It takes a particularly strong and determined woman to take complete charge of her child in hospital. This is in no small measure responsible for the lack of confidence, the insecurity and depression many women experience on returning home with a child they have not grown to know and respond to naturally. They can then only cope by copying the strict hospital structure with its four-hourly schedule, regardless of the baby's needs. A theoretical timetable replaces intuitive responsiveness and communication.

Martin Richards, who has done research on early infant development, describes the situation in America (where hospital practices in maternity wards are unfortunately not altogether different from those in England): 'If she does not see her baby for a day or so after delivery and then only at a brief feed each four hours (as is not unusual in American hospitals) the mother may then leave the hospital with the idea that this is the natural and expected pattern of the relationship which she should continue when she gets home. After all, the hospital is run by paediatric and obstetric experts so it is reasonable for her to conclude that the pattern of contact laid down there is what modern science has "proved" to be best. Most mothers could hardly be expected to analyse the situation and conclude, as some social scientists have done, that the hospital routine is a product of the institutional structure and the convenience of doctors and nurses and has very little to do with the interests of either mother or baby.'[5]

Such a rigid pattern of interaction with the baby and times of feeding is one which makes it most difficult to establish breast feeding successfully, even when this is wished for by the mother. When the mother is not certain that she wants to breast feed, this rigid pattern and its accompanying problems will almost inevitably mean that the attempt to breast feed is doomed to fail.

I asked Barbara to do a drawing of herself at the moment (a procedure I was to repeat at most interviews during her pregnancy). While she drew she went on with what she was saying:

Barbara Oh well, at the moment I'm pretty depressed. I couldn't draw a mental state but if I was having a laugh I would draw tear drops all over the side because I will keep grizzling for nothing. Probably I'm worried still . . . things get on top of me much more easily than they used to. It comes and goes in phases; for the last four or five weeks I wasn't so bad and now I've started grizzling again. I told the midwife I'm not taking any tablets or anything, it will pass off again, but I expect it's because I do worry about . . . probably delivery . . . and so I make my home environment hostile and I take everything my husband says the wrong way. He's quiet usually and quite moody, and normally that goes over my head, but now I take it personally and I get depressed and think I don't know why I put up with it. But once I've had the baby I think it will be OK again.

Dana Did you feel like this with the first one?

Barbara No, I wasn't depressed at all when I was pregnant. I had a bit of postpartum depression but it didn't last – a week of good howling and that was it.

Dana How do you feel about the idea of having two children?

Barbara He won't be the baby any more. He's not a baby really. I don't look at him and say: 'Oh dear little baby' but – I don't know if I've done it, but he's very shy. I feel he is quite dependent on me, on Mum, and I feel a bit sorry for him really. I think it might do him good. He keeps saying that he wants us to have a little girl but I don't think that it really means anything, I don't think he knows that there is going to be any difference. He wants me to hurry up – we told him that Mummy will get very very big, the baby would have to grow a very big bump out here before the baby could be born, and he thinks because I'm this size this is it, it's going to come any day; but we told him a bit longer. I think he'll be pleased, sometimes he'll probably be jealous; all children must be jealous sometimes but I hope he'll be pleased.

Dana Have you got any brothers or sisters?

Barbara No, I haven't. My parents were divorced. They are both remarried. I have a half sister and two step brothers but I never see them.

Dana If you have never experienced having a brother or sister
maybe it would worry you more for Peter, since you don't
know what it feels like, having a younger one.

Barbara I don't know, I can't really imagine the situation.

The relationship with a first child is felt to be a very special and
intense one, like the relationship one had or wished one had had
with one's mother, unspoilt by the presence of rivals. A woman's
position and experience in her own family of origin will colour
which child's plight she can most readily empathize with – the
one who is born already or the one who is coming into the family.
Her own jealousy of a younger brother or sister, relived when she
is giving a brother or sister to her first child, can accentuate her
wish to be rid of this baby and consequently her feelings of guilt
and concern.

I have met a number of women who have felt more anxious
during their second pregnancy than their first, and particularly
have worried more about the baby. Jane said: 'All the time I was
pregnant with John [her first child] my husband kept saying you
shouldn't be so sure he'll be all right; he might be deformed, he
might be dead when he's born. And I was doing it all the time I
was pregnant with Jill [her second child]. When she was born I
had her stripped, examined all over.'

Sometimes the sex of the child is more important than the birth
order. Susan says about her daughter: 'I think there's something
very special about having a girl, partly I think because my firstborn was a girl and we're very close.. I have always been closer to
women than to men, closer to my mother than to my father. I
don't know if I would have felt so close had I had a son rather than
a daughter. Yet when I was pregnant, I really didn't know what I
wanted. In fact perhaps I thought I wanted a boy.'

In our society, women – and even more so men – wish to have a
boy as the first child, and an American study found that women
more often dream of baby boys during their first pregnancy.[6] The
wish to be reborn a boy, the wish to have an intimate male–female
relationship, the wish to be the centre of a little boy's attention, or
the fear of rivalry with a daughter can lead to a woman's desire
for a male child; the wish for immortality is a factor in men's
desire for a male child. The higher status of men in our society

25

(and by extension, of mothers of sons) is yet another aspect.

Adrienne Rich describes her feelings that having a son would compensate for certain qualities denied to women: 'I wanted to give birth, at twenty-five, to my unborn self, the self that our father-centred family had suppressed in me; someone inde-pendent, actively willing, original – those possibilities I had felt in myself in flashes as a young student and writer, and from which, during pregnancy, I was to close myself off. If I wanted to give birth to myself as a male, it was because males seemed to inherit those qualities by right of gender . . . I wanted a son, also, in order to do what my mother had not done: bring forth a man-child. I wanted him as a defiance to my father, who had begotten "only" daughters.'[7]

In wanting a daughter a woman may want to be reborn, to get something she felt she missed out on in her early life. Susan dreams that she gives birth to a kitten with red hair. She then tells me that she has just used red shampoo on her own hair. The dream expresses her wish to be reborn, through this new baby, into what she calls 'a real family', the family she herself never had because of the war. The 'real family' is also one she feels is only possible now with Paul, her second husband – and he too has red hair – so the baby/kitten is clearly his.

During pregnancy many women are reluctant to express a preference as to the sex of the baby; they fear their disappoint-ment could harm their child or that they would feel they had failed if the child was of the other sex.

I asked Barbara what sex she imagined the baby to be.

Barbara A boy. First because it is very much like Peter. Peter never stopped kicking from the time I got up until the time I went to bed, and this one is similar; the feelings are so much alike; and secondly because I think I'd really like a girl. I'd really like a girl, but I don't want to be disappointed if it's a boy, so I think it's going to be a boy so that I shan't be. That's a lot of it. But I don't feel it's going to be a girl any more; I don't know if I've brainwashed myself, but I think it will be another little boy.

Dana Do you remember what you thought the first time?

Barbara Yes, I thought . . . I was sure it was going to be a boy the first time, but I didn't dare think it in case it wasn't, because I wanted a boy last time and I was delighted that I got one. I thought it was wonderful. I thought I was going to, but when everyone asked me I used to say: 'Oh I don't mind, I don't know,' but I did feel it was going to be a boy, I just didn't like to say it; but this time I think it will.

Dana (*Looking at her drawing*): It's quite defined, except the abdomen is a bit fuzzy; perhaps you're not sure how big to make it?

Barbara No, my husband said this morning: 'Look in the mirror and now turn sideways' and I said 'Good grief' . . . it shouldn't be allowed, should it! It looks very much like when you see the charts of development of the child. I know what you're supposed to look at is how it's all developed [inside] but what I always notice is this big lump [in the abdomen]. With this pregnancy, to start off with I wasn't as big as when I was expecting Peter, then all of a sudden I was just like the diagram. That's what I feel like, having had a good look, but it probably goes out even further than that.

Dana The rest of you is very straight.

Barbara No, not really, I just can't draw how I look, I'm going out all over the place, I'm just getting fatter and fatter, dreadful. . . .

16 December

After I left, Barbara realized that her difficulty with the drawing had to do with her feelings about her body. She had, some time ago, been overweight at a time when she was depressed. She saw a psychiatrist then and realized that the depression was connected with her parents' divorce in early adolescence and her father's departure. She went to find him and now they meet occasionally. When she started feeling less depressed, she lost weight. Now that she was pregnant and putting on weight it made her feel fat again, and very insecure.

A woman's feelings about her parents are crucial in colouring her feelings about her pregnancy and in her ability to deal with having a baby. In particular her relationship with her mother, now and in childhood, will come into every stage of the child-bearing process.

Linda describes this in relationship to her difficulty in conceiving. 'It was two years after fairly regular intercourse that I conceived; the funny thing was it was just after Mummy died. It seems odd. We'd lost Daddy when I was twelve, and she'd remarried, and she died of a broken heart I think. She was a constant worry to us, myself and my sister, and perhaps it was just some sudden curious reaction – release really; not that I wished her not around, she wasn't demanding really, she was depressed, but it was difficult for me that I should have conceived then, not having done so for two years. Anyhow, when I was pregnant, I had no idea I was and I thought I had glandular fever. My sister gasped when she found out I was expecting a baby so soon after, it almost seemed as if I'd done it on purpose – as if had I been on the pill, stopped the pill and there was my replacement.' It is as if Linda can only allow herself to have a baby when she no longer needs to look after her mother; she cannot 'replace' her mother, and have a life of her own as a mother, while the latter is still alive, and yet being pregnant immediately after her mother's death feels uncanny and worrying.

Women who cope well with the experience of having a baby tend to have a positive image of their own mother and feel themselves to be similar to her. They also tend to have worked through some of their conflicting feelings about their fathers. In this interview Barbara made me understand why her second pregnancy was such a worry to her beyond her own conscious fear of having a difficult childbirth. She described her mother as a very anxious person who needed looking after rather than being able to offer a supportive and mothering image. She told me that her father had reacted to her pregnancy by saying he didn't believe she was pregnant because in their family 'women can only have one child'. Mother and grandmother had had one child only and it had been a major bone of contention between her parents. She had asked her mother about this and was reassured to find that it was not for physiological reasons but from choice. Nevertheless she *did* wonder if she could have a second child, the second child which in a sense her father had wanted her mother to have and which he was telling her she could not have. Had her mother had a second baby, her father might not have left them.

28

Being pregnant with a second child had thus a very special meaning for her.

Another aspect of this situation is the not uncommon fear women have of being punished for surpassing their mother if they have more children than she had; it is likely that Barbara imagines that her father is saying, 'Women in our family *may* only have one child'. The idea, too, of being creative at her mother's expense (being young and fertile when her mother is getting old and sterile) is also felt to be worthy of punishment.

Similar fears of punishment are present in women who have had an earlier abortion – an 'eye for an eye' retribution involving the baby's death or deformity.

Such are the thoughts which contribute to the food fads or other rituals during pregnancy, designed to keep at bay the poisonous, destructive forces threatening the body. Such too are the thoughts which lead some women to follow superstitiously and without questioning the words of books or doctors.

CHAPTER TWO

Two of us

8 January

BARBARA is now thirty-two weeks pregnant. I had not seen her for three weeks because of the holidays and she expresses in this interview a radical change in her feelings about herself.

Barbara My father says he doesn't think I can be this size for another eight weeks. Actually I don't feel as big as when I had Peter. Well, I know I'm not. We have photos and you can see I'm not so big; I was right out this way (*pointing outwards*). It's probably because the first time you can – well, I did – just sit down for most of the last four months, and now I'm busy all the time; so I haven't put on half as much weight as when I had Peter.

Now I'm this far on, I can feel the baby and almost tell you which way round it is all the time; this last week it's been doing somersaults – there is hardly enough room and you can feel every inch as it moves around. Instead of just feeling this big lump now, I rather feel as if it's me and somebody else, not just me and a lump. Before it was just a big tummy, but now I rather feel it's somebody as well. Oh yes, with two hands round the front, that is how I spend all my time. Every time I stand up, I think: There it is. I've just started feeling that there are two of us, possibly because I know that once you get to about thirty weeks or thereabouts, then the baby can be born and have a chance of living. Before then I was rather: 'well I'm jolly well not making too many plans because . . .' I never had any threat of abortion or anything, it was just that I didn't like to tempt fate.

Dana Can you remember feeling a change like this from one person to two with Peter?

Barbara No, I definitely didn't. When I was expecting Peter, when I was in labour I forgot I was having one, it was just a lump that hurt then; the rest of the time he kicked and moved a lot but I didn't visualize a baby as I do this time; probably because I didn't know what to imagine and this time I imagine him [Peter]. I don't feel the baby is as big, but I remember with Peter I felt from my ribs I came right out [sideways] and this time . . . perhaps it's just that it will be another four or five weeks before I feel like that, but I remember feeling like that from about April and he wasn't due until August. I don't know if it's because I was generally heavier then, so I spread more, or what.

Dana Last time we spoke you felt you were enormous, do you remember?

Barbara I'm sure that's why I became so withdrawn to start off with – because I started spreading. Now I feel more happy because I really look pregnant, I don't just look as if I'm getting fatter and fatter. Everybody knows why I look so huge, so I'm happier about it. Does that make sense to you? Before, you are just spreading and spreading . . .

Our ideas about the shape and size of our bodies are very subjective. Women, in our society which places such an emphasis on certain norms for the female body, are particularly prone to misrepresentation and negative feelings about their bodies. But it is not just a question of norms. Psychoanalysts have come to understand basic fears in the little girl about the intactness of her genitals which cannot be seen as the little boy can see his. She may have wished to hurt her mother and kill her babies and in becoming a mother previously unconscious anxieties about the state of her internal organs and babies may become more conscious with the reality of the pregnancy. A preoccupation with the 'outer' body can cover an unconscious preoccupation with the 'inner' body. Feelings about one's body are also linked with the sense of worth. Sometimes a beautiful outward 'shell' is needed by a woman to cover what she fears to be her awful inner self, a mask behind which she can hide.

Pregnancy also brings into focus an organ little thought of before, the womb. Inside the womb is now a representation of the sexual partner, and the fear of being fat rather than pregnant can express a woman's anxiety about her sexual appetite.

Whatever her feelings about her body, a woman cannot remain unaffected by the massive physiological changes which take place during pregnancy and childbirth. These may awaken feelings she had during bodily changes at puberty. How she feels about her body will also reflect her feelings about and idea of the baby at any one time.

Many first-time mothers do not really believe they are carrying a baby: 'When I first felt her move, I knew there was life inside me. But I didn't realize I was having a baby until my doctors literally pulled her out of me upside down and she sneezed, and then she lay next to me, and I felt her tiny breath on my fingers.'[8]

'I'll tell you something. I never really believed I was pregnant; until I had him I never believed I was really pregnant' (Bridget). Even Susan, who is expecting her third child, says: 'I find it difficult a lot of the time to realize there is a baby there . . . I mean you know there's something there, but to associate it with a baby when it comes out I find very difficult. I have to concentrate on making myself think that it's a process of which there is a baby growing, more than just an odd state in itself.'

This uncertainty about what is going on inside leaves room for fantasies and fears. Barbara talks about having to get rid of the 'lump'. A common fantasy associates childbirth and defecation, originating in the little girl's confusion between anus and vagina. Children associate the baby 'inside the tummy' with the food 'inside the tummy', both leading to 'big tummies'. The baby is thought to be a product of a feeding relationship. (When I was expecting my second child, my two-year-old daughter kept talking about 'Mummy and Daddy eating in bed all day long'.) Giving birth is then like getting rid of the contents of the stomach. These ideas persist in adults, and childbirth has been described as 'shitting a pumpkin', an image which comes from the actual sensations in labour when the baby's head presses against the rectum in the second stage.

When giving birth it is frequent for a woman to fear she is going to soil, to make a mess. Instead of pushing the baby out, she contracts her muscles; the midwife's order to push reminds her of her mother's orders when she was on the pot – should she give in or on the contrary be defiant?

The fantasies and anxieties about what is inside the body during pregnancy are most often unconscious. Anxieties about what is inside the body are probably universal and stem from childhood fears and fantasies. One woman, while suffering from a postnatal disturbance, expresses directly the fantasy of a single internal cavity filled with different things. Pregnancy, she said, was being 'filled up with semen and blood and milk'; her increasing size had meant she was becoming 'more and more full'. 'It's the one time I was completely full'.[9] In a less extreme form many women feel that pregnancy fills some void or emptiness inside them; that they are finally satiated, replete or complete. The pregnancy or the baby then represents the previous missing part, often linked with what has been long desired from a parent – the never-ending supply of milk from the woman's mother (as in the above example); the baby wished for in childhood dreams from the father; the baby stolen from the mother; or the potency taken from the father. The new mother feels contented with this baby who represents a part of herself, to whom she offers and with whom she relives vicariously the perfect union. Lesley describes going to a strange place for a few days without her husband: 'I felt I wasn't alone, I wasn't lonely; it seemed extraordinary to experience the feeling that wherever I went I wasn't alone, the baby came with me; that I carried it around wherever I went; that I would not and could not be alone.'

If the baby is felt to be stolen from one of the parents, the damage it will cause that parent is feared. Lesley, eight months pregnant, has the following dream: 'I was getting pains in my pelvis and my mother also had a swollen abdomen. The dream had to do with one or both of us being pregnant, and with a diagnosis for my mother which was either infertility, menopause or pregnancy. At one point a nurse took one of my dresses to give my mother and I got angry and took it back.' Clearly this dream expresses a confusion between who is pregnant, mother or daughter, and a fear of what Lesley's pregnancy might be doing and whether it is taking her mother's fertility away. There is a reversal of what she fears she may have done (in the dream she doesn't take anything from her mother, her mother takes something from her, in the form of a dress). Reversal is also expressed in a dream reported by another pregnant woman: 'I'd wake up in the night and think people were going to come in and take things, take the baby from me.'[10]

The baby may also be felt to be a danger to herself. This idea originates in a woman's relationship with her own mother and her fear of what she may have done to her mother when she was herself a baby. Susan fears that both she and the baby cannot be healthy; that one of them will be damaged. She dreams: 'Something terrible was happening to the baby – like mongolism; the dream then switched and I felt that something terrible would happen to me if the baby was not removed.'

To Margaret whatever is inside her can only be bad, the representation of all her nasty thoughts and feelings; she feels possessed by the devil. Lesley feels contented with a baby inside her; wherever she goes she has the comfort of this intimate presence. Claire is frightened by her body, which seems to her to be doing mysterious things of its own accord – things which she feels are totally out of her control and follow a course she can no longer put a stop to. She wonders if this is her body or someone else's.

The passage of time is felt acutely during pregnancy. Barbara talked about a significant landmark, the moment of viability of the baby separate from her. Now she can let herself make plans, truly anticipate the birth of her child.

Abigail Lewis describes her changed sense of time during her pregnancy: 'Were I to lose consciousness for a month, I would still tell that an appreciable amount of time had passed by the increased size of the foetus within me. There is a constant sense of growth, of progress, of time which, while it may be wasted for you personally, is still being used, so that even if you were to do nothing at all during those nine months, something would nevertheless be accomplished and a climax reached. Death has never seemed so far away, because growth, which is life, is so obviously occurring. The sun that rises tomorrow cannot be the sun that rose yesterday, because the foetus is a millimetre and a half larger; and though you may be engaged in repetitive tasks that dull your own sense of time, the foetus is not repeating. It stretches and turns, its movements gain in power and direction. Whatever may be your own doubts about where mankind is heading and what maturity is, the foetus seems to feel no doubt at all as to what it wants; and in all that curious, segregated, seemingly static chunk of a year, you become aware of a new kind of time; the foetus's time, the slow pushing time of growth. . . .'[11]

Pregnancy is part of sexuality and women's feelings about their pregnancy are often linked to their feelings about their sexuality, past feelings or new feelings. Three women express positive feelings about this sexual side of pregnancy: 'Being pregnant meant I was a woman. I was enthralled by my belly growing.' 'It gave me a sense that I was actually a woman. I had never felt sexy before. I went through a lot of changes. It was a very sexual thing. I felt very voluptuous.' 'It meant I could get pregnant finally after a lot of trying, that I could do something I wanted to do. It meant going into a new stage of life. I felt filled up.'[12] For a woman who hasn't come to feel relaxed and accepting towards her body and sexuality, being pregnant can be accompanied by a painful sense of shame and exposure. She feels embarrassed and guilty, she stays at home to hide her body, and sometimes does not admit even to herself that she is pregnant until a very late stage.

Barbara, on the other hand, described her relief at being visibly pregnant. She now did not mind being seen by other people.

Adrienne Rich enjoyed this too: 'As soon as I was visibly and clearly pregnant, I felt, for the first time in my adolescent and adult life, not guilty. The atmosphere of approval in which I was bathed – even by strangers on the street, it seemed – was like an aura I carried with me, in which doubts, fears, misgivings, met with absolute denial.'[13]

I was struck by how Barbara had now represented the baby in her drawing and was clearly for the first time aware of its presence as another person.

Dana   Maybe being able to think of it as two people during pregnancy, to feel one is carrying a baby, makes it easier when the baby is born, because one doesn't have to adjust all of a sudden to having a baby.

Barbara   It's true with Peter it was quite a shock when they said you've got a son, and I thought: Gracious, I forgot I was doing that! It took the week in hospital to get used to having him at all, and even afterwards I didn't associate . . . Because my tummy was going flat again I didn't think: Well here is the baby outside. It was as if the pregnancy and the baby were two completely different things, but this time they have started to be the same. I was reading a book called *Painless Childbirth**

---

* By Lamaze (Burke 1958).

and it said that if you needed a picture so that you didn't get frightened during the birth, while you were busying yourself doing the different levels of breathing, you could imagine the cervix opening over a baby's head. If you think of a baby's head then you must acknowledge that there is a baby. Until you start thinking about that, well it's as if you're just a lump, not two people at all. I thought next time I must jolly well remember this is all to produce this baby, instead of just lying there wondering whether it's going to end.

This time Barbara has already begun thinking about the baby. She talks for the first time about how it will be when I come to see her and there is a little one 'fast asleep'. She starts thinking about what her baby will be like. She tells me a dream:

Barbara   I was standing at a bus stop with Peter, who was about six. He didn't look any different, but he was taller, and a little boy. I was talking to somebody, another woman in the bus queue. She said, 'Aren't they alike?' and I said, 'Yes it's amazing, isn't it?' and the little one was fourteen months – well, that's too much age difference anyway but this is in the dream – and he was talking just the same as Peter. I know what started the dream: we got out our old tape recorder and we had it repaired, and we found an old tape of Peter when he was about one and he'd just started to talk and we've got him going 'Mumumumum' and all this, and I imagined it was the second one doing this all over again.

Here Barbara imagines the new baby to be a repeat of the first one, while her first child is pushed into being very much older, making it clear that he is no longer the baby. During my second pregnancy I found myself saying one day to a friend, 'This time I'll dress her differently', and realized as the words slipped out of my mouth that I was talking as if my first child was to be reborn.

Barbara had told me her dream quite spontaneously. One preliminary study[14] suggests that women have a special interest in their dreams during pregnancy and that they can sometimes remember them long afterwards, even linking the dream with a particular pregnancy.

A study of dreams during pregnancy[15] reported that 40 per cent of the dreams were about the baby (as opposed to 1 per cent in non-pregnant women). When the sex was specified, it was twice as often about boys, and often the children were past infancy. The dreams were often of misfortunes and harm, and the babies were often abnormal. Anxiety generally accompanies such dreams, and the dreamer somewhere inside herself cannot help but fear that the dream is a premonition; that it is based on reality rather than fantasy. Another study[16] also mentions themes relating to feeling unattractive and the fear that the sexual partner finds other women more attractive, and themes relating to conflicts over dependence and independence with the subjects' own mothers.

Pregnant women's dreams also revealed a greater percentage of architectural references than the dreams of non-pregnant women. These architectural references can be interpreted as representing concern about the 'architecture' of the body. Lesley (two months pregnant) has the following dream: 'Some friends had bought a flat in a rather crummy area. The outside was dreadful but when I went in I realized that it was really quite special. There was a large square with grass inside (similar to a cloister); it was like a garden, only *inside* the flat, and there were lots of nice rooms. In fact I could see that it was quite a find.' The architectural reference here links with a reversal: what should be outside (the garden) is inside and the focus of interest; the niceness is now inside (the baby), and what is outside (the outside world) becomes 'crummy', unimportant. The idea of the cloister adds to the dream's reference to the state of seclusion and withdrawal common in pregnancy, during which a large amount of communication and interest is directed inside – to the baby and to inner feelings and fantasies. This tendency to self-absorption is one which some women fight against for fear of becoming totally cut off from the outside world, and it may be particularly difficult for women who are involved in a professional activity which they have always valued and fear losing interest or involvement in. The withdrawal or self-absorption is one which also threatens relationships with other members of the family, and the woman may resent what she feels to be excessive demands made on her by the rest of the family – demands which may in reality be increased during her pregnancy at a time when she feels a greater need to be looked after herself.

Lesley's dream also expresses the idea of self-sufficiency: all the goodness is inside, even the garden is inside; there is no need to go out, nothing to be looked for outside. And she says: 'A few weeks ago I started feeling less like arranging to see my friends. I just wanted to stay at home, or very near home . . . to stay "here" rather than go out and do things. I also find it hard to talk to friends at the moment; I don't really feel like it.'

Dreams about what the baby will be like are also frequent during pregnancy. Marion dreams that she gives birth to a wooden doll, 'rigid, absolutely rigid . . . like a piece of wood my husband has carved; he's just carved the face and the rest is the body'. In another dream she and her husband take the baby out to have a look at it but then they cannot put it back in again; she feels anxious. It is as if the secrecy of pregnancy which hides the sex and any knowledge of the baby is sacred: curiosity is punished, just as curiosity about what goes on inside Mother's body is felt to be prohibited to a child. (In particular the body is just the rest of the wood so that the sex of the child is not defined.) Marion's husband is intimately involved in both dreams: the wooden doll is *his* doll, he has created it – and not yet finished it. Here again the image of a doll emphasizes the link with childhood.

For some women, on the other hand, the baby is very much their own baby, almost born out of parthenogenesis; a reproduction of themselves rather than a joint effort. In other dreams the baby resembles another important member of the family such as brother, father, or mother: a person the woman emulates, dreads or would like to have a child by.

And then there is the problem of how the woman will relate to and cope with this new child. Lesley dreams that 'the baby is kept in hospital for four months without my being able to care for it, and when I meet the baby again there is no relationship between us'; she is then five months pregnant and worried about 'meeting' the baby in four months' time. Sarah has a recurrent dream concerning: 'the sudden realization that I'd had a baby, and I was doing what I used to, and I'd forgotten about him. I would rush upstairs and dread going into his room. I was afraid of what I'd find, afraid that he would be dead because I'd forgotten to feed him, or he'd be wet because I hadn't changed him and he'd been sobbing. In fact I always manage to open the door and find him asleep. It's never as bad as I thought it would be.'

Yet Sarah coped well with her baby and felt at ease as a mother. It is a paradox that to be able to deal well with a difficult situation it is often necessary to worry about it beforehand. The woman who can worry about how she will cope with her baby is also the one who is aware and realistic – who will not be shocked, bewildered and taken by surprise when faced with problems, and will therefore be better equipped to tackle them. In a study of sixty first-time mothers I found that the women who were most likely to experience difficulties with the physical and emotional side of having a baby were those who during pregnancy expressed either extreme anxiety or on the contrary hardly any at all. In other words, to experience and express a fair amount of anxiety during pregnancy turned out to be a healthy sign.

Fears during pregnancy are not concerned only with the baby. A major preoccupation is the actual birth. Childbirth is after all a normal event (though quite a rare one for each individual woman, and in our present society one which we rarely have a chance to witness even with friends or relatives), and the fear of it must in part relate to irrational feelings. Of course, childbirth is not without dangers, but then neither are many other normal events. Most other normal functions can and do go wrong; medical intervention helps to reduce the risks and heal the damage. But childbirth is the only *normal* event which takes place in a hospital and is surrounded by a host of strict practices and procedures. In one of his articles,[17] Peter Lomas, doctor and psychoanalyst, looks at the similarities between the way women are treated now in childbirth and the rituals associated with childbirth in primitive society, which include such things as the segregation of the woman, and the husband's imitation of childbirth and his submission to various privations and duties (a practice called 'couvade'). He suggests that whereas in couvade the husband is made the important figure, in our society it is the doctor who takes control. This means that the physical is emphasized at the expense of the psychological and the mother is treated as someone who is sick. The medical authorities advise her on what to do and not to do during pregnancy, she generally gives birth away from her home, she is treated like a child, and her baby is separated from her and looked after by the staff. 'Much of what is done in the name of medical necessity has the consequence of preventing the mother from regarding herself as a mature human being, from participating actively and fully in the birth, from loving and caring for her baby and from taking an uninhibited and triumphant joy in the occasion.' And, as Lomas goes on to say: 'The most convincing explanation for this relative failure to meet the mother's needs is that there exists in society an antipathy towards childbirth.' Why this ambivalence? Lomas suggests, following Melanie Klein's ideas, that envy of a woman's creative success is the motive behind the need to put her down. By having the birth taken out of her hands (through the use of anaesthetics, inductions, forceps, and so on), the woman is in a sense robbed of her creativity and the doctor is the one to give birth. That the woman often willingly submits to this treatment, Lomas suggests, is linked with her own fear of other people's envy and her inability to be 'triumphantly creative'. I would add that one aspect of the help offered by natural childbirth classes is in allowing the woman to take full control of her body and, amid support from the teacher and peers, to be joyful in her creative success. In such an atmosphere, obstetrical procedures can even be welcomed when necessary, rather than accepted as punishment or resented as control.

As in any other situation which is felt to put in question personal worth, a woman's feelings about how she coped with childbirth can colour her future feelings about herself. The birth of Barbara's first child was very traumatic and she lost confidence in herself as a mother. A vacuum extraction in a situation where she was alone and mystified and felt totally out of control of what was happening to her left her feeling inadequate and insecure.

Barbara At the hospital I was induced the first time and it had frightened me and I really would rather avoid induction if I could. And they said: 'These days we don't induce until you are ten days late.' It's only three and a half years since I had him so it must have changed in the meantime. I suppose they review their attitudes all the time. That would be towards the end of March; I was rather thinking it would be like him [Peter] – the thirty-ninth week they said: 'Oh he's big enough, come in' and you rather think: I hope they don't do that again. I felt a bit happier about that. But she said: 'You can always refuse an induction you know,' and I said that would be a very silly thing to do because if they thought it was the right thing they must know. I don't want it done because they're not busy, but if they say it's necessary it's not up to me to say no. It does give me ten days grace at least, perhaps.

Dana   When is the expected date?

Barbara   Well, I've been very cunning; I've probably been much too clever. I told them three or four days after the right date because I didn't want to be started off slap on the day, and so they think it's 10 March, but actually it's the 6th. There's only four days in it, so they'll start me off if it's ten days afterwards – that's 20 March; it will actually be fourteen days late then, so it should be pretty well ready. I'm not sure about the day of conception, so there must be that many days difference in every pregnancy, and I thought; It won't hurt I shouldn't think: not three or four days.

Dana   Do you have regular periods?

Barbara   No, I came off the pill and they were mainly thirty-two days, you see; that's why I allowed myself four days, because they always take you as a regular twenty-eight and I wanted it to be as near to the right time as possible. It's naughty, you shouldn't be having to do this sort of thing, you should be able to reason with them. But they tend to say, 'Look we know best dear, leave it to us.' And it worried me so much about being induced this time: I don't want to be induced and find that it's perhaps a week early, because I'm sure a child must start just when it's ready and not when they think.

There is a current debate about the advisability of inducing labour for other than very specific reasons such as a dangerous rise in blood pressure. Evidence has accumulated that induction carries a risk for the child through possible prematurity and through the high doses of drugs administered. The timing of a spontaneous labour is controlled by mechanisms which are not yet fully understood. Induced births can be more painful; they often require greater amounts of pain-relieving drugs, and epidurals (which in turn often require the use of forceps) are more frequently necessary. The psychological effect on the mother and on the baby should also be taken into account. Certainly many women regard induction as unnecessary and intrusive; they feel their body is being treated like a machine which must produce not when the baby is ready to be born but according to a standardized timetable. The mother feels robbed of her creativity. She no longer gives birth according to her own spontaneous body processes and rhythm; instead the birth is monitored and conducted by the medical staff and their machinery. She becomes only a piece of machinery herself, strapped in, hooked up and injected into, standing between the baby and the outside world, obstructing its passage and made to eject her own creation or have it scooped out of her. This is the opposite of slowly helping her baby into the world at its own pace and her own pace, and thereby confirming the goodness and competence of her body. Most women react negatively to having their labour induced. The procedure seems to violate an intimate sense of inner body-time which emerges in pregnancy. 'For the first time in my life I'm in step with the world. It's rather peaceful to have staked out a piece of time for oneself. It has a beginning and an end and it belongs to you. It makes you feel at home. I suppose dates are essentially feminine, our need and our fate.'[18]

One must, however, be careful not to idealize the body and must accept that it does not always work perfectly if left to its own devices. A woman who assumes that she can give birth naturally and unaided may be quite shocked and unprepared when obstetrical intervention is necessary. Foreknowledge of all eventualities can only mean better preparation.

The same procedures will be experienced differently by different people. A woman's reaction to any intervention will depend on her feelings about herself: one who is confident, trusts her body and has experienced support from other people in the past will be only mildly troubled by an induction even though she would have preferred spontaneous labour; one who deep down feels very inadequate and incapable of achievement, and who has been in great rivalry with her mother or other people will react with a sense of total failure, resentment, distrust and depression. However, such a woman may also opt for the sort of birth which is taken out of her own hands, because she trusts science and the doctor more than herself.

42

One of the problems for Barbara, as for most women who would like a natural birth, is the aura surrounding medical science. In discussion of the advisability of induction in specific cases, it is assumed that such cases are clear cut. Yet a doctor who favours induction will interpret any minor sign as support for what he already prefers, and few women will resist when he describes the dangers involved in not following his advice – dangers which might belong only to extreme cases. Few doctors explain the risks involved in the induction itself, and very few take into account the psychological risks. Our society emphasizes physical health and the role of the doctor as master and magician so much that even to balance the psychological against the physical components of well-being has come to seem absurd. The question is not whether babies should be left to die rather than be induced (the counter-argument is generally given in an extreme form), but whether so many inductions are necessary, if the premise is accepted that inductions carry a physical and psychological risk for mother and baby; and whether it is possible to reduce the need for intervention by good psychological preparation during pregnancy.

Apart from feeling that she is being robbed of a fulfilling and precious experience when her labour is induced, a woman can feel that she is being robbed of her baby. Such a fear is often present during pregnancy or postnatally. Lesley insisted on keeping her baby next to her in hospital. The nursery was far from the ward and near the street, and she noticed that at times the babies were unattended. She feared that anyone could come in and take her baby, and hardly dared to leave her for a minute, out of fear that someone would steal her away. Birth is a traumatic separation for mother and child; it is natural to want to regain some of the closeness which has been lost. An enforced separation for a woman who seeks this closeness can only be experienced as the threat of having the being she most wants to be united with taken away from her.

Being robbed of the baby is not just a fantasy in the mother. Envy of the imagined blissful state of the baby in the womb and envy of the pregnant mother's completeness which lie dormant in all of us may have its part to play in the medical practice of inducing labour when there is no real emergency. Some women's anger with inductions for 'the convenience of the obstetrician' is referring to more than timetables.

One midwife revealed the possible unconscious significance of such procedures when she asked a woman to take pills to speed up labour, telling her that they were 'male hormones, also used for abortions'. This woman's labour lasted only two hours and a half, in spite of her refusing the pills.

CHAPTER THREE

Just knowing somebody is there

13 January

BARBARA had told me about her fear of childbirth and her wish to find support with her second birth. I told her about classes of preparation for childbirth, and gave her the address of the nearest teacher working for the National Childbirth Trust.* She had read a book about preparation for childbirth during her first pregnancy, but not known of classes in her area.

Childbirth is a biological event. It is also a psychological and a sociological event. Like other biological events it takes meaning in a social context. Karen Paige found with menstruation that the amount of anxiety and physical distress experienced was related to women's attitudes and to their cultural background. The women who suffered tended to be those who considered menstruation to be embarrassing, unclean and an illness; they also tended to be the ones who espoused the more traditionally feminine role in the sense of having no personal career ambitions and feeling that the woman's place is in the home.[19] Similarly we may assume that the amount of pain experienced in childbirth will in part relate to a woman's expectation, knowledge and interpretation of the situation. If a woman has no idea what to expect, is in the dark as to what is happening to her and has grown up to believe that childbirth is a time of suffering and expiation, she is very likely to find childbirth exceedingly distressing.

There are different sorts of classes of preparation for childbirth, but in all of them the basis is a thorough knowledge of every

---

* Information about classes in different parts of England can be obtained from the National Childbirth Trust, 9 Queensborough Terrace, London W2.

phase of the childbirth process and the possible procedures which could be used. In most classes the woman is taught how to relax the muscles which are not being used, and to control the muscles around the perineum so that she can relax them in the second stage of labour. She is shown different ways of breathing, helpful at each stage, and taught the positions she might find most comfortable. Her attendant is shown ways in which he* can be most helpful to her. Practice in spreading out her legs is no small part of the exercises in a society that is so strict in teaching girls to keep their legs closed or crossed, and talking about her genitals is a way of helping her accept the process without embarrassment.

But these classes do more than teach specific skills. They encourage a woman to feel that she can actively help herself through labour in a state of complete knowledge. Her labour is less likely to feel interminable if she knows what to expect and is on the lookout for signs of progress from the first to the second stage. Rather than tensing her muscles when a contraction begins, she relaxes and breathes through it; rhythmic breathing helps to relax but also requires a certain amount of concentration, alleviating panic and pain.

Some classes are also involved in teaching a new philosophy of childbirth. Childbirth is described as a joyful experience (which does not mean that it is without pain for most women). The different phases are redescribed so that, for instance, the birth is 'the vagina opening up like a flower making room for the baby's head', or 'like a tight rollneck sweater fitting over the head', instead of the 'shitting a pumpkin' mentioned earlier (page 32). During labour, instead of thinking of suffering the woman can picture what is going on (the cervix stretching, etc.) and may find pleasure in this purposeful activity – the more it hurts the sooner the cervix will be dilated and the sooner the baby will be born.

Another aspect which Sheila Kitzinger[20] puts emphasis on is helping a woman to listen to and control in the sense of actively 'going along with' her body. (Such an approach is very different

---

* In our culture it is generally taken for granted that if there is an attendant it will be the sexual partner. If he is unable or reluctant to be present at the birth there is no reason why the attendant should not be a friend but this is not automatically accepted by all hospitals.

from the mechanical one used particularly in the second stage of labour when the woman is ordered to push strongly, irrespective of the strength of a particular contraction.) Her aim is 'childbirth in which a woman finds delight in the rhythmic harmony of her body's functioning' and in surrendering to primitive instinctual pleasures. This is not always possible: 'A woman who is resisting and fighting her body can never feel delight in the tussle of labour. She lies in stoic patience and endurance, taut with anxiety, determined not to give in, even though there may be little or no real pain. She wants labour without sensation. For some reason which may have its origins in her own childhood, and which is probably linked with the quality of her marriage relationship, she is blocking her knowledge of herself and retreating from the overwhelming reality of the childbirth experience.' Sheila Kitzinger calls her method of preparation for childbirth 'psychosexual' because childbirth relates to a woman's sexuality as a whole. She writes: 'Moreover, in describing the feelings and behaviour of a woman giving birth to a child it is important to remember that labour is but one part of her whole psychosexual life. Puberty, ovulation, menstruation, love-play and intercourse, birth, breast feeding and menopause – there is a flow and rhythm about her life bound up with her sexuality. The things she learns about herself, sensations of which she becomes aware, rhythms to which she is able to surrender herself, whether in reaching orgasm or in the remarkably similar urge to bear down in the second stage of labour, for instance, are interconnected. Where there is non-comprehension, or muscle spasm, or frigidity, then there tends to be a carry-over into other aspects of her psychosexual life, and I have known women who have discovered something about themselves in relation with their husbands afterwards.' One difference, though, I would add, between sexual intercourse and childbirth is that there is not the same possibility of trial and error in the latter, so that the opportunity to learn to enjoy childbirth through experience is almost non-existent.

Barbara I went to the first of those classes. It's very interesting; I shall definitely go to all of them; it struck me how much support they give, compared to normal antenatal services.

Well, I've already had Peter. There was no . . . I can't think of any other word than support. They tell you the mechanics of it all but apart from that, that's it, and the people that are talking to you aren't going to be there at the time; they just say this will happen and that will happen. This time [at the NCT classes] I just went in and was introduced to the girl in whose house it was and J. the teacher; it was before anyone else arrived, and one of the girls said: 'We come if you can't stand it any longer,' and the other one said: 'You mustn't say that, you mustn't give that impression'; and the first girl said: 'It's OK, Barbara has already had a baby.' So I said: 'It's something to know if you need someone you can call them'; if you're getting out of control. Just knowing somebody is there if you need to lift up the phone, that helps a lot. I thought: Good grief, you can't imagine the National Health Service running anything like that.

Barbara was also pleased to find that she was given practical advice about such things as backache or cramp during pregnancy. There was only one unpleasant note about this first class. 'I think everybody's husband turned up except mine – that was a bit offputting; you felt he should be there.' Her husband had refused to come.

Beyond the learning of skills which facilitate childbirth, the teacher and the class function as a good and supportive 'mother' who helps and allows each woman to have a good experience in childbirth. For a woman to feel herself to be a good mother, she needs to feel that her own mother was good and there is often during pregnancy a 'pattern of reconciliation'[21] with her mother or at least with an 'internal image' of her mother (that is, with her idea of her mother). This internal image can become modified through a relationship with a helpful antenatal teacher or midwife, who can contain her anxieties without brushing them aside, and gives her 'permission' to have a baby. The teacher also provides a model she can identify with. Peer group support further changes her attitude, if necessary, by helping her to think of childbirth as an important and positive experience, an experience where mastery comes into play.

In order to give birth naturally and in the best conditions for mother and baby, a woman needs to be active, in control and able to participate in the birth while at the same time able to surrender to her body processes. The problem can come from two sources: total loss of control often accompanied by panic and therefore pain or, on the contrary, tensing up (also leading to pain and a more difficult progress of labour).

The use of drugs, far from helping, can increase the loss of control. As Sheila Kitzinger aptly puts it: 'Just as one would not attempt any skill one had acquired, such as driving a car, whilst semi-conscious or under the influence of powerful drugs, so in a straightforward labour a woman should not attempt the important business of having a baby in a doped state if she wants to use all her powers efficiently to put into practice all she has learned during pregnancy'.[22]

Not all childbirths can be natural. Births may be particularly painful if the baby is not in the optimal position, and complications require special measures such as caesarian sections. And some women prefer to be numbed in childbirth. That is a legitimate choice which must be respected.

Helene Deutsch[23] has talked about women's innate masochism. I certainly do not hold the view that a woman who takes pleasure in the act of childbirth is masochistic. The pain in childbirth is pain *with a meaning*. And if the birth has been a good experience, the pain is felt to be an unfortunate aspect which soon fades into the background. Sheila Kitzinger talks about the 'exhilaration which comes in a creative experience of completely harmonious psychophysical functioning, where pain may or may not occur in the background – but if so, is willingly experienced as something that can be controlled, or else is brushed aside as being not nearly so important as the business of having a baby'.[24] Adrienne Rich speaks of childbirth as 'one way of knowing and coming to terms with our bodies, of discovering our physical and psychic resources'.[25]

There are women who do feel they *ought* to suffer in childbirth, according to the commandment in the Bible. They feel they must not enjoy themselves in a sexual relationship, and they must not enjoy themselves in childbirth. They feel guilty if they receive an anaesthetic; they feel they have cheated. In such cases it is legitimate to talk of masochism. These women are also often the ones who will feel that they must sacrifice their life for their children.

Pain generally comes to the foreground only when the experience has been a negative one as, for instance, when a woman felt alone in labour, when she felt mystified by what was happening to her, and afraid in unknown surroundings, or when the labour was a particularly difficult one and she was not prepared for this possibility. One such woman I spoke to was deeply shocked and relived the trauma in her dreams for many months.

Of course some women are able to tolerate pain better than others in any circumstance; and some labours are more difficult than others. The interchange between Barbara and one of the helpers is misleading in that many teachers do not (certainly they should not) minimize or hide the difficulties.

Charlotte describes being taken by surprise as the most upsetting aspect of her experience: 'The pregnancy was very straightforward and I didn't have any trouble. I started labour and my waters broke. When I got to hospital I remember them saying I was so many centimetres dilated; I remember thinking: Good Lord that's really good, and they gave me the same impression; but I didn't make any progress and I was in labour for ten hours. Then they started getting a bit concerned and his heart started to fail which I heard because I had a microphone on my stomach. There was then quite a panic and people rushing around, and they took a blood sample from his head and they took me to the theatre and it was an emergency caesarean. That was a great shock. It was something I had never contemplated. I had contemplated all the other things . . . I went to all the classes at the hospital and I can remember forceps are used 90 per cent of the time with first babies, and most people have an episiotomy, and I thought that's bound to happen to me. And then they told us about epidurals and I thought I'll probably have one of those, and whenever caesareans were mentioned I was always under the impression that one knew beforehand because of the way the baby was lying or because of something that was known before the baby was due. I think it would probably have been a good thing if they had mentioned emergency caesareans because I know so many people now who had that and who were absolutely shattered by it, and their husbands especially. My husband was ill; he lost a stone as a result of the experience.'

But perhaps it never is as one expects it, especially with a first baby. It is a novel, unimaginable situation, in which one's body is carried away by a mysterious inner force, faster and faster, with no respite, no possibility of stopping for a rest, and with an intensity, and for most women pain, quite unlike any other.

Having to go into hospital during their pregnancy also takes women by surprise. It is not something which is usually given any thought beforehand, and yet it is not an infrequent occurrence, whether for a short period at the end of pregnancy because of high blood pressure, or for longer periods and at other stages. In some unfortunate cases (for example that of placenta praevia) a woman must stay in hospital for months until the birth of her baby.

Being in hospital is emotionally taxing at any time. In pregnancy, hospitalization is often for preventive reasons, and there is a curious ambiguity in feeling quite well and yet being a patient in a bed in a nightdress, removed from one's normal habitat and one's family (including other children one usually cares for), sometimes on total bed rest and quite helpless and dependent on the nursing staff. A pregnant woman's anxiety is of a special nature as it relates not only to herself in hospital but also to her unborn baby. Anxieties about life and death centred around the survival of the baby are at their height at this time. But in the words of one woman (who was in hospital with her third pregnancy, her second having been stillborn), part of the experience can be reassuring: 'One feels very safe in hospital; it is a very comforting thing sitting there knowing that however much you hate it and you resent it and ask: "Can I go home now?" somebody is coming to feel the baby twice a day, your temperature is being taken and your blood pressure is being taken so that you're constantly being reassured that the baby is still all right . . . But it's the imprisonment that is difficult. Most conditions in pregnancy just require rest and it's the most depressing sort of thing, there's nothing specific. Even after a caesarean or something you get better every day and you think tomorrow you'll be better, but when you're sitting and you know you've got to last out for twenty-six weeks or so there is a time span which you've got to survive; you can't say: "Well in a few weeks it might be better" because you know you won't be able to go home. . . . You start

51

building a little world in the hospital after a while, and you build a terrific routine and mealtimes become fantastically important, you work the day through bit by bit. You get very involved in other people's lives.'

Coming home after a long stay in hospital to the tumult of everyday life with a newborn baby whose demands are without respite can be another shock. It is going from the extreme of being like a child to that of having to look after a child, with no transition time between the two.

CHAPTER FOUR

It's too late to change my mind, isn't it?

20 January

THE reality of a baby is getting greater for Barbara, and with it the worries and practical problems.

Barbara I had an off week; I don't know if all expectant ladies go through that, a sort of anti-babies week. I actually managed to get the energy together to change all the rooms around. I moved Peter's bits and pieces (all the toys are in his room now); got the baby's things in our room ready, and that's why I thought: Ohhhh!! It's not quite so bad now as it was. I wonder if other women get like that. I feel it's an awful shame . . . here we are, the nice routine, all is calm . . . and we're going to be getting up in the middle of the night all over again. . . . Oh well, it won't be long, I expect. I shouldn't have got everything out; if I'd put it off for another month it would have been a better idea.

I just got tired of thinking about babies, talking about babies, hearing about babies, and I'm still a bit like it now. This one particularly. Don't let's think about this one for a few days. I knew eventually I had to get the carry cot out from the loft and start getting the things together; it says really to have them ready by thirty-six weeks. I thought: I've got a fortnight, so I'd better start getting them ready now; and once I started getting the table out on which we used to put the carry cot I thought: Oh no . . . It's so lovely putting Peter to bed at seven o'clock and that's it for the night, and he comes and scrambles in with us in bed in the morning at about seven again for about half an hour and we read or mess about; and I thought: Now I'm going to have to haul myself out of bed at six o'clock, and two o'clock in the morning . . . It's too late to change my mind now, isn't it? (*laughs*) It's partly now I suppose the time is dragging; such an effort now, being down, and things are difficult. I tend to think it's so many weeks, give or take a fortnight, whereas before I used to think it's months yet. It's only getting the things ready, starting to do something about the baby, that's made me think it's this amount of time. The days go slowly. Not as slowly as they did the first time. I've got Peter to keep me busy now. Everyone says how quickly it's gone except me.

Barbara is aware of what having a young baby will mean but first-time mothers don't generally imagine beyond the delivery in any concrete way although they know theoretically that having a baby will change their lives. They wonder if they will be good mothers, but they don't often wonder how they will deal with the physical strain and sleepless nights. Specific problems are not imagined.

Barbara I went to another class and they had a breast-feeding consultant there. Everyone kept very quiet. Everyone said they were going to breast feed but there was no great enthusiasm about it from anybody. I don't know if half of them will. They just didn't seem at all keen, or perhaps they'd decided to do it and didn't think there was anything to it. Nobody asked anything, nobody discussed anything much. There was a girl called Jill and it was her second baby as well, so she and I both tended to speak about it and everyone else was very quiet.

The first-time mother is very hazy about the period after birth and her relationship with this new, unknown being. Her main concern, if she plans to breast feed, is with herself, with her body: how will she look? How will she feel about having her breasts used in this way? How does she feel about the substance which will come out of her body? Some women find the thought disgusting, like that of other excretions. Other women feel their breasts 'belong' to their husband or partner; the sensuousness of breast feeding disturbs them. The woman who never considers breast feeding and the one who is determined to breast feed rarely have problems. But many women are not so clear. Perhaps they should . . . maybe they will try – they are influenced by the advice and opinion of family, friends and medical staff. Many of these uncertain women try to breast feed but give up very soon. It takes a determined and self-confident women to persevere when faced with problems, and to go on believing that her milk *is* good and satisfying to the baby. Unconscious fears about what the baby might do to her breasts – devour, bite or destroy – combined with her own wishes as a baby may make a woman reluctant to breast feed. (Such fears are reflected in the common belief that breast feeding must stop when the baby gets a tooth.) Fears about the goodness of her breasts, the quality of her milk, make her give up her attempts. The success of breast feeding is often undermined by the very people who recommend it. One woman says: 'When my daughter was a few weeks old my health visitor told me that because very frequent feeds were being demanded, I didn't have enough milk. She then squeezed one of my breasts, looked disapproving as there was no response, and said cheerfully: "Don't worry dear, it's not because you can't breast feed your first child that you won't be able to breast feed your next one," and departed. My confidence was somewhat shaken, and I wondered if I was starving my poor child, though she was pink and plump. But I carried on and breast fed her for nine months. It had never occurred to this visitor that my breasts might not yield any milk when *she* squeezed them, or that they had recently been emptied by my daughter; or that if my daughter looked healthy she must be getting enough; or that it is possible to increase the number of feeds in order to increase the intake of milk if the mother is happy with such a regime.'

There is now evidence that women who adhere to a four-hourly schedule, as generally instructed by the hospital, often fail to breast feed because their breasts do not receive sufficient stimulation, especially in the early weeks, and that breast-fed babies require more frequent feeding than bottle-fed ones. Far from being a sign of insufficient milk, it is quite normal for a baby to require frequent feeds.

Barbara had hoped to breast feed her first baby. She found the plan was jeopardized almost immediately, partly through her own insecurity and the difficulty over taking charge of the care of her child.

Barbara I should say that out of about six (women in her class), half of them won't have bothered. Because you've got to be really keen, you've really got to put your foot down in hospital to breast feed. Well, I found this with Peter anyway. I wanted to breast feed Peter and it was entirely my decision – they said they had on my papers that I wanted to breast feed and he was being cot-nursed, and they said did I want to feed him and I said 'No', I said 'Give him a bottle. I'm too tired' – and then I just didn't have the nerve, I just didn't, to sit in hospital all undressed and have somebody come and show you how to do it . . . so I wasn't terribly keen then.

Dana You didn't feel you could ask.

Barbara How old was he then? – Six hours I suppose, and they said, 'You can either start feeding him yourself or we'll give him a bottle with some water.' And I said, 'Oh that's all right, give him a bottle,' and after that I didn't like to say 'come and draw the curtains I want to have a go.' And the time goes so quickly that it's too late. The first few feeds I thought I must ask someone, and I didn't and didn't, I put it off until it was too late. When I got home I regretted that.

Dana In hospital you didn't feel you could just pick up your baby and have a go?

Barbara If you wanted to feed, you didn't have a room you could feed in, and I didn't fancy stripping off in front of a roomful of women; and if you wanted to feed just off your own bat like that you'd have to draw your own curtains and get on with it, and I just didn't have the nerve.

Dana It shows how intimidated one gets in hospital.

Barbara They never spoke. There was one girl there who . . . we were complaining . . . not complaining but saying it's uncomfortable, and this one girl didn't even know what we were talking about, didn't realize apparently that she was going to get any feelings or different sensation when the milk started coming in. This girl just didn't know and said, 'Well it sort of gets tight and full up and it goes off quickly.' She was quite worried; she was asking the nurses if she ought to take some medicine or something – there is such a lot of ignorance – and they didn't tell her, they didn't say anything to her. But now they wouldn't get away with it so easily because I've done this once and I've got more firm ideas now. The first time you go in and you're shoved from pillar to post and you do just as you're told.

Dana Were there other people breast feeding?

Barbara One. She used to get teased. You get your one moment of decision and that's it. From then on you don't get asked again. I don't know if they can't be bothered perhaps, or they don't want to pressurize you into anything you don't really want to do, but having had it down in my notes they might have asked again. I guess they don't have time.

In hospital bottles are often brought as a matter of routine, and many women fear that they may not match up to this man-made feeder. This was Marion's experience: 'With the first child I was so uptight about the whole thing, it was all so new and I didn't know enough about breast feeding. I didn't know whether it was going right or wrong. My husband had flu and I was exhausted and it was just easier to give up. Physically I could have managed it but emotionally I couldn't cope with it. I had a great trauma of failure – I looked at it as a failure – I wouldn't now. I said with the second one, "Well I'll see when he is born; I won't make any decisions, they're both available", and I wasn't going to pin myself down. All the little booklets I'd read had said how good it was, how it is best for your child. I thought automatically how I would do it with the first child; that I could do it, that there was nothing to stop me – When he had jaundice in hospital, when . . . well things didn't run how the books said – I didn't expect anything like that.'

For Marion, being in hospital meant being under scrutiny, being put to the test. Like many other women, she felt there was great pressure to breast feed and when she didn't she felt she had failed, she was inadequate. I think there *is* pressure to breast feed, and disapproval of the woman who does not manage to do it, but at the same time everything is organized in such a way as to prevent breast feeding from being successful, for instance by the setting up of rigid timetables described on p. 23. Double pressure may well contribute to the 'blues' often experienced after the birth.

The actual decision to breast or bottle feed is influenced by a woman's own experience in infancy and by her feelings about an intimate bodily relationship. These can vary depending on the sex of the baby.

During pregnancy Lesley dreams that, after being sexually aroused, her breasts secrete a substance. Her dream depicts the sexual aspect of breast feeding and the unconscious equation between the feeding breast and the penis, both of which penetrate and link with the partner.

Barbara felt that it was more than just breast feeding that was inhibited in hospital.

Barbara The babies were there all day for you to see to, but they don't like you cuddling them. They'd wheel the bottles in at feeding-time and there was each baby's bottle with a name on. According to how old your baby is and how much it weighs there is something in the bottle, either milk or water, and there's a certain amount of it and once that's gone that's it, the baby can't have any more. That's terrible because if you've got a baby like Peter, he'd finish that lot in two gulps and then wanted to know where the rest was, and he'd start yelling as soon as the bottle was finished and they used to say, 'Oh it's wind' because he was only three or four days old, but he was so obviously hungry. They used to keep on giving me water and more water and more water and all I *got* was soaked nappies; and there's nothing you can do – you can't go and make up more feeds, you see. I felt so frustrated about the whole business. I'm lucky this time. It's a forty-eight hours delivery, and I've already told the midwife who is coming here that I definitely want to breast feed and if I'm sitting around looking at the bottles she's to tell me not to and I'm to get on with it and have a go. Because I said, 'If I have a go and don't like it, fair enough, I've tried; but don't just let me give him a bottle or her a bottle or whatever'; and she said that we'd do our damnedest to get me feeding successfully before she finished coming, which is ten days, a pretty good start.

Dana You said they didn't like you to cuddle the babies in hospital.

Barbara No, they didn't. I don't know how they put it. I couldn't hold Peter when he was first born because I was flat on my back and I think they put him in a nursery just down the corridor and took me back to the ward, and then Patrick came. It was about two in the morning and he went and had a look at him, and about four o'clock they said they would just put him in the other nursery with the other babies because he was sleeping quite well, and they picked him up and gave him to me to hold. I remember them saying: 'For Heaven's sake don't tell Sister' because they're not supposed to take them out for twenty-four hours, and I sat there feeling quite thrilled, for a little while anyway. I had about ten minutes I suppose, and then I went back to sleep and they put him in the nursery. And the next day I fed him in the cot thing which they just tip up and you stick the bottle in. They don't want them picked up. And then I went back to the ward and there you don't actually get a set lecture on it, nobody comes and says: 'You pick your baby up and feed him, burp him, change him and put him back down.' I used to sit with Peter – I couldn't put him down. But if you sat for very long, they'd say: 'You're going to have a lot of trouble when you get home.' And if the baby keeps crying then they say: 'Oh so and so's baby, why don't you put him or her into the nursery?' They don't tell you to pick him up and walk up and down and cuddle him, you see, which is the obvious thing to do, especially in hospital when you've got all the time in the world. And they say: 'You should be resting, there's nothing wrong with the baby' and so on and so on. That's what I mean; they don't actually say to you you mustn't pick the baby up. Peter and I found that 'meal times' went on for ever – as long as possible anyway.

Barbara describes vividly in this passage her insecurity with her first child in the face of experts, her inability just to be natural, her fear of being ridiculed or teased in her clumsy efforts to breast feed. But also she aptly conveys the atmosphere in postnatal wards, where indeed the norm is to leave babies in their cots except for feeding and changing. Some mothers would rather not have the baby with them all the time, and regard the constant demands of the newly born baby as impinging on their need for rest. But for those mothers who feel that a strong unity with their baby is vital the experience of a hospital ward can be upsetting.

One woman described her first birth like this: 'I was told that I held my daughter in my arms too much. One day a nurse came in while my baby was in the bed next to me (a frequent occurrence when we were both awake) and snatched her from me, telling me that I mustn't put the baby in my bed. This was two days after the birth and I was feeling quite tired and emotional and burst into tears rather than fight back. Had I been in the ward it would have been more difficult to pick the baby up again when she had gone.' When I was in hospital myself, having my first child, I rarely saw a woman holding her baby for more than a few minutes, generally at feeding-time. In fact, the whole layout of the ward was such that to do this could have been physically difficult. The beds were high and the cots low, making it impossible to pick the baby up when in bed; there were no comfortable chairs permanently next to the bed (chairs were mainly brought near to the bed for visitors), no privacy for a woman to be with her baby on her own. Such a setting makes it very difficult for a woman to learn to know her new baby intimately and may contribute to mothers' attitudes in the ward. One baby was crying desperately; reluctantly, the mother went to pick him up. The baby stopped crying instantly, to which the mother said, putting the baby back in the cot to cry: 'So that's all he wanted!' Hospitals are intimidating places. The staff feel they must run an orderly regimented unit, and in some cases, for their own personal reasons, find difficulty in allowing close mother–baby relationships. Babies are removed from the mothers part of the time, fed according to rigid timetables, and washed at set times. Implicit and explicit rules of child care are set out. It is difficult to have a close, intimate, subtle and developing relationship between mother and baby in a hospital ward. The atmosphere is very hard to fight because a woman in hospital has few rights and little power. I went to visit a friend of mine, usually a strong-minded woman, after the birth of her son, and was surprised to find her alone in her room. I inquired where the baby was, and she told me he was in the nursery because this was 'resting-time'. I conveyed my surprise that she had not asked to keep her baby with her, as I knew that had been her wish. She looked at me with near bewilderment and said: 'You think I *could* ask to keep him with me during the resting-period?' I wondered what had happened to the woman I had known before she entered the hospital. (She did keep the baby with her on subsequent days, which was possible because this was a 'progressive hospital' – but she had to ask *permission* to have *her* baby with her.)

One woman describes the hours after the birth: 'I remember feeling very strange, to have experienced the most remarkable of all things, the birth of my first child, and then to be left all alone. First they took the baby into the nursery. Then I was wheeled into my room, where my husband was able to stay and chat for a while. But he had to work the next day, so he needed some sleep. I was tired, but too excited to sleep. So there I was, alone, remembering the experience full of wonder and amazement that we had all shared. But for the next few hours we were not sharing. The hospital had separated us.'[26]

The argument given to justify removing the babies at night and for parts of the day is that the mother needs to rest. But one of the reasons it is difficult for the mother to rest is that she has to follow a rigid timetable. It is natural for the mother to sleep when the baby sleeps (whether during the day or the night), and to be awake when the baby is awake. This is not possible in hospital. My daughter had a habit of waking up many times during the night, which was tiring. Her best sleeping-time was in the morning. In the morning, however, when she and I wanted to sleep, I was ordered to take her to the nursery for washing and dressing. Then I was told I had to wake her up at specific times because this was when she ought to be hungry and the paediatrician would be coming around tomorrow and would want to know that she had been a good baby and fed at the right times. This was both tiring and unnatural.

Nothing can replace a home birth for a woman who wants an intimate relationship with her child from the beginning. Although hospitals can be improved, it is not possible to run a unit with individual timetables and the privacy of home. Women who have had a child at home will rarely have a subsequent child in hospital; they describe the relationship with this child as very special, and different from that with a child born in hospital.

Marion describes how she was able to breast feed her second child after a natural childbirth at home: 'So much was different the second time: my husband was there, and I was at home and I didn't have any drugs, and when you've had one you do feel more relaxed. I can remember when my first child was born (in hospital), he was put in a cot, one of those goldfish-bowl things, and he was at the end of the delivery bed and I thought: What if he cries, I won't know what to do, what shall I do? . . . not knowing anything, the uncertainty which wasn't there with the second child to the same extent. Having him at home, being responsible for him from the moment he was born – in hospital I didn't feel responsible, there was always somebody who'd take over, the so-called professionals who were there to do it, whereas with him the midwife left at three and we were on our own. They came in every day but not on the same basis. It was much more natural to breast feed because one was at home. It was much more natural to feed him when he cried than to go and get a bottle.'

It must be added, though, that women who choose to have a home birth generally have a supportive and helpful home environment, and feel confident in themselves. Few first-time mothers, even if they have the support, feel confident enough.

During pregnancy women are hypersensitive to their physical selves. They are preoccupied with what they should or should not eat, with their weight gain, with the changes in their skin, hair, bodily secretions. Every sign is scrutinized for what it might reveal about the baby and about the woman's own body as a suitable or unsuitable container for the baby. She strokes her abdomen, feeling the shape of the baby, or enters into private conversation with her baby. This continuous double interaction with outside and with inside worlds characterizes pregnancy.

While drawing herself, Barbara describes her feelings about her body.

Barbara I just feel more and more huge . . . it's past the stage of trying to cover it up.
Dana Do you think that being pregnant is ugly?
Barbara Not now, no. To start off with I did; but when I was depressed I felt very different from how I feel now. I felt everything was wrong then. I think it embarrasses other people more now. People tend to be careful . . . how should I

say? . . . perhaps people are naturally more considerate when pregnant women are around. I feel as though everything is so stretched and so tight and so big that it's quite surprising to me. I'm trying to draw me feeling really physically big; I feel every part of my skin is stretched almost as far as it can go. I feel not so much 'baby and me' because I've got past that being so new; that doesn't mean that I've lost the conception that there's two of us: I still think of this person and me, and even more now this one as being separate because I'm getting all the things ready for it and it seems so funny to think of a little one again. This is the feeling, so tight and so big, but I can't draw a baby like I imagine mine's going to be. I would only draw one like Peter. If I could draw I would draw a little Peter upside down here. Last time I'd definitely have drawn a . . . how do you draw a boy or a girl, they look so alike when they're little? . . . but the only thing that's changing is that I absolutely don't know which sex it is. I've been wavering all the week now about it being a little girl, I don't know why. I came home from hospital Friday . . . I don't call it Christopher any more . . . it just suddenly changed. All these months I've been sure it's a boy. I'm not quite sure it's a girl now but I'm not so positive that it's a boy.

Perhaps I feel more of a mess in a way; my complexion has completely gone to pot this week. I feel . . . not ugly, just . . . I spend all the day in various shades of pink and red. I know when you're pregnant you're supposed to look all beautiful and in bloom but I didn't get it. So I don't draw a nice neat and tidy me. I don't look in the mirror and think: 'Oh no!' now, which is odd because now is the time when you really might think it, isn't it?

27 January

Barbara's experience of doctors is very negative. She complains that they don't listen to her and don't answer her questions. She says: 'I think they gang up against you; there is a complete wall of silence, isn't there?' I suggest that often they do not know the answer. She has never thought about this possibility, so much has she expected and hoped for them to be all knowing and powerful.

She does a drawing of herself:

Barbara You know we were talking about different concepts. . . . For weeks I just thought of *me* pregnant, singular, and it's since I've started going to the National Childbirth Trust classes that I thought I do rather feel there is me and somebody else; so I thought I would draw me in the middle and one National Health Service lot on one side, and all the other people that have been more help on the other. Me very large in the middle. Perhaps other pregnant women don't feel as alone as I did when I first started – it was a terrible feeling; I was going from one place to another trying to find reassurance. At our clinic classes . . . after they'd all finished I waited till all of the first-time ones – I didn't want to sit there and say 'I'm petrified' when they all keep turning to me and saying 'What is it like?' – after they'd gone I said to her: 'To tell you the truth I'm really frightened, there's no other way to describe how I feel.' I shan't be at all relaxed when I go into labour because I'm just expecting it to be a dreadful experience. So I said 'I'm really frightened' and she said 'What of?' and I couldn't put my finger on it exactly and I said something about being induced. She seized on that and said 'Don't worry about that, we don't do that so much these days, dear,' and that was that.

Dana You feel she tried to get rid of you.

Barbara 'Don't worry,' everything is 'Don't worry.' When I was about four months pregnant I was at the antenatal with our doctors, and the regional health visitor came around and said 'Is everything OK?' and I said then 'I've got no clinical problems at all but I'm really worried about delivery,' and she said 'Well if you're still worried nearer the time we'll tell the hospital and they'll be extra kind.' I said 'I've got no complaints about the hospital being cruel at all!' Nobody understood . . . After you've had that sort of experience you give up, quite honestly, and you think: Well you've just got to put up with it and hope for the best.

Dana What was the worst aspect of the first birth?

Barbara The feeling of being helpless [she had to lie there with a drip in her arm, unable to move for hours on end]. Those hospital classes were useless. I already knew how to put a nappy on before I went there. Perhaps they think they have to run classes for expectant mothers and they have to visit for ten days afterwards and that's it, beyond that there's no responsibility at all.

Dana I think people are afraid of other people's fears. They don't want even to listen to what you've got to say; they don't want to hear.

Barbara A lot of women, especially first-time labours, go into it thinking they're going to sail through it without any effort at all, and it doesn't seem to happen very often, does it? I don't know very many women that can just say, 'Oh well, I didn't know I was having a baby.'

Dana But one of the problems is also one of information. As you said, some people don't know that it is likely to last a long time; no wonder it's going to appear particularly dreadful.

Barbara There's a wall of silence in hospitals. When I had Peter, the other girl in the next bed (she was induced at the same time) . . . we were lying there chatting and suddenly she called the nurse and said she felt quite peculiar and she must have been in transition stage by then . . . she looked a bit worried during the afternoon, and they whisked her up to delivery and I said to the nurse 'Was that quick and how much longer will it go on now?' and she said 'Oh we'll have to get a doctor to examine you dear . . .' You see, just pass it on, don't directly answer. . . . And when he came he said that there was very little dilation at all and it would be hours yet and it's just . . . you know there's no . . . I don't know the words for it, support I suppose. I wanted to know why I wasn't dilating and they couldn't tell me why. The doctor said the contractions were lovely from their point of view, the contractions were lovely, they were nice, strong, regular contractions which should be working.

You asked me what was the worst part, it was feeling helpless; at least this time I can try the breathing, even if I find it is only of limited help it's something to do.

Helplessness is not an uncommon feeling during pregnancy as well as during the birth. Helene Deutsch puts it as follows: 'This knowledge of an event that will happen on a certain date upon which one depends, and which nevertheless one cannot influence, this mixture of power and submission, has something fatal and inevitable about it, like death.'[27] There is no going backwards or backing out of the situation or even slowing down the regular and inevitable progress towards labour. 'Last night its kicking made me dizzy and gave me a terrible feeling of solitude. I wanted to tell it stop, stop, stop, let me alone. I want to lie still and whole and all single, catch my breath. But I have no control over this new part of my being, and this lack of control scares me. I felt as if I were rushing downhill at such a great speed that I'd never be able to stop.'[28]

Not all women find this lack of control distressing. Hermione Demoriane enjoys the feeling of abandon: 'My body has taken over my life. It is no longer mine. I am on a lead to it and must follow where it goes. I feel passive, acted upon, invulnerable, voluptuous. I could walk from here to Chelsea blindfold. The Magical Mystery Tour is waiting to take me away. I am glad.'[29]

A woman can only happily give in to this feeling of abandon in pregnancy and childbirth if she can trust herself and people around her. Basic trust stems from her experience of being cared for as a helpless baby and as a child. Her feelings about her mother, coloured by this experience and by her capacity to modify the relationship between them during pregnancy, are crucial. If her mother is not available, in reality or psychologically, other women or her partner can be used to represent a good mother. But the importance of the actual environment in childbirth cannot be minimized. Childbirth is the only intimate situation which it is taken for granted will take place amongst strangers and with little concern for the mother's wish for privacy, intimacy or affection.

The now common practice of partners being present at the birth is a move in the right direction, but often it is just a question of men being tolerated there and asked to leave if there is any technical intervention to be made. And not all men wish to participate. Barbara's husband refuses to attend the antenatal classes and has mixed feelings about being present at the birth:

Barbara He hasn't got anything against being there for the sake of it, but he's worried that it's going to be a very gory experience that's going to make him feel ill.

Dana Have you seen a film of a birth as part of your classes?

Barbara They had one for the previous course. I saw one at the clinic, and they did show it for husbands one evening and I think that about two turned up . . . *that* would finish him! If he saw that film that would be it; he wouldn't go because they showed it from this end of the bed (the bottom) and actually you don't see it from that end, the delivery of the baby; from your point of view you can't see everything that's happening.

Dana Some men find the films reassuring; it's not as bad as they imagined.

Barbara On TV about a month ago . . . it was only in black and white, no glorious technicolour . . . there was the same thing that I'd seen. I said to Patrick, 'Oh dear,' thinking Here we go. He didn't say very much and he didn't say 'Oh my goodness' or 'Oh how dreadful' . . . so . . . I don't know. I'll tell you something that did occur to me – at this hospital they're terribly keen on sending people out as soon as there's the slightest . . . if there's forceps or anything . . . and I thought 'I'm almost bound to have some stitches, am I not?' because I had them before. If they're going to cut, wouldn't they send him out?

Although Barbara says that her husband would not like to be present at the birth, it sounds to me as if *she* was not so sure that she wanted him there; that perhaps *she* feared it would be too gory and messy. She rather seemed to be hoping that 'they' would send him out. Some women feel that childbirth is undignified or unladylike and they would rather set about it in private; that their genitals must not be exposed in this way; that their behaviour must always be controlled and composed; that their husbands will be revolted with their body and will no longer desire them sexually if they see them in childbirth.

Barbara I influenced him a lot because after I had Peter I said 'Well, thank goodness you weren't there for that,' because he definitely wanted to be there for the whole thing with Peter, and then, one thing and another, he wasn't there at all because he had an accident, and I said 'It's just as well because I wouldn't really have wanted you there for that.' He couldn't have been there, it was in the operating theatre.

Most fathers who have been present at the birth talk about it as a very welcome and exciting experience, however. One study of a hundred fathers present at birth found that ninety-three of them said they would like to be present at the next birth.[30] There is the occasional man who finds the experience disturbing (perhaps especially when he is not able to help and feels himself to be only an onlooker), but most find it disturbing *not* to be there. Presence at the birth also helps a man to feel that it really is his baby, and that he can be the first to greet his child as he/she emerges into the world, after all those months of pregnancy when he was an outsider.

CHAPTER FIVE

It's a funny shape

FEARS and fantasies about what is going on inside the body are frequent at all stages of pregnancy. Lesley worries because she cannot feel all the baby's limbs; Susan about the jerky, rhythmic 'spastic' movements; Kate about the very long periods of immobility, while Marion feels angry and trapped when the baby kicks her to the point of pain.

Every detail of a woman's body takes on a great significance to her, and she worries about everything that she thinks is strange. Does this mean something is wrong with the baby, with the baby's shape or state; does this mean her body is not functioning properly? At this stage there is no real separation between fears about her body and fears about the baby; they are part of one whole: the baby is a part of her body.

Barbara I did read that the advantage of a vacuum extraction is that you can use it before the cervix is fully dilated, which is what they did. But I don't know if they actually cut the cervix or just pushed it back. Mine does seem particularly lopsided instead of being regular; it has a peculiar shape now. Still I dare say if I ask someone they'll just hedge around the subject. I just don't know what they did with it. I've asked and asked. I asked my own doctor, the midwife, the health visitor and the midwife at hospital. When I was eighteen weeks pregnant I went to my own doctor for an antenatal, and you could feel as this lump is growing it was this shape inside (higher on one side), and always the baby lay here because there was the most room. My doctor said he thought it was twins; well, I didn't think so, but he said he could feel so much . . . it was so high up here, you see (on one side) . . . and then the midwives both had a go, and he said 'No, it's the uterus that's a different shape', it's got a corner, and he said probably when it's little it just goes round like this; it probably just goes up in a little bump, and it's like a balloon when you get more pregnant, it goes up more and more . . . now it takes up the whole space and the corner has gone round here (side), so I get kicks under the rib here and it comes up the front here . . . I can still feel the shape of it and I've asked if it will make any difference in labour; if something completely round will give a better push, if you like, or pull, than something that is irregularly shaped; and no one will say a word. In fact at hospital when I said it's a funny shape – and especially when I have a contraction you can see it, it's not an oval or circular at all – she said, 'It's just the way the baby is lying, dear' . . . Oh I thought nobody would tell me!

Dana I can vaguely remember with me there was one side higher than the other.

Barbara Really? With Peter he was always regularly in the middle.

Dana I can remember it was a corner.

Barbara That's right, this one's the same; he came up this side and then having run out of room, it ran there (side). This side is always stretched much more. Oh well, thank goodness somebody else . . . and it made no difference in the end? The uterus functioned just as efficiently, being that shape?

Dana Well, I didn't have any problems anyway.

As is the case with Barbara, the present pregnancy is often compared with the previous ones. Anything which is different is considered suspect or, if there were complications or a miscarriage or abnormalities before, it is the similar signs which are suspect. If the first baby was late, the next one will be expected to be late.

Barbara felt her body had been irreparably damaged during childbirth. Such a fear is especially common in women who have had an abortion and who also fear that they will be punished by having a deformed baby. One study found that women who had had abortions were more often depressed and anxious than other women during pregnancy (which was not the case with women who had had miscarriages).[31]

Previous good experiences are not necessarily taken as a positive sign. Susan worries about her third child because she is much older now, but also: 'I guess it's partly superstitious. I've had two healthy children, a boy and a girl, and I feel I'm pushing my luck.'

In a first pregnancy, the comparisons a woman makes will be with her mother and sisters (though even with later pregnancies comparisons will be with her mother's subsequent pregnancies). It is almost invariable for a woman whose mother has had very difficult pregnancies or childbirths to fear that she must be the same, and that if she has had a younger brother or sister who was stillborn or born with a defect she has no right to a healthy baby.

We see again in the previous conversation how Barbara assumes that the medical staff know all the answers; that, although they know, they will not tell her and that they can predict what sort of labour she will have. She thinks she is the only one to be left in the dark, afraid of the mysteriousness of her body. Barbara described earlier (pp. 64–5) her terror of being helpless. Her need to think that somebody, somewhere, must know the answer may be her way of avoiding this feeling of helplessness and her wish for a powerful all-knowing figure who will take over and make everything safe for her. This image is a mixed blessing. On the one hand she believes that the doctors possess all the knowledge, which relieves her sense of helplessness in the face of unknown and unforeseeable bodily events, but on the other hand she resents it when they take over and she is then made to feel helpless again at their interference.

How a woman feels about being passive or active, in control or totally dependent, in charge of herself or in the hands of an all-knowing expert, and how she feels about her body processes (confident or intolerably helpless and frightened), will largely determine the kind of labour she will seek and appreciate. If she cannot accept being taken care of, she may wish to be totally desensitized and unaware, so that things can just be done to her, or on the contrary, she may feel that she has to give birth absolutely by herself without human or non-human assistance of any sort. Opposite reasons can make different women opt for a particular sort of childbirth. One woman wants a childbirth in full consciousness, using psychoprophylaxis,* because she feels this

---

*Psychoprophylaxis: method of preparation for childbirth involving using the mind to prevent excessive pain.

is most natural; one because she cannot bear somebody taking over her body; another because she cannot bear to be looked after; another still because she is afraid of what might happen to her or be done to her if she should lose consciousness, and yet another because she fears she will lose control and make a fool of herself under the influence of drugs. Similarly one woman will ask for an epidural and forceps because she feels there is no need for her to suffer in childbirth; one because she is terrified of her body processes; another because she fears losing control, or because she feels the experts can do it better than herself, and yet another because she is afraid of pain and the unpredictable.

4 *February*

Barbara is now thirty-six weeks pregnant. She is beginning to feel the weight of the baby.

Barbara With this baby I'm much more uncomfortable than I ever was with the first. My ribs ached for a while and seemed to have opened up and made room. This time . . . perhaps it's because my abdomen isn't so strong this time: I can't actually lift it in very much; it makes my back ache a lot more than before in this pregnancy or with Peter; but I can't grumble, I've had a lovely time until now.

I've tended to sit down more because I noticed at the weekend I seem to get little bits of swelling in the ankle and I thought: Feet up in the air before anyone sees that. That's the difference in a week: last Wednesday I went into Birmingham shopping, and I could do up one of my jackets that I've been wearing and now I can't – when I stand up, I used to have a controllable lump at the front and now, it's almost a central part of me; it's really heavy. I'm sure it's going to be a great big baby – nine pounds or something like that! I can't remember this part last time. I can remember up to thirty-two weeks. But I can remember going out the weekend Peter was due, not feeling terribly huge. I was with friends going out, now I'd rather not . . . it sits on my lap, this one; it really is enormous. I don't think it could turn round now if it wanted to, it's jammed up under here (the ribs) and up under here (her side) and everywhere . . . it must be pretty big. I spend so much of my time leaning back to give it room. I don't know which is worse, when I stand up and it aches under here, or I lie down and it comes back here and my cup of coffee decides there isn't room for that then. All through this pregnancy I haven't felt as big as last time – and now – Oh, now it seems to have suddenly grown.

Women distance themselves from their bodies when they are pregnant. They often describe their body as if it were an object, not really part of themselves, or as if it had a life of its own. They point to parts of their abdomen in a way they would never dream of doing if they were not pregnant. It is 'me' and at the same time 'not me'. Other people too feel they have a right to stroke the pregnant woman's abdomen and talk about her body.

In her bath a woman watches with fascination the moving bumps. She touches the fleeting limbs and talks to her baby. It is both her body and not her body, inside her and yet not her. What is this peculiar bump which sticks out of the water? No, she is not just bloated and fat, it is moving, expanding in all directions like an amoeba. And it punches and kicks. It hurts. She thinks: 'Wait till I get you, you little rascal. . . . But will you ever come out? How can such a huge lump get out of such a small opening? It will surely rip me to bits, I mustn't let that happen. Stay inside for ever! But then I will just grow and grow until I burst. You had better come out. But how will it happen? Does my body just decide to push the baby out, evict it from its cosy habitation, or does the baby decide it's had enough, it wants to see the world and be set free? And where will it happen? Will the waters break one day in a crowded shop? If I asked to be induced, wouldn't it be safer? I could go into the hospital calmly, prepared, no embarrassments, no surprise. But perhaps I want the surprise, the romantic mystery, the drama of the unexpected and unpredictable. I am not a machine.'

Barbara I have on the top of my suitcase the ambulance number and everything like that and I honestly don't believe it's going to be that sort of hurry. Peter was so long, I can't believe it's going to be so quick. I should be so lucky! My mother is so worried about this baby. Already she is telling me to get plenty of tuppences, and have I got the number of a taxi – I haven't.

(*Laughs*.) I'm sure it won't be such a rush. She's getting quite concerned. There's another month yet! Oh dear! I said to my mother, 'I shall probably wake up in the morning or afternoon or evening, and there'll be plenty of time for Patrick to come home from work; we'll probably be able to go to bed for the night before it arrives; I don't expect to have to say, "Oh cut the dinner" and rush off.

A friend of mine started at home, and very early on she went to hospital because she thought she was starting, and I'll bet you anything within five minutes she was full up with drugs. That's half the trouble . . . they put you on a drip then. What worries me if I go in a little bit too early is that they're going to go sticking needles in me.

Dana Yes, I reckon that many labours start very, very slowly, with contractions on and off sometimes for days; in fact it is arbitrary what is called the beginning, but if you're very worried you go into hospital, and they don't want you hanging around for three days so they put you on a drip. But it may be much better and more normal for things to progress on their own very slowly, and if a woman isn't worried and can deal with the contractions this is no problem.

Barbara If I could manage it at home I would, I really would; but I'm worried that if I should deliberately stay at home then something might go wrong. I wouldn't do that, but I shall wait until I'm really going strong. My friend up the road, she was off and on in labour, she had contractions for a day and then during the night they became quite strong, and she went in in the morning and the contractions stopped . . . and she was put straight on to a drip. One of the girls at the class said she absolutely quails before hospitals and doctors, and she wants her husband there to do all the fighting for her (she also doesn't want to be induced). I'm the same, I tend not to argue. That's why I shall leave it so late I shan't be in a position to argue; I hope it will be straightforward then.

Like many women Barbara would choose to have her baby at home if she thought this could be done safely. For many women the choice is not open because of the present policy in favour of hospital confinements. When the choice *is* open (when she can find a sympathetic doctor, and she has had no complications in previous labour), a certain amount of conviction, confidence and determination is required of a woman before she chooses a home birth, because she feels a hospital confinement is the safer of the two. A point generally omitted is that errors, omissions and unnecessary standardized procedures are more likely when a woman becomes part of an institutional setting with its greater diffusion of responsibility. Also, a woman having her baby in the familiar and natural surroundings of her home requires fewer drugs, and is certainly offered fewer drugs. Jill Tweedie draws attention to the confusion between normal and abnormal in the area of childbirth: 'Is this then, the dilemma? Either go to hospital to have your baby; feel frightened, isolated, or, at best, dependent; endure all the solutions to problems the hospital itself creates but at least feel you have done everything for your baby that doctors tell you you should? Or stay at home, give birth among familiar faces in the way that seems best to you, have a joyful and memorable experience but risk a sudden emergency that may end in death? Personally, I think we have stood the problem on its head, that normal delivery has been ignored in the concentration upon the abnormal.' And she quotes Dr William Silverman as saying: 'With both birth and death, we face the question of how far we are willing to go from the natural process just to protect us from risk. The agonising experience of having to make difficult decisions is part of life. The whole quality of life today is interfered with because we attempt to avoid experiencing parts of life and to lay down blanket rules about what is and what is not an acceptable risk. I think the price that has been paid for attempting to avoid all risk is a dehumanised birth.'[32]

In the present climate a woman even fears that she will be punished by something going wrong for choosing to have her baby at home – imagining a parent/doctor-figure saying 'I told you you couldn't do it on your own.'

If childbirth were thought of as a normal process in which there are some exceptional cases requiring obstetrical interventions and sometimes hospitalization, home births would at the same time become safer (through greater emphasis being put on the training of district midwives and doctors).*

This is not to say that all women would welcome a home birth;

for some women and some families it is important to separate this frightening experience with its messy and powerfully emotional aspects from the setting of the home; the stay in hospital after the birth can also be a valued respite from the drudge of the daily routine and unending tasks, and an opportunity to be looked after rather than have to cope with the needs of the family. On the other hand a woman may feel better looked after at home, in an emotional sense, by the midwife and the doctor she may have known for a long time. In hospital the staff is always changing and there is rarely a continuing relationship with a member of staff who will have known her for any length of time. I still think very fondly of Mrs Jones, the midwife who looked after me when my second baby was born at home and who listened to me without imposing her ideas, but I have no recollection of the names or the appearances of the many midwives and nurses who came into my room when I was in hospital with my first baby.

Whether or not a home birth is possible will ultimately depend on the partner's feelings (conscious and unconscious) and the atmosphere in the home.

---

*A leaflet on home births written by Sheila Kitzinger suggests that good reasons for having a hospital birth are: *toxaemia of pregnancy* (the signs of which are raised blood pressure, protein in the urine, and water retention in the tissues), *breech birth* (bottom-first position of the baby), *a previous complicated birth* (especially a caesarean section or a birth followed by a lot of bleeding), *a premature birth* (more than three weeks early), or *placenta praevia* (the placenta lying in the lower part of the uterus).

CHAPTER SIX

Just given up, just standing there waiting

18 February

BARBARA The hospital will love me, I finally did it; they examined me because the head was engaged, they called another midwife and said 'What do you think of this?' and nobody would tell me anything. It's just the same, they never will discuss it with you. It's unusual, isn't it, from what I've read? Well, they said it's definitely engaged . . . no answer, you see, then. . . . Oh I've forgotten what I was going to say, I'm like this all the time. A lot of women I've spoken to have found that with the second pregnancy they got much more . . . they call it amnesia, don't they. . .?

Dana When you can't remember things?

Barbara Yes, when you can't remember anything, you can't concentrate. I think it's because you have a first one: it's a defence mechanism a lot of the time; you just can't concentrate all the time.

Dana You said you'd won.

Barbara Yes, they don't want to see me again till 14 March, so that's nine days grace, they can't possibly get me in before then. They think I should be four days late then – it will actually be nine. It does actually give me a few extra days to start on my own. Also I told them about the natural childbirth classes. Well, it wasn't greeted with a great deal of enthusiasm. I told Patrick he will have to fight for me and he is quite prepared to do it.

I wrote in my diary the day that the baby engaged was the 9th, a week ago Sunday. I was getting very bad indigestion and I was really fed up with it, and I couldn't stand up because it ached, and I couldn't sit down because I got indigestion. Walking around made me tired. Then on Sunday it was just like a miraculous cure. It was suddenly out here (low down), but it felt so much better and Patrick said it looked very much lower. I look a lot bigger, a lot lower down, so that must have been it. I was very excited because I thought the baby would arrive. In the books it says that second babies don't usually engage till term or the beginning of labour. But nothing happened so the excitement subsided. On Sunday I had strong contractions every twenty minutes for about four hours, but I didn't take it seriously; Patrick did, though.

Barbara seemed much more subdued to me, more resigned. Although she said she was very impatient and expectant it felt to me more as if she was in a timeless state, a state with no real progression: there to stay. I was struck by her drawing:

Barbara   The other drawings are all probably trying to say something and that one's just given up: just standing there waiting, that's all. In the others I felt something; now I'm past anything. (*Laughs*)

Dana   It seems more solid, more one piece. You look very determined here – because on the one hand you're just waiting, but you look as if you're waiting in a very determined fashion – that's what comes across. I don't know if it's purposeful or accidental.

Barbara   Well, I rather feel that it's my husband and I against the rest of the establishment.

Dana   That's what it looks like. It really looks as if you're saying 'I'm here.' You're not hiding, here. You look like someone who is saying you're not going to let yourself be . . .

Barbara   Pushed around.

Dana   Yes, pushed around. Also the pregnancy is not . . .

Barbara   It's not the main thing in the picture, is it?

Dana   Well, it's there, but it comes across more as the whole thing, as opposed to just the pregnancy. [I felt she was putting herself forward as important, not to be dismissed.]

Barbara   I'm quite expecting it to be late.

Dana   You seem less worried than you did.

Barbara   Oh yes, the classes . . . I felt better as soon as I went there. I do still have moments of panic when I think: Oh, supposing it all goes wrong, and they do suddenly say: 'We're going to induce you' and that's it. Last time I was quite confident, quite cocky, that's the only word for it. I went to antenatal classes, and everything you are taught is: 'Don't believe everything you hear'; if you relax it won't be unbearable, nobody is going to let you go through anything that is absolutely awful,' and I just put all my trust and everything into the doctors at the hospital. They could have done just what they liked and I'd have . . . I let them. I was trying to explain to the midwife at the hospital about the classes I go to. I told her I was going to do the breathing. She said 'Fair enough . . .' ('Ha! ha!' – you could almost hear it.) She said did I have my last baby there and I said Yes and she said did I feel cheated because I'd had an induced birth and an epidural. That's not the feeling at all, but I can't explain how I feel about that. She was saying a lot of women feel if they haven't started on their own they haven't experienced childbirth; but it isn't that; I feel I experienced it, I just don't want *that* experience again, thank you.

Some women have an idea of the kind of labour they feel they ought to have. They set themselves high standards. They must 'do it well', or they must not have drugs, or they must not scream, or they must do it alone without their husband. For Barbara the question is, can she rely on her husband or is it safest to be independent?

Barbara I'm more dependent on my husband but that's probably because he is more forthcoming towards me, so I tend to rely on him more. The first time I wanted to do the whole thing on my own.
Dana Do you find it difficult to take help from other people?
Barbara Support? I did before but not so much now. It always seemed, you see, without sounding self-pitying I hope, that it was rather a risky thing to do, to rely on people, because you get let down at the last minute. In actual fact that's just what happened. If I'd relied on Patrick, he wasn't there just when I needed him, but this time I keep saying 'Don't have an accident or anything.'
Dana Now you want him there.
Barbara Yes.

Dana You didn't before?

Barbara No, not really. But I thought he'd get cross if I became unreasonable, and last time when I was in labour I remember feeling quite cross with people that were visiting. In the end I said to the nurses: 'Will you please tell visitors that I don't want to see anyone.'

As well as feeling cross with visitors we can guess that Barbara was cross with her husband the first time for letting her down. This may well have increased the displeasure she experienced. I wondered if she feared that this bottled-up anger could come out during the coming labour, and thus felt the need to deny the anger in advance. 'I said to Patrick, "I'm liable to get quite unreasonable and tell you to go away. Don't take any notice." '

At the same time Barbara feels that her relationship with her husband has changed during this second pregnancy:

Barbara You see, before, Patrick and I were getting so far apart that I couldn't say that to him; the whole relationship has changed such a lot the last few months. I don't know why. It's annoying that I don't know why. It's since I've become so obviously pregnant, and the other day he said up until now I haven't put on any weight except on this big lump on the front. He said once I've had the baby it shouldn't be too bad to get back into my clothes again. So I said, 'I don't know; I was all right until about now; now I'm really starting to spread.' But he said, 'No, it's mostly hanging on the front. I shall watch you afterwards.' And I wondered if maybe he thinks I'm not attractive to anybody else, perhaps he's jealous in a way, perhaps he's . . . I don't know.

Dana So when you're pregnant he's not jealous.

Barbara He needn't worry. But I don't give him anything to worry about. Gracious, I take it for granted that he's not going to go off with other women, and I expect him to do the same for me; but perhaps he doesn't, perhaps he does think that I'm here all day on my own. But now he's saying to me 'Don't eat too much and don't drink too much, don't have lots of salt or lots of sugar, because I want you nice and slim again afterwards.' One thing conflicts with the other all the time. I shan't know until afterwards. I shall be heartbroken if it all starts again. I'm hoping that the last few months have given him enough confidence to carry on in the same way, because he likes it that I'm not so independent. I've always been very independent. I do everything for myself. My next-door neighbour was talking to me Sunday and she said, 'If you need any shopping or anything, then let me know,' and I said, 'OK thank you' and just left it at that, because if I wanted I wouldn't ask anyone to do shopping. I'm quite capable of walking down to the shops. But if there's anybody that's going to do it, I'd ask Patrick now, and he likes it that I ask him. He says: 'If you want anything done don't ask anybody else, ask me.'

Dana So maybe he's quite pleased that *you want* him to be there at the birth.

Barbara Yes. Whatever's changed him, I think it's wonderful, whatever's done it. Oh, it's not as if life is one huge bowl of roses; life is just normal now. We still disagree and we still have a fight about things occasionally, but not very often, and he's not moody and miserable like he was.

One study of sixty couples expecting a first baby[33] found that there was an indication of improved husband–wife relationship during pregnancy in most cases, the couple drawing closer as they shared in planning the future, and supporting each other at times of anxiety. At the same time, though, there was a tendency for the woman to shut her husband out of her inner preoccupations and for the husband to leave his wife to her own resources to deal with her conflicting feelings. The way the husband responded to her, and to her pregnancy, did not seem to affect the way the woman adapted to the pregnancy. After the birth of the baby, however, there was a connection between the woman's acceptance of the maternal role and accommodation to the baby and the quality of her relationship with her husband. It was also found that in many families the relationship between husband and wife deteriorated in the postnatal period 'doubtless due to the strain of trying to adapt to the infant's needs and to the unfamiliar roles of mother and father'.

Not all couples, of course, become closer during pregnancy and further apart postnatally. Lina finds that her husband withdraws during her pregnancy and she feels she has to support him as well as deal with her own conflicting feelings. She resents this and yearns for more tenderness.

Reactions of detachment in men during their wives' pregnancies can relate to their envy of the woman who is able to create a baby in her body and to their jealousy and exclusion from the 'perfect' prenatal union. In turn the woman feels unloved and abandoned at the time when she most needs support. Such feedback reactions can appear incomprehensible to the couple. Some men are so unable to tolerate their wives' involvement with the baby during pregnancy that they choose this time to leave or to enter into relationships with other women, as retaliation; or they become angry and rejecting.

During pregnancy there is also often a decrease in sexual activity, with one or both partners being afraid of harming the baby. Such fears are increased by the negative feelings which always exist in conjunction with the positive ones. Sometimes there is uneasiness at having intercourse 'in the presence of the baby'. Some women become temporarily frigid; but others on the contrary feel more sensual during pregnancy.

In the latter months of her third pregnancy, Susan describes how she feels: 'Not very interested in sex now. I feel much more a mother, a mother-figure, than a wife-figure or sex-figure at the moment. The other two pregnancies I wasn't interested in sex at all from the moment I knew I was expecting them; but this one – whether it's being with another man or what, I don't know – this time I was still very interested in sex at the beginning. It increased it if anything, but now I find . . . I think maybe if he didn't go to work all day . . . The trouble is you tend to meet in bed at night when you're feeling tired and fat and everything . . . When I make love I like to be thoroughly absorbed in it, and I find suddenly the baby starts moving or kicking or something like that, and it takes your mind away; you think again about that, and I find I'm very easily distracted although I still enjoy it at times, whereas before I felt I just didn't want to know at all. It must be difficult if you've got a husband that doesn't understand, or finds it difficult to cope with, himself. I felt slightly guilty at first or slightly wishing it wasn't so but now I don't. Or if you had a husband that demanded it as such . . . I miss it in a sense, I feel very close to Robert and I wish that I could express it physically more often, because I feel exceptionally close to him.'

A single woman says: 'I felt very ambivalent about making love. I had miscarried several times. I wanted to make love and I was scared to make love. As a single woman it was hard to find men who found me attractive with my belly so big. I had no sexual contact at all the last two months.'[34]

Lesley during her first pregnancy becomes particularly aware of her pelvic area and finds that being pregnant is almost like a 'permanent coitus'. Psychoanalysts have described how pregnancy can have the unconscious significance of possessing a penis, the permanent coitus Lesley talks about. Lesley, who is not formally married, also becomes aware of feeling tied down to her partner with the coming birth of the child. In the last months of her pregnancy she dreams of former boy friends, one whom she gives in to, another whose advances she turns down – because, she says to him, 'I'm going to be a mother now.'

Another woman says: 'If pregnancy meant anything, it meant being married. I no longer felt it was easy to get out. It was like a seal on the marriage.'[35] And with such feelings can come painful doubts about the relationship; doubts the woman may hardly dare admit to herself, with a baby on the way.

Similar doubts are present in the man who finds his relationship threatened by the mixed feelings he harbours towards his wife in her new condition. His feelings about her pregnant body can vary from enthralment to disgust: 'Sometimes I thought you were very beautiful and your belly was beautiful. And sometimes you looked like a ridiculous pregnant insect. Your navel bulging out looked strange.'[36]

Some women fear such a loss of attractiveness during pregnancy, and permanent body-changes after the birth of the baby. The birth of a first child symbolizes the passage from childhood to adulthood. In our society, where youth in women is so much prized, having a baby can be experienced as the beginning of the decline, the beginning of 'getting old'. In the fifth month of her pregnancy, Lesley has the following dream: 'I dreamt of a pregnant woman, but it was a caricature; she was little with a huge round stomach and huge breasts pointing out with very long nipples. Later in the night I dreamt that I was looking old and thinking that my husband was finding me very old-looking.' She enjoys sex less now that she is pregnant, and feels the baby is robbing her of youth and sexuality. She fears her baby will sap her energy as she fears she has sapped her mother's in the past. And what if she were to have twins? she thinks to herself with horror; that would be more that she could possibly cope with.

While one woman enjoys her pregnant body, another makes every effort to hide it. One feels creative and full of life, another fat and ungainly. One stands straight and proud; another slouches miserably. For most women all these feelings are mixed together.

Susan, in her third pregnancy, says: 'I feel as if my body takes the wear and tear of it a bit . . . every baby you have, you're never so young again afterwards . . . but I don't mind, it's worth it. I haven't got good veins and I know they get worse all the time. I sometimes feel it would be lovely to feel slim and energetic, to be able to move quickly again and to feel that the real you is still there underneath the bulge somehow; but on the other hand you feel a certain loss when you've had the baby . . . you feel empty, somehow. A friend of mine said: "If I thought I was pregnant again I'd die; I couldn't go through that again." But I can't imagine, you know I'd really have to have four, five or six before I thought that.'

Lesley, five months pregnant, notices a man looking at her: 'Is he looking at me because he finds me attractive and he hasn't noticed I'm pregnant, or is he looking at me because I'm pregnant? Maybe he finds me attractive *and* pregnant. That hadn't occurred to me before . . . one is so used to separating mother-hood from sexuality.'

The breasts become focal in a woman's awareness of her body. One woman is pleased that her breasts become rounder during pregnancy; another hates this new expansion, which she is determined to conceal. Feelings about a new aspect of her breasts emerge: for the first time the breasts will become functional. In her second month of pregnancy Lesley has the following dream: 'A little girl wanted to suck my breast but I couldn't do it. I had no milk because I hadn't had a baby yet. But I had very big breasts like a wet nurse I saw recently in a film.' And the next month: 'I was having a sexual relationship with a woman and I touched one of her breasts which became erect. When I woke up I was struck by the penis-like quality of the breast.' This last dream reflects again the unconscious connection between breast and penis.

Whether all these tremendous bodily changes fill her with awe or fear, pride or shame, each woman has to integrate and come to terms with them if the pregnancy is to run well.

CHAPTER SEVEN

Really miserable

28 February

BARBARA has just finished her series of classes. She is feeling somewhat depressed. The ending of the classes before the birth of the child can engender a sense of loss and abandonment at a time when a woman feels the need for maximal support. This loss can parallel the sense of loss when the baby is born.*

Barbara We finished our set of eight classes at the National Childbirth Trust. It was an awful feeling when everyone had finished; nobody wanted to go home. We were discussing it, saying that you feel quite supported until they've finished, and then you're on your own. We decided to meet next week, but now we won't. We're going to meet again in April, by which time even the last baby should have arrived. One girl's had hers – it wasn't due until about the end of March, it was very early. . . . I shall be late! I had all the spring cleaning, I was gardening Wednesday . . . I never garden . . . I thought: This is it. I'm getting depressed days now. I can't say it's painful: it's so *uncomfortable* this baby, a little pest; this morning the tops of my legs kept going dead and you think: Oh heavens! and in bed he will not let me go to sleep – I get quite cross . . . quite cross . . . fed up! Its head's engaged now; it came out at the weekend and that was wonderful, I could walk about. I go shopping and get stuck halfway down the road and I have to crawl along with one foot in front of the other, that's what gets me down . . . never mind. When I get really fed up, then I think to myself I should make the most of it, because it's the last time I shall feel anything like this; you can't really

* The need for support in the postnatal period has recently been recognized and postnatal groups have been set up in many areas. But it is still rare for the same group to start with pregnant women and continue after they have had their baby.

imagine it when you're not pregnant . . . it's not a lot of consolation really!

Well, next week I shall be really depressed, if I'm like this now. I found this with the whole group. My baby was due first. Myself and the girl that's due on the seventh (the next one), both of us were really miserable. It's a whole week before it's due. She was so fed up she was even saying there might be something in all this induction business. I'm not that far, I wouldn't think that, but . . .

Dana One always hopes it will be early.

Barbara Yes, you do. You read in all the books thirty-eight to forty weeks and you hope to goodness it will be thirty-eight. This is like a first labour for me. I don't know what signs I would have had if I'd been left alone, or how late he would have been. I get days when I think it's going to start any minute. Yesterday was one of those days; I had a backache all day and I thought: There is something happening down here. My mother-in-law is quite affronted that I haven't had it yet. She said: 'Come on, come on, none of this hanging about.' I don't feel much like visiting, it isn't really like me. You always have to put a smile on. They say: 'How are you?' and you say: 'Fine'; you can't say: 'Oh I'm fed up' . . . you *can*, but . . . It's not even due yet, I shouldn't be getting fed up yet but I am. All the way through until the hospital said: 'It's head is engaged, have you got your case packed?' I was OK until then, and then I started thinking: Any minute now. That's wearing off now; anticlimax now. If I get twelve hours when the baby doesn't move about a lot, I think: Oh that's nice and quiet, and perhaps it will start; or like yesterday, I had a lot of backache, and last weekend, Saturday afternoon and Sunday afternoon I had contractions beautifully every twenty minutes for about four hours and it's only because I'm sitting down doing nothing that I notice them.

Women frequently get depressed in the last weeks, especially when 'the day' passes with no sign of labour. The date given is only an approximation based on a statistical calculation, of course, but it is often taken as a magical figure. Throughout labour that date has symbolized the culmination of the pregnancy; when it passes like any other day, a feeling of let-down and anxiety is experienced. Clinging to a particular date is a way of removing the uncertainty; when the date passes, the woman is reminded that her body is not under her control, and she has to live with her anticipation, concern, and doubt. Concentration on the actual delivery-date can also be a way of avoiding thoughts and fears linked with what comes after: the new baby, and life with a new baby. I asked Barbara if she thought much about the baby.

Barbara Hmm . . . not really. I don't imagine it blond, and Peter was, but there's no logic behind that either. It should be blond; both my husband and I are and Peter is, but I don't . . . probably because I've thought too much about the delivery. I didn't see Peter delivered. I can't say I wanted to, but I saw him going upside down across the room by the side of me, and then I saw him two or three minutes after that and he was already wrapped up, so what colouring he had didn't strike me; but this time with the pushing for delivery . . . you're upright almost, and I think it is most odd to see its head, because I didn't with Peter and I don't expect to see that blond. It will be wet anyway so it will look dark. I think it will have a little broad face because Peter did, but apart from that I haven't got any ideas. I haven't any concrete ideas what sex it is any more.

Dana Do you worry about the baby?

Barbara No. I think a couple of times, perhaps in the last fort-night, I've thought: Oh I don't know what I'd do if there was anything the matter with it, but that's as far as it goes. I don't actually worry about it.

Dana Did you worry about Peter?

Barbara No, Peter I took a lot more for granted. This time it's occurred to me more often. It's no good saying that I wouldn't be able to look after a baby that was handicapped, because you can't tell when you haven't had one; but with Peter I assumed right from the beginning that there wouldn't be anything wrong with him. But I did ask afterwards, as soon as I had him I said: 'Is he all right?' I think it's automatic.

Many women find themselves more apprehensive with a

second and third pregnancy than with the first one. With a first pregnancy, the main concern is the actual birth. With a subsequent pregnancy the woman is acutely aware of the delicacy and complexity of the baby, and she fears that she cannot create again such a perfect being. Also for a number of women the first pregnancy is the long-awaited fulfilment of some deep wish. Feelings about a second or subsequent pregnancy are more often tainted. For Barbara, for instance, the decision to have another baby was not an easy one and, as she later told me, it was made on her husband's insistence and in order to save the marriage. Fears about the baby reflect concern lest these rejecting thoughts could cause harm.

Such fears, conscious or unconscious (and expressed in dreams), are almost universal in pregnancy – even if each woman feels she in particular has special reasons for being worried. What is this growth that I have been carrying for such a long time inside my body? Will this being whom I have come to cherish turn out to be some sort of monster with no arms or legs? What if the accident I saw the other day affected the baby, if that article on mongolism I read in the newspaper was a premonition, and if my dream of a baby with the ears of an animal was showing me my baby?

Such thoughts are not surprising. Birth and death *are* mysterious, and all civilizations have tried to understand and deal with these phenomena in their own way. Each pregnant woman must make her own sense of them, and her magical thoughts only parallel the apparently magical nature of the creation of a new life inside her body.

Sarah worked in a hospital with severely handicapped and deformed children. This exacerbated her fears. 'I used to worry a lot about the baby having either a cleft palate, a hare lip, or a port-wine stain on its face, or a club foot. People say the palate is the last part to form and to join. It would be a perfect baby *but* at the last minute it could go wrong. I guess the fear of the stain was to do with my own failure showing. These fears had to do with me, with myself, what it would be like if it were me. There is something horrific about never being able to buy shoes, but needing someone always to make up special boots. Another thing I worried about was a mongoloid child, but through my experience of mongols . . . I found that reassuring; I could cope with it, I could accept that.' She wondered if she could be as good a mother as her husband's first wife, who had produced two healthy children.

Psychoanalysts see some of these fears originating in the little girl's relationship with her mother: in the destructive feelings she at times has towards her mother, in her jealousy of her father and brothers and sisters, and in her wish to steal all the good things from her mother for herself. According to Marie Länger, it is her feeling that these wishes and thoughts are monstrous which make the little girl, now become an adult woman, fear that she is carrying a monster inside her. In the same way that she wanted to destroy her mother's capacity to have more children, she now fears that the birth will harm her and make her infertile, a punishment for her childhood fantasies.[37] (Earlier on (pp. 28–9), Barbara feared that because her mother had only had one child, she might herself be unable to have a second child.) The 'monster' inside comes to represent all the monstrous feelings, and an atonement for these feelings. 'I'm not allowed to have a healthy child; I'm not capable of having a healthy child because I'm such a bad person; I will be punished by carrying a monster inside me; it will be my penance' is the unconscious thought-process. The little girl's anger and rivalry with her mother was expressed directly by Sarah's stepdaughter, who said to her: 'What if you had a monster?'

One woman puts it like this: 'When I was about six months pregnant, and Dick was starting (University) again, I was home alone, isolated for days at a time. My nightmares and daydreams started around then: really terrible fears of the baby being deformed. All my life I've always been the good girl. I knew I wasn't really good. I knew I had bad thoughts, but I was never allowed to express them. So I thought that my baby's deformities would be the living proof of the ugliness and badness in me.'[38]

We may suppose that being left alone and isolated while her husband started a new career led this woman to resent him and the baby who was keeping her trapped at home – her unconscious wish to be rid of the baby leading to her fear of the baby being harmed, deformed, abnormal.

In the sad cases when there is an abnormality in the baby, or in those of a miscarriage or stillbirth, it is as if such fears are given confirmation and the woman feels she really has been 'bad' and destructive. On the other hand the birth of a healthy child is a reassuring experience, leading to an enhanced self-confidence and sense of wellbeing. Similarly a delivery in which a woman is able to participate in full awareness, and without too much pain, or a sense of being torn apart, can help absolve her from old feelings of guilt in relation to her mother.

One author suggests[39] that the unbearable need to find out if the baby is normal, and its opposite, the escape from the proof which the birth represents, can be one of the factors contributing to shortening or to lengthening pregnancy. (From the physiological point of view little is still known about why labour begins at a particular time.)

This factor seems a possible one in the very slow progress of Bridget's labour. Having adopted two children, she gives birth to what she calls her 'home-grown' child: 'I wouldn't watch him being born; I chose not to because I was so frightened there was something wrong with him, I think because I felt I'd been so lucky having got my children so soon after going on the adoption list, much quicker than I ever expected we would; and then I got pregnant, which I never expected. I thought my luck really can't hold out; there's going to be something wrong with it. I was actually thinking this during the labour. Before he was born I can remember saying to the midwife: "Is the baby going to be all right, I'm really scared now . . ." I was really frightened before he was born. It was quite a relief when he was lovely and normal; he cried as soon as his head was born, before even his body was born.' This woman had no spontaneous contractions at all; after her waters broke she was put on a drip in order to produce contractions. 'I don't think my uterus ever contracted by itself. Before he was born I remember saying to the doctor, "If they put me off the drip now would I stop contracting?" and he said Yes.'

With the approaching date of birth, women also have to come to terms with the baby being outside rather than inside and with the sense of losing a part of themselves which can be felt to be very precious. Elenor describes the feeling of being 'physically complete' when she is pregnant: 'I didn't know what it would be like when I had her, whether I would really want her or whether it was being pregnant that I wanted.' If childbirth is experienced as a loss of part of the body, it will be a traumatic event.

Women also have to come to terms with losing the illusion of self-sufficiency which has developed during pregnancy when they contain within themselves both the person who provides and the person who is provided for, experienced as a part of the self. If a woman experiences the baby as something good inside her which fills her and makes her feel satisfied, then the birth will mean emptiness and deprivation. Susan found that pregnancy was the only time she felt free from depression. In such cases eternal pregnancy is unconsciously wished for, even if consciously the physical discomforts lead to the wish for pregnancy to end.

Although Barbara is feeling very despondent about the baby ever being born, she does now seem more prepared for the event. She talks about the baby as a person for the first time, and twice she links the baby inside with the baby outside. The first time is when she says that she doesn't get much sleep because the baby kicks, but that it's no different from me, because my daughter gets me up in the night – 'It's no different, the baby is just inside instead of outside' – and later, again referring to my daughter she says: 'The only difference is the lump on the front,' and we joke about how she, at least, doesn't have to get out of bed for the baby, whereas I do.

Some women prepare themselves in the last months of pregnancy for bringing the baby into the world. The boundary between inside and outside the body becomes more fluid. Six weeks before the birth of my daughter I had the following dream: 'For the first time I could grab the baby's arm through the abdominal wall – I was so excited I called my husband. But then the baby's hand and nails got stuck in the skin and I panicked before being able to release it.' That night I woke up several times and felt my abdomen and thought that the baby was much nearer the surface than ever before.

Lesley wished at times that she could keep her baby inside for ever, yet at other times, towards the end of the pregnancy, she wondered if the baby was all right, inside for so long. One night she dreamt that a dog was drowning. When she woke up she remembered that the dog in the dream was curled up like a foetus and she realized she must be worried that the baby would drown inside if it was not born soon, as the expected date of delivery had just gone by.

Fears of damage in childbirth may also contribute to delaying the time of the birth and are common in late pregnancy. Lesley, in the last month of her pregnancy, after a visit to the delivery room at the hospital, had the following dream: 'I was in a train with my husband and we realized that we were at the very front; that is, in the most dangerous position; we overheard the drivers talk of sick and hurt people who were in the last carriage.' In another part of the dream 'there was a human being, adult but the size of a child, covered in blood and wrapped up in white bandages.' Another woman has 'a dream in which a china cabinet was smashed and a dismembered infant was wheeled out of a bath-room. To the china cabinet being smashed she associated fears of an episiotomy* which, in turn, reminded her of having a penis ripped off. To the dismembered baby being wheeled out of the bathroom she associated long forgotten fantasies of anal birth. As she understood more of her fears about the delivery, she was able to consider pregnancy more as a process which would lead to her gaining a baby, and less as one which would lead to the mutila-tion, soiling and loss of a fantasied penis.'[40]

Not only damage but death itself is feared in childbirth. At the present day it is a very unlikely occurrence; still the fear remains, as if the birth of one being is inextricably linked with the death of another; as if a new self emerges from the old one, leaving it behind like a disused shell; as if the soul is being reincarnated.

The fear of dying can stem from a need to be punished for being successful, for usurping Mother's place, surpassing Mother, for 'being God' and creating life. The fear of damage to herself or to the baby can stem from a woman's feelings about childbirth as the first separation of mother and baby, a symbol for all future sep-arations.

Barbara's feelings, in this interview, soon after the end of her classes, are a mixture of depression, anger and apathy. She gets very impatient with her mother and with Peter:

Barbara I'm quite cross because . . . it's probably not very justifiable, but I do think she (her mother) could have offered

---

*Incision into the perineum, the area between the vagina and the anus.

to take Peter for a walk or something during the last couple of months. He does get on my nerves a lot more than he used to – through no fault of his own; he's no different. I just feel I'm so tired that having him all day every day really wears you out, and the only time he is really, really happy is running around outside and I do feel she could have offered. She doesn't work and she does nothing else all day except chat to the neighbours. I have said I wish somebody would take him out for half an hour so that I could put my feet up and the whole place would be nice and quiet, and she says her arms hurt her too much and he might fall over, and I get quite cross. She comes here and doesn't mind how much mess she makes, but she doesn't actually do anything to help. Perhaps I'm just peeved because it's the end and I'm getting fed up. If I'm not being kicked to death, I'm absolutely dead to the world.

This feeling of being 'dead to the world' is characteristic of the latter months of pregnancy. The woman is increasingly involved with the baby inside, whom she strokes and pokes to make sure he/she is still alive. Previous passionate interests seem to fade out of existence. The outside world (including other children) only appears as an intrusion between herself and the baby.

Barbara describes her drawing: 'It looks like a little doll. I'm so vague I just can't think of anything to draw. I haven't got any concrete feeling . . . depressed that's all.' She used to dream (p. 22) that she would give birth to a doll. Now she feels she *is* a doll. Could it be that she fears her own aliveness and her baby's aliveness at a time when uncertainty, anxiety, a feeling of not being able to control her body and the course of events are maximal? She deadens herself to these feelings. A doll has no life, let alone the ability to give life.

3 March

Barbara's depression was greater still today. She managed to communicate to me a feeling of almost unbearable hopelessness. She made me feel as if I too were in an intolerable state of waiting, where the anticipated event was never to come. She also felt angry – angry with her mother who doesn't help with Peter (perhaps there is also a feeling that she ought to be able to make the baby come); angry with Peter who is being demanding and difficult; and maybe angry with me for not being more helpful. She feels *somebody* ought to be able to do something, *somebody* must be responsible for this delay. She asks me when I think the baby will be born, as if someone (perhaps a mother-figure) must know the answer; someone must be controlling all this. She watches out for every possible sign of labour and, like most women at this stage, keeps thinking labour is beginning. Because she is determined not to go into hospital until the last minute, she sticks it out, and the contractions stop again.

Barbara I thought I was off yesterday; for four hours every ten minutes . . . I went into the shops very slowly and I got everything done, and I thought: I'll phone Patrick this afternoon once the contractions get a bit closer . . . and they all stopped at half past two. Oh it will be late. After a couple of hours of it I thought: Oh this must be it, I'll just keep holding on until I feel a bit panicky, I'll wait until the very last minute until I think: I must go now. I shall be delivering it on the floor in here. (*Laughs*) I think the baby will be born on the 9th. I've realized why. It's because all the shops have got 9 March – it's Mother's Day, so probably I've been shopping and seen the 9th so often. Its head engaged on a Sunday, so I imagine it's going to be born four weeks after that to the day. I don't really mind so long as I don't have to go into hospital before; *that* worried me. I'm in a better mood than when I was waiting for you to come, I don't know why – this little one hurts so much, that's why, and when it does I feel quite anti babies altogether.

Dana It makes one very angry.

Barbara Yes.

Dana Waiting for me to come today when I was late was a bit like waiting for the baby. You felt annoyed; you felt I was never coming.

Barbara I just can't think of anything to do. I wish the calendar was late. You know these tables where they give you the expected date, they should add a couple of weeks so you don't . . . I'm fed up just hanging about indoors, yet if I go out I feel really bad. Even if you sit down in a chair like this there's a terrific weight, and lying in bed is uncomfortable. I found just about with three cushions that I can fall asleep quite easily, but it seems not very fair because I'm taking up three quarters of the bed with padding and Patrick is right out on the edge. I can't eat anything much because I get indigestion, in fact from now on it's impossible eating or drinking anything, virtually impossible at this time of day. I go to sleep almost sitting up. Everything is just – Oh . . . if I could only think of one thing that was comfortable and happy!

Barbara's drawing today I found most striking though she said about it: 'It's just a pregnant lady, nothing spectacular, I don't think there's any vital difference.' To me there was a vital difference – the eyes were empty, there were no pupils, no actual eyes. I pointed this out to her, but she didn't go back and fill them in, she seemed unmoved by my comment. I found the drawing quite frightening. I felt it reflected her sense of being totally cut off from the outside world, from the other members of her family who make demands on her; I felt that she had become totally self-absorbed and inward-looking? Could it be that she is now only relating to herself, only looking inside?

CHAPTER EIGHT

Feeling quite hopeful

11 March

BARBARA's mood is very different today. On the surface things are still the same, waiting, wondering if labour is starting.

Barbara I had a marvellous morning, I washed all the curtains. Well I was wrong (about the 9th), wasn't I? It wasn't. I could have told you about Friday it wasn't going to happen then. In fact now I just don't know. All this morning I felt sure it was going to start today or tomorrow . . . I feel finished now, I don't think so any more. I had the bursting enthusiasm and I can't . . . I think Here goes; for no reason at all. I hope that when I actually start labour I feel a bit more comfortable. I don't know if the baby will turn round, or what he's doing, but my goodness he hurts. He seems in the most odd position. I keep getting very sharp pains across here (the lower abdomen) and . . . if it's not that, then it's the same sort of pain but up here (upper abdomen). I can't work out what it is and the doctor couldn't care less. The contractions I've had are getting really strong now, they pull now, and I can cope with those easily, but sometimes the pains that I get make me shake and I get very cold and they're really bad. I just can't move once they start. The baby kicks a lot, and then will lie in a particular way and until he moves I can't move. They're not contractions. Contractions are lovely, when they come they spread all the way up and really pull inside and those I can cope with, it's these . . . the doctor won't say what it is. I said I was getting the most peculiar pains and I said not contractions, definitely nothing to do with labour. They don't know. They say it can't be anything much, it must be too big by now. I don't feel very well when the baby is this particular way which is so uncomfortable But sometimes the baby will curl up in a neat little ball

97

and I feel wonderful, I start working and then he fidgets about
and I'm stuck again. I don't dare mention it to the hospital.
Apart from that I've cheered up a lot, since the actual due date
passed, I cheered up quite a lot. I thought: Well now it's going
to be within the next two or three weeks. I think I was depressed it didn't come early, but after it was late it didn't
matter so much. This pregnancy is the opposite to Peter. I
haven't minded being pregnant all the way through. I haven't
been sick or anything until the last couple of weeks I get these
inexplicable real pains. I can understand when my legs go
dead or . . . I can understand because its head must obviously
be pressing on one of the nerves but what this feeling is I just
don't know. It feels as if the bones around here (the pelvis) are
being pushed really hard and something between them really
hurts, but there isn't anything between them that can possibly
hurt. If I'm having a contraction when . . . the baby always
moves when it hurts and the contraction will stop. Anyway as
long as he gets nice and comfy ready for delivery I don't mind.
That was a contraction and that was beautiful. Since about one
o'clock this afternoon they've been coming about every
quarter of an hour. When I started getting these pains in my
tummy they stopped. It's not – well yes, it is my stomach,
which is very squashed up here, I suppose. Perhaps it's caught
a piece of intestine or something and that's why I get these
terrible pains. It's the baby's movements that cause those, and
the contractions I can deal with beautifully.

Behind talking about the painful sensations, Barbara is also
expressing her anxiety that something may be going wrong, that
unusual things are happening inside her body, that the baby is
doing something to her, inside, and that it is impeding the normal progress of the contractions and the dilatation of the cervix.

Barbara The other night my husband was saying you could see
the baby moving; he hasn't moved much for the last couple of
days, but you could see him moving, and once his head really
engaged; if I sit down, his head seems to bob out – you can see
the whole uterus move up slightly and his head seems to come
out of the rim of bones and up slightly, and then once he starts
moving it's really . . . it's excruciating painful. Patrick was

quite worried because I just couldn't stop shaking; it was a terrible pain and I was so cold and he said to me, 'Do labour pains get worse than that?' and I said, 'Well really they don't start like that; this suddenly goes wallop and you just don't know what's hit you.' The contractions I get now, they're what I call nice contractions because it feels quite warm being pulled and I actually feel it's doing something so I'm not worried. Well, they're not very long. What was that one, perhaps twenty seconds? Not much more than that, but if they were every ten minutes for a minute and a half I might . . . I'd go in then, but otherwise I think I'd wait until I was really nervous and thought it can't be much longer. And I might get in there and be completely wrong; it might be hours, but there is no way of knowing. But I had them every ten minutes last Monday. That was for a long time – I started thinking I'll phone Patrick, and then they all stopped. They weren't very strong – if they had been I might have done something about it. It'd be lovely if I could have it on the kitchen floor!

Peter (*butting in*): Are you soon have this baby?

Barbara You're fed up with it, aren't you? Yes we're all a bit fed up with babies at the moment. I've had to ring up all my friends to tell them I haven't had it. One day I wake up and think I've got beautiful backache or something and I'll think: This is different, perhaps something's going to happen today. But as the days go I just get more and more depressed. And I always think something's going to happen during the night and it never does. I'm sure it's a girl now, because Peter wasn't so uncomfortable. No logic behind any of these feelings.

The whole family is 'expectant'. Men often develop physical complaints during their wives' pregnancies. One study of sixty couples found that 65 per cent of the expectant fathers developed 'pregnancy symptoms'; their complaints were generally similar to the complaints of pregnant women and included such things as fatigue, nausea, backache, and vomiting. Many of them gained ten to twenty pounds, which they lost after the birth of the baby; some stopped drinking coffee and began drinking milk; some stopped smoking 'for the baby'.[41]

Barbara Do you remember that I told you that Patrick had a rash; he went to the doctor's again today because it's getting worse. The doctor's given him tablets, and he can only take one: he's got to take it in the evening because it's going to knock him out completely, and I said to him: 'For goodness sake don't you go to sleep when I start in labour.' He doesn't know whether to take them or not. Oh dear, what a performance this is going to be. He takes the first one tonight so . . . if I can't wake him up I shall go on my own.

Peter (*singing*): I'll go on my own! I'll go on my own!

Barbara These things always happen at the wrong time. Apparently these tablets are going to make him feel a bit groggy. I said it will be fine if I say to you 'I want to go now' and you can't find the car or something.

(Peter decides to draw a stork.)

Barbara I can't draw anything today, I can't even draw me expecting any more. Good grief I can't! Oh let's have a big tummy for heaven's sake. It doesn't even look like me. I can't do it, isn't that funny?

I told Patrick, I said you were coming and at dinner I was feeling quite hopeful, 'It'd be lovely if she's here and I start.' You can have it all down on tape for posterity, the first moments . . . (*Laughs*) Oh it doesn't look like me (the drawing). Oh it's absolute rebellion, I'm fed up with the pregnant drawings and I can't do it.

Dana It doesn't look pregnant.

Barbara No, I keep adding an extra line to the dress but . . . it doesn't look anything.

Peter (*singing*): Anything but you!

Barbara Patrick seems quite interested in being there at the birth now. I said to him, 'You're funny; you don't discuss it, you just suddenly . . . from the conversation I assume you're going to be there.' He said, 'Well I don't think it's worth worrying about.' Is there still an atmosphere of waiting (referring to my comment last time)?

Dana It seems very different from last week. It feels more imminent. Last week it felt hopeless whereas this week it feels hopeful.

I was indeed very struck by the atmosphere today, which

seemed one of great excitement. I found it extraordinary that she no longer drew a pregnant woman – I thought that to her the baby was more out than in – and almost did expect her to give birth there and then. I felt that psychologically she was giving birth.

It was no surprise to me when her baby girl was born two days later.

CHAPTER NINE

Like a grapefruit

CHILDBIRTH is probably the most intense physical and emotional normal experience in a woman's life. It is recalled with terror or with joy, but most often its vividness is forgotten. For one woman it is a time of frightening loneliness; in this strange and aseptic hospital setting, she imagines the worst. She feels abandoned, prey to strange sensations and excruciating pain; nobody cares, nobody will come if she screams for help. For another woman this aloneness is welcome; she wants to deal herself with the important task ahead. She feels alone in spite of those around her. 'I thought beforehand that this would be a wonderful time to have my husband with me, but I found that when the labour pains came I was all wrapped up in me.'[42] And Elenor, a single mother in her late thirties, feels she can cope well on her own: 'I had quite a lot of thought about whether I should have somebody there, because the baby's real father had said for about one day that he would, but then changed his mind, which I can understand, and three other people had offered to be there. The first one was my old boy friend I'm friends with now, he's the one I really had to decide about. I partly thought he would be somebody that I could not worry about, take for granted, but I finally decided that it would be an ambiguous start to her life because it was another man and somebody I'm not really involved with emotionally. The other people were two women. I suppose it's just that somebody said it would be such a help having someone there, because in fact I didn't really need anyone.'

The partner's presence, which can feel like an intrusion, is for most women reassuring, as is to some the possibility of having their baby at home in familiar and undramatic surroundings. In turn many men welcome the possibility of participating in, and, in a sense, experiencing through their wives, giving birth to their child. If a woman wants her partner with her, desertion, emotional or actual, is an added stress in labour.

Each labour is different; each woman lives childbirth differently. 'Everything inside me exploding', 'a feeling of splitting', 'like an orgasm', 'a terrible loss of control', 'animal-like': these are only some amongst the many expressions which have been used by women to re-evoke their experience of childbirth.

One woman describes her second stage of labour thus: 'I asked for my first shot of pethidine at this stage as the pains – in my back – were getting a bit excruciating, though not unbearable. With the second shot, about 15 minutes later, which I didn't ask for, I went off into a kind of drunken stupor, which I regret. The drugs seem to release rather hostile feelings towards the midwife and nurse for not allowing my husband to be there, and I even took a perverse delight in not pushing when they were telling me to. I had negative rather than positive feelings, which probably slowed labour down. I certainly wasn't at all inhibited emotionally in the labour ward and called variously on God, James and the baby – to get a move on. "It's no use you telling the baby to get a move on" the nurse reproved me. "It's you who should be getting a move on – come on, push!" "I am pushing" I roared, so loudly they must have heard me at home. I suppose there must have been about 20 of these monumental pushes, in which I felt as if my whole body was converging on to the birth canal and trying to get out through it. And then suddenly it was over. I opened my eyes and there was the little blue bottom slithering out into the midwife's hands, trailing the blue cord with it.'[43]

The first and second stages are often felt to be quite different: Lesley was 'struck by the total contrast between the first and second stage. Towards the end of the first stage of labour I felt as if my body was slipping away from me, that the contractions were getting stronger and stronger, and nearer and nearer, and that there was nothing I could do about it. I didn't know where it would all end up – something like falling down a slope and not knowing if one will ever stop, or the feeling of being on a horse which suddenly galloped off when one was a very inexperienced rider. The end of the first stage felt like a terrific surrender to a powerful force inside me. In marked contrast, in the second stage I felt as if it depended on my will whether or not this baby would ever come out, and I feared I might not manage to do it. No longer the sense of being carried but the sense of enormous effort.'

For some, the use of spinal injections which paralyse the lower part of the body marks the way for the true liberation of women. Others advocate an understanding and acceptance of the full force of their body-processes. I personally believe that a natural (or near-natural) childbirth can be an enriching experience, because it is so uniquely powerful and releases such extreme body-processes, and that this experience can become uniquely cherished.

For births which are particularly long and painful (as when the baby is not in the more usual position), the possibility of pain relief is essential. So is it also for women who do not want, for whatever reason, to experience childbirth. Liz, for instance, would like to have a baby but she is terrified of birth; she is in her thirties and finally decides to have a baby when her doctor assures her that she can have an epidural. Childbirth experienced in terror and excruciating pain is a poor start to a mother's relationship with her infant.

Unfortunately there is a tendency for dogmatism on all sides. In some hospitals it is very difficult for a woman not to receive at least a shot of pethidine, even against her will, while in other hospitals women have to fight if they want an epidural. It is also unfortunate that women who wish for a natural birth feel they have failed if they find they need some pain relief. Bridget describes this feeling: 'Because I wasn't contracting and because my waters had gone, they put me on a drip at eight in the morning; the dreaded drip which is absolutely horrid. It really is awful and of course once your contractions come they come very fast and very strong, so they fiddled about with it, up and down. I'd done the psychoprophylaxis classes, which I thought were really good, and I coped until six in the evening with the contractions and I really was getting very tired. I wasn't coping at all well when they examined me, it was hurting, and they wanted to give me pethidine and I didn't want to have pethidine, because you know this big thing about natural childbirth – 'Thou shalt not have drugs' – and then the midwife said I think we *would* like you to have pethidine. So I thought Right, if she'd said it's going to be a couple of hours, no, I can cope. But I thought in no way can I cope for at least another twelve hours or longer. By that stage I wasn't even coping with the contractions, I was letting them hurt. I'd said to my husband before going in, 'I don't want any drugs,' and when I agreed to have the pethidine I really felt that I'd failed and so did he. After the pethidine I felt terrible, I can remember talking absolute rubbish but it helped in that I couldn't feel any more pain; in fact I went to sleep. I couldn't have coped without it. I felt that I'd failed but I'm glad that I had it. I had one more shot of pethidine, maybe two, and then in the middle of the night I had an epidural – they don't like to give you too much pethidine because it affects the baby, which apparently the epidural doesn't. I thought the epidural was excellent because from my waist down I couldn't feel any pain. When I woke up at half past six I was lucid, which was such a contrast to the pethidine. In the morning a doctor examined me and said, 'You've still got a rim of cervix left, I'll top up the epidural,' which she did; which in retrospect was very unfortunate, because about twenty minutes later his head was below the rim of cervix, so I could push out, but by this time the epidural had taken effect; I couldn't utilize the pushing contractions fully.'

Bridget humorously describes the new commandment of those who advocate natural birth: 'Thou shalt not have drugs.' She has a point, and creating guilt is certainly unhelpful, but it is important to stress that the objection to any drugs whenever it is possible to do without them is not just an arbitrary, extremist position. It is linked to the fact that even a small amount of, say, pethidine can greatly impede the woman's ability to cope with her labour. There is also the fact that 'some' drugs lead to 'more' drugs; Bridget describes how she would rather not have had her epidural topped up, so that she could have pushed the baby out herself without the need for forceps. Finally the increasing evidence of possible effects of drugs on the baby and on the development of the relationship between mother and baby, through the drowsiness of both partners and lack of immediate contact, should make one cautious in their use.

Childbirth is frightening because it is an unknown physical and emotional experience (even when it is not the first time) and because of the possible dangers to mother and to baby. Many mothers' first question is: 'How is it?' or 'Is the baby all right?' In some cases the baby is not all right. A stillborn baby is a great shock. This death, as in the case of a miscarriage, is one which is especially hard because there is 'no tangible person to mourn.'[44] 'If your mother dies you may recall with tenderness a small woman with a shopping bag. If your brother dies you can remember the childhood fights, rivalry, companionship, (but) when a child is born dead there is nothing. The world can remember nothing. I felt that I had failed as a woman – hating my body as a defective machine. The anger was frightening.'[45] There is no one to talk about the baby with because no one knew this baby. There is only the guilt about having produced a dead baby, the depression at feeling 'rotten inside' and unable to produce life, the anger at being robbed. 'Such a large part of me had died . . . all the hopes, plans, proffered love, with no one to give it to. My arms, my belly were empty. I felt like an empty shell, making only the motions required by the rest of the family.'[46] One author suggests that 'A way to overcome some of the obstacles to normal mourning that result from the emptiness of stillbirth is to make the most of what is tangible and can be remembered. Bereaved parents should be encouraged to look at and if possible touch or hold their dead baby. They will then have someone to remember. Parents should also be persuaded to take an active part in the certification of stillbirth and should name the baby and try to make the funeral memorable. The family should be encouraged to attend the burial or cremation and to know of a marked place or grave.'[47]

Other people may be reluctant and unable to bear the bereaved woman's feelings: 'I went into the hospital for the birth of my first child. I never saw him. When I began to return to myself I found that despite all those times I had told myself that nothing could really happen, I had but an empty belly. I don't know if we should be told ahead of time to worry needlessly about something that happens to a very few women, but as one of those women, I definitely needed to feel some sense of sharing with others in the same position – not to cry over what had happened, but to work out how to face other people. That's the hardest part – nobody wants to deal with death, especially when your friends are at the child-bearing age themselves and can't help being afraid of you for what you stand for. I found that my friends wanted me to pretend nothing had happened – that there had been no pregnancy even . . . And so my fantastic pregnancy, in which a lot of things went on in my head and body that helped me to change and get myself together, had to be buried. Even now, after a year, I can see their pain and fear for me as I start into my eighth month of pregnancy with my second child. I have to be the one who keeps them calm, and I especially must assure everyone that this one will be okay.'[48]

It is important to stress that what is frightening in childbirth is not only the pain, not only the fears for the baby and for oneself, not only the uncertainties about one's adequacy to meet this situation. What is frightening is also giving birth to a part of oneself and becoming transformed through giving birth. One woman describes her fears in labour: 'I was frightened thinking that it would never end and that the birth would be difficult. I focused on a spot on the wall and I focused on the breathing. I was afraid to hope that a baby would come out. I remember thinking "What comes out of people? Nothing but shit, mucus, urine, blood. Just ugly things come out of people. What can ever be beautiful that can come out of me?" I just could not believe that there was really a baby in there. I mean there was some part of me thinking that I was just getting fat and just eating too much. And I was getting very fat anyway. So I looked at the spot on the wall and I did my breathing.'[49]

Adrienne Rich describes the feeling that the child can be like an 'enemy within' when there is a feeling of opposition between motherhood and being an individual, between motherhood and freedom. She writes: 'The depths of this conflict, between self-preservation and maternal feelings, can be experienced – I have experienced it – as a primal agony. And this is not the least of the pains of childbirth.'[50] 'What is going to come out of my body?' and 'What will *I* become?' are the emotional birth-pains which come to exacerbate the physical birth-pains.

Barbara describes some of the methods which helped her cope with the physical birth-pains.

Barbara I went to the doctor on Thursday morning because it really got me down, I couldn't walk or anything; and he said 'They'll take you into hospital and induce you' and I was terrified. Oh God, I thought, no; I was really frightened about this labour, right up to the last minute I was frightened about it. And I was lying there and I had cushions all over and the waters broke . . . I shook absolutely all over, I thought: Oh my goodness – it was so unexpected. My husband was ever so shaken too, he didn't expect it either. This was half past eight at night; we were just here watching television. I just couldn't think of anything. I said 'Oh my goodness, I think the waters have broken!' 'I think!' – there were gallons of it everywhere. Anyway after the first shock I didn't know whether labour was going to start straight away or not, so I said I thought he'd better tell his mum in case it did. I didn't intend to rush into hospital straight away. I thought in hospital they don't worry for about twelve hours so I'd leave it for a bit. Well then the contractions started gradually, I was getting changed and ready to go. My parents-in-law arrived to stay the night and look after Peter, and I sat and chatted with them until ten forty-five when the contractions were noticeably stronger, still regular at five-minute intervals, but for fifty to sixty seconds, and I was beginning to use levels A and B breathing and keeping a picture of riding a wave surfing-style in mind, to keep calm. By eleven I could feel a lot more, so I said 'We'd better go I think', and the labour was, I guess, like any other labour, just ordinary contractions that got closer and closer, and the hospital didn't think I was in labour because I wouldn't admit it. I went in and said: No, nothing hurts me, don't worry, I'm all right. I'll just go and lie down, ignore me, go away. I was so frightened about them putting me on a drip, and then I told them that yes the contractions had started and they seemed to be coming a bit more regularly. We were both keeping ever so calm: 'Don't worry, we're fine,' and then I explained to them that I wanted to try the breathing after I really thought contractions were established, and I was very lucky, I had a cooperative midwife who was interested and joined in. About three in the morning the contractions got really bad. They were without a pattern; that's what I found disturbing; suddenly wallop and you were in the middle of one. I worked through to level C by about two a.m. and found that using level C and drumming 'Come away, come away with William Tell' just rhythmically on the bed I was doing well. I didn't mouth the words, just kept up the rhythm and kept in my mind a picture of the cervix opening to a larger circle and the top of a baby's head pushing towards the rim. The contractions were very strong. I could breathe over the height of them, but after them I had a real ache over the lower abdomen which I couldn't breathe through, round or over, or massage in any way. I didn't need or like any sort of back rubbing and didn't find effleurage* any help either during contractions. I mentioned the ache during a chat with the midwife, who said it would be probably the cervix stretching after the uterine muscles had contracted, so I wasn't too worried. At least I felt the ache had a purpose. By three a.m. I was up to level D and only just in control and I asked for an internal as I said I didn't think I could keep up the breathing if the contractions got very much more painful. The contractions had no pattern. They would either begin slowly or at a terrific speed, and I was having real difficulty in keeping relaxed at all. I said I didn't think I could keep it up for very much longer and did she have any idea how fast I was dilating so that I'd know whether I was going to have to have loads of stuff or not. From what she said my husband and I both thought that she expected me to deliver some time the next morning – sort of eight o'clock – so I said 'Well I'd better have something because I'm just getting frightened.' So I had half what they usually give one at the hospital of pethidine and that was smashing. I managed to get back to breathing and relaxing again, and that was OK. That went on for about one hour, and then all of a sudden I started sitting up during contractions and I didn't know what was happening, I didn't have a clue. When I started sitting up I got really upset because I said 'I don't know what I'm doing' and I was saying to my husband 'I just don't know what to try next', so I lay on my side. We tried anything I could think of but I still couldn't help it. Instead of just flopping down I kept going up to sitting position, and the next thing I said was 'My God, I'm pushing.' That's what I was doing. So that was that. I said 'You'd better call the nurse' and I was trying not to push because I didn't know if I was fully

---

*Rhythmical light stroking of the lower abdomen.

109

dilated and having heard so much about anterior lips I thought I'd better not. So there I was trying not to push and panting and getting in a right state for a couple of minutes and they rushed me to the delivery room; it's mad, isn't it?

Dana Patrick wanted to stay by this time.

Barbara Oh yes, he was all right by then and I was saying 'Don't you go away.' So he came down with me and they gave me the gas-and-air mask in one hand and I held on to him with the other. I found that I didn't have time to explain to them then that I wanted more cushions behind me and this sort of thing; it was too late then; so I delivered on my back, which wasn't the way I'd been taught, but still . . . I said I'd rather have an ordinary delivery and if she shouted 'Pant' I'd try, but at the end the midwife said she thought the head would deliver in about two pushes and I would probably tear; she said the muscles were getting very stretched and very thin, so she thought she'd better cut it; she didn't want to cut it either but she did. It wasn't as bad as when I had Peter and I had stitches everywhere, this was just one line which healed up quite quickly. And there she was. She was yelling before the rest of her head was delivered, she was yelling. The second stage took one hour. I knew what to expect as far as feeling the head coming was concerned – the teacher's description of a grapefruit was very accurate. Beatrice was laid on my tummy still yelling and gradually turning bright red. The third stage took about five minutes and one nurse cleaned up Beatrice a bit while the other delivered the placenta. That was much thicker and more red than I'd expected and I had a good look, determined not to miss any detail, as I wanted to remember this experience, not forget it as I had my first delivery.

After delivery the midwife came back and said did I regret having the pethidine? She said she was sorry she didn't realize I was going to dilate so quickly, and did I regret it? I was getting frightened anyway and it helped me relax so I didn't mind and I wasn't so dopey that I didn't know what was happening, and I saw her born quite normally, and then they said yes I was fine, and I went to have a shower. I found that the pain I've forgotten altogether, I've forgotten it now. I know it hurt but I've forgotten it, whereas with Peter I used to wake up and think Oh my goodness; it was awful. But this time I haven't, and now I wouldn't mind having another one, whereas after Peter I said 'Don't you ever talk to me about having to go through this again.' My husband was a lot . . . it's changed . . . he can't leave her alone. He's more fussy about her than I am. It does change your attitude a lot, that experience, compared with the first.

I couldn't believe it. In fact, I don't think I got over the excitement afterwards; the emotional reaction after having a baby that way is completely different from having this sort of delivery (with Peter) where it's all done for you. With Peter I couldn't believe it, I still couldn't believe there was *my* baby at the end of it; but with this one I was so excited afterwards, I couldn't sleep for about four days; I just couldn't believe it, I simply couldn't. I spent nine months being frightened to death about this delivery, and I was so thrilled afterwards. I can't say it was painless. The end of the first stage was jolly painful and I was shouting: 'It hurts' . . . I wasn't any hero. I told you I thought it was a girl, but when they said it was, I was so pleased I nearly cried.

I was absolutely dependent on Patrick during labour; every time there was anything, he was the person I grabbed for. Well, it was great that he was there. I felt so much better because he was there this time and it was a relief too. You see I expected everything; everything in my first labour seemed to go wrong. I can't explain it any other way – I hadn't done the classes, I hadn't any preconceived ideas about labour before, but I didn't expect it to be quite like it was, and everything went wrong. He wasn't there and the baby wouldn't come and just everything went wrong from beginning to end. This time everything went right and the only muddle there was, if you can put it that way, was when they thought it was going to be a long time and it wasn't, and they couldn't believe I was so relaxed. They kept taking my pulse and saying 'She'll go to sleep in a minute' . . . My friends come and I say it was terrific and they say 'You didn't feel anything?' And I say 'Oh no, it hurt, of course it hurt, but it was a terrific experience.' And they don't know what I'm talking about, and so I must curb so much enthusiasm that I'd rather not see them at all; I know my next-door neighbour is going to say 'Was it terrible, dear?' And I get quite impatient, I don't want to see people.

The ability to relate immediately to her baby varies from one woman to another and can be greatly impeded by obstretrical procedures. Women who have had caesarean sections and a full anaesthetic often describe a difficulty in experiencing the baby as belonging to them. Miriam describes how on waking from the anaesthetic she thought her baby was really nice, but could not feel the baby came from inside her; it was more a question of feeling lucky at having been given such a nice baby. And another woman, who nevertheless welcomed the anaesthetic, comments: 'The only trouble when you are put out is that you cannot connect the baby with yourself. It's like going to a place, you go to sleep and the next day are given a present of the baby. I could not put the womb and baby as part of each other because I did not see it happen, I suppose. That's the only thing I sort of regret. But I would much rather endure that than worrying about being around . . . It was very difficult for me. I kept on looking at the baby and saying "I cannot believe it, I cannot believe he came from me." '[51]

As is the case with drugs, women can experience an induction of labour or a caesarean section as a failure. 'I felt terrible, I felt I couldn't even give birth, I felt a failure! I didn't realize in fact so many women are induced.'[52]

For another woman it is her very person and particularly her femaleness which is put into question. 'I was so confused and distressed when I woke up in the delivery room around eleven at night. I was not prepared to have my baby with a caesarean. The idea of not having been able to have my baby the natural way was unbearable. I felt like a cripple. I didn't even want to see the baby. I wasn't at my best to meet her. Slowly I reasoned with myself that all was fine because I have a lovely baby girl. Lying in the room, all night I was hearing this baby cry. I asked the nurse if it was mine and it was. Finally, at five in the morning, I asked the nurse to bring her and it was a happy reunion. When I saw her everything went away even though she looked red and blue.'[53]

Preoccupations about what could have happened if it had not been for medical intervention can also come to the fore, and the feeling that the doctor had to rescue the baby from her body can lead a woman to feel that she is bad for her baby.

Not all women feel distant from their baby after a caesarean section, however. Charlotte said: 'I felt I related to him straight away, inasmuch as I felt he looked really like the image of my husband, and much more handsome than I thought he would; I was really prepared for the worst. All babies born by caesarean there looked beautiful, and they look mature somehow when they're born. He looked as if he was about a couple of months older to me.'

A problem Charlotte did encounter was one of helplessness. 'Everybody I was surrounded by in the hospital, some within a matter of hours, others within a matter of days, was up and around and looking after their babies which in no way could I do. I couldn't lift James, there was no way I could physically lift him, and seeing everybody else doing it and me not being able to I felt it was all wrong, it made me very unhappy. I didn't feel that I had failed personally. I think I felt very envious of the other people being able to do this for their babies and me not being able to, although once I was up and around I thought: I wish I was in bed. And all the nurses were running after me and being so kind to me. I didn't like this helpless feeling. Every time it was time to feed him I had to ring the bell for the nurse to come and pick him up and hand him to me.'

This feeling of passivity and helplessness during the birth and in the first week in hospital is one which can jeopardize the longer-term well-being of the mother and her relationship with her baby; it becomes more difficult for her to feel confident, creative and able to follow her feelings. Other circumstances can of course affect a woman's reaction to her baby. Jane, who became very depressed after the birth of her first child, describes a similar feeling of passivity. 'My mother wanted a boy desperately and gave me hell because I wasn't; I was the last one. And all my life she said: "You should have been a boy, you should have been a boy", and I think I wanted to have a girl to make up for the fact and say: I'm glad it's a girl. Also all my husband's family wanted a boy, and my mother wanted a boy and when he was born I thought: Now you've got him; I've never felt he was mine, he was everybody else's baby; I never felt he was anything to do with me.'

She was not depressed after her second child, a girl, was born: 'I feel Jill is very much mine.' In a sense, with her first child, Jane had produced the goods her family had ordered; her body was the vehicle for all their wishes and expectations. It is in this sense that she feels passive; she merely executes their order. When the baby is born, it is their baby. 'Where do I fit in all this? I just felt as though my life had gone, as if that was it, and it took a long time to realize that I was still a person.'

The birth of a healthy baby can bring great relief to the woman who feared that her baby would not be normal, though it may be hard for her to shake off this idea she has nurtured for nine months and she will look out for any sign of abnormality. It takes some time for Bridget to accept that her child is healthy: 'Ever since I knew I was pregnant, I was afraid there was something wrong with the baby. I was still worried when he was born, really until he smiled . . . he smiled when he was four and a half weeks old, and when he smiled I thought: Oh yes, you're going to be all right.' Other women are disappointed that the baby does not match up to the perfect baby they secretly imagined they were carrying, the sum of all their hopes and ideals. They are shocked to find their baby ugly, or that they have no feeling of 'love at first sight', or that the baby has a minor imperfection. 'I don't think I was prepared at all, because you read in books and you talk with people and you think that all of a sudden there is going to be this motherly surge of love which is not true. In my case it wasn't. I had this colicky baby that spat up and we had to stay home. It took me a long time. I don't think motherly love is automatic as a lot of times you are led to believe. I think you should be prepared for this because you think you're unusual. There is a lot of guilt.'[54]

The sex of the baby can also be a great disappointment. As we have seen, it is common for women (and even more so for men) to wish for a boy as their first child, particularly women who find their own femaleness difficult to accept. Lesley realized when her daughter was born that she had been assuming the baby was a boy. 'I think it's partly because culturally the blueprint is male: the baby books all say "he" about the baby . . . but I was pleased to have a girl. Having a girl seemed extra-ordinary, literally out of the ordinary.'

With subsequent children it is often, though not always, a

question of wishing for one of opposite sex. Bridget, who has two boys already, desperately hoped for a girl: 'I cried a lot after he was born; I think it was the relief. I also cried because he wasn't a girl. I don't mind now, but at the time I was very disappointed; my husband was, as well. It shouldn't be important so long as they're healthy. I can remember when I went to the clinic and saw all these pregnant women, I thought: I wonder how people are lucky enough to have a girl. I did think I would be very lucky if I had a girl. I never really believed that I would; I always thought he was a boy. We've always thought of a girl's name and had to dash around at the last minute thinking of a boy's name.'

On the other hand Mary, who has a boy already, hopes that her second child will also be a boy: 'I feel I couldn't cope with a girl, because I felt I was so horrible myself as a child.'

And Erica says 'I'm glad I've had boys rather than girls. Boys are less problematic. People expect them to be active and aggressive. I feel that if I had an active and aggressive-type girl I'd all the time be feeling that I wanted to push that, but that other people didn't want it to be pushed. Also I think I quite like the idea of being the only woman in a house of men . . . an ego-trip thing: having always been one of three girls I quite like the idea of having nice big sons when I'm old.' And this relates to feelings about her own femaleness. 'I feel I'm still working out what I am as a girl or woman or female: what is important, what bit of femaleness is important to uphold, and what bit isn't. It never occurred to me, although I must have heard it said, that women were at any disadvantage till I had kids, so it's been a terrific reorientation for me and a terrific refinding of what I am in that process – just being female and being expected to be certain types of people.'

CHAPTER TEN

I'm not very clever yet, but we'll learn

THE first weeks are emotionally turbulent. Mismatches between what was imagined and what now is have to be accepted, or at least tolerated. The experience of childbirth, with all it represents of success or failure, power or powerlessness, loss and gain, must be come to terms with. Some women feel haunted by their experience, others feel exhilarated, but none remains unmoved. This experience and the first meeting between mother and baby will leave a lasting impression on both.

The French obstetrician Frederick Leboyer has emphasized the importance to the baby of this first meeting, and has devised ways of making the passage from life inside to life outside the uterus as smooth as possible. 'I sought to make the transition from internal to external life a gradual development by prolonging some of the sensations felt in the uterus, and by slowly introducing the baby to the new ones. All new babies are, in fact, hypersensitive through the skin, the eyes and the ears. They are in a raw state.' Through his method Leboyer helps the baby deal with the different new sensations (such as light, breathing, sound) slowly and gradually. For instance: 'It is considered normal to put a baby into cloth wraps straight away. But, after having been in such a slippery environment, the contact with clothes for the infant is as if he were being scorched. I put the newborn on the mother's abdomen, naked, since only skin is alive and sensitive enough to be bearable. He first lies on his tummy, so he will open very slowly from the fetal position, following his own speed and rhythm. The mother puts her hands on his back and so does the father (or myself) and the newborn feels security, being held closely once again as it was in the uterus for such a long time. The baby, once outside the uterus, suddenly feels that nothing is holding him together and has a sensation of bursting at the seams. Figuratively speaking, we are holding all of the pieces together. When he begins to stretch, I turn him on his side and only once he is comfortable in that position do I turn him on his back. A little later the mother props up the baby in a sitting position. His internal attitude has changed in some way.'[55]

When it comes to the realm of infants' experiences we can only talk about hypotheses based on intuition and observation – observation, for instance, of the way in which a baby is soothed by being held closely, or, on the contrary, the way in which a baby screams when undressed and not held, as if a protective layer were being removed. The mother herself has been described as being 'a protective shield against stimuli' which are too intense for the infant to process adequately. She recreates, as it were, a womb where the newborn baby's needs are met as they arise, and where the outside world is absorbed in very small doses during the short waking periods.

Margaret Mahler and her co-workers make a distinction between biological birth and psychological birth, which, they point out, are not coincident in time. 'The former is a dramatic, observable and well-circumscribed event, the latter a slowly unfolding intra-psychic process.' At first the situation is one which approximates the prenatal state. Gradually the infant builds up an awareness that there is a source of supply which satisfies his or her needs, but it is not yet experienced as a separate person. It is only, they suggest, around the fourth or fifth month that the infant begins to 'hatch', to emerge from the symbiotic fusion with the mother. 'The hatched infant has left the vague twilight state of symbiosis and has become more permanently alert and perceptive to the stimuli of this environment rather than to his own bodily sensations, or the sensations emanating within the symbiotic orbit only.'[56]

Although authors differ in their construction of the earliest stages of childhood, most authors and mothers alike describe how the infant gradually seems to emerge from a self-enclosed state where *apparently* any caretaker will do, to become more of a 'person' in a relationship with others and reacting differently to familiar and unfamiliar people. I say 'apparently' because marked reactions to strangers around seven or eight months have tended to obscure the more subtle signs of growing recognition of the mother, which research findings are now bringing to light. For instance one study has found that very young babies could recognize their own mother's smell. As early as ten days after birth infants would more often turn their head towards their own mother's breast pad than to another mother's breast pad (which was not the case at birth).[47]

Such rudimentary awarenesses come together to build up over the first months of life a total image of the mother as primary caretaker. Concomitantly with the infant's growing awareness of the mother, in a different way the mother has to learn to know her infant.

Leboyer was asked why *he* often does the massage, and not the mother. He replied that many mothers were too apprehensive and emotional after the birth to be able to massage with calm and confidence. One may question the intrusion of a stranger in the intimacy of the relationship, however skilled he may be at being a substitute mother. But this does draw attention to the point that although mothering is thought to be instinctive, in fact it may require a fair amount of learning. Even when the mother does have an immediate and powerful feeling of love, knowing how to handle and respond to her baby is not something which automatically follows. A good deal of trial and error may be needed. This requires time and psychological space.

One study found that the mothers who were allowed extensive contact with their baby in the first days after birth related more positively to their child even a year later. We can see that this would have long-term effects on the relationship.[58] Mothers who have had a home birth and therefore could hold, fondle, explore, their baby as much as they wanted and at their own pace describe the relationship as quite special compared with the one resulting from a hospital confinement. At the other end of the scale, mothers whose babies are born prematurely and have to start life in an incubator face the greatest problems of relating to their child after what is often felt as a hiatus and loss of the baby for a period of time.

Erica describes this poignantly: 'Alan was five weeks premature – it's quite a lot. He couldn't suck so he had to be fed by tube, which is a bit offputting when it's your baby; he went downstairs instead of being next door so that it was a big effort to go and see him – in fact I couldn't see him for about twenty-four hours, maybe even longer. I couldn't understand why, although it was obvious that I had to go down in a wheel chair, so until somebody could take me I couldn't go. Once I got used to going down there, then I could go down whenever I wanted, but I kept trying to breast feed him, which was stupid, because he couldn't, and I got all upset about it. It's very strange leaving hospital and not having a baby. I waited about five days because they said "He might suddenly develop this sucking impulse and then you could take him home with you," but I think they only said that to cheer you up, because other people who were being a bit more realistic said "It will take a month – he'll make up his five weeks and then you can take him home." So then I went home after five days. They gave me a breast pump; I pumped for a month, I took the stuff down there. It was amazing; I had so much milk I kept the whole prem. unit going. They taught me how to sterilize it in the end and I used to sterilize it and freeze it and go down with this great pile of bottles. It was horrific, ghastly, absolutely terrible. Then I breast fed him until he was about five months. When I look back on it it seems an incredible performance for not much end, but they encouraged me at the hospital. I'd breast fed my first child for seven months and I wanted to do it again. I was determined he wouldn't miss out on it because he was premature. But it seems crazy – this great big machine: I'd get up at six in the morning and plug the machine in and produce all the stuff. The thing is, the more you use it the more milk you produce. It came gushing out.

'The worst problem was making a relationship, which really I think took about a year . . . ages . . . especially with a second one, because when they come home – you're so used to dealing with babies, and you just sort of feed them and tuck them up, and he was very good and just used to go to sleep and you shut the door and that's it. He was very little trouble the first two or three months so it was almost as though he wasn't there. I think once you break that link immediately after birth it's very hard to make it again. You suddenly realize at about six months that you're fond of him and you realize that you hadn't been before. I don't really think I found it difficult at the time to look after him, it was just very much a business, you know, a job; I think I'm much more aware with him of how sometimes I do feel more fond of him and how at other times I don't. Also he was a very difficult baby and I don't know if that affects you in all kinds of different ways. He used to be very grumpy and he wouldn't sleep. He was very good for about two or three months and I think once he began becoming a bit aware of what was happening he realized he couldn't do anything, he started crying and he never slept through the night. Going twice a day to bring the milk to the hospital was like going to work in a sense: it wasn't really anything to do with having a baby, it was very odd; and coming out of the hospital and being up in the ward without a baby was terrible because you feel a sense of loss but you're not quite sure what it is you're feeling, because you haven't met this baby and you don't think: Oh I'm missing such and such; it's not a defined personality you can miss. Something's not there, and after a while you forget what it is that isn't there. I think you still feel a sense of loss but in a way the baby doesn't replace it when the baby comes back because there's such a gap, such a hiatus, nearly a month . . . very peculiar sensation, and I can well understand how those babies get battered if some mothers are very busy or not able to talk about it. I never felt like battering him but I could always feel a difficulty, and I think Jack as well found it difficult. He was much less interested in the second baby, partly because he was premature. It took him three or four months to come round to noticing him, but second babies I suppose are at a disadvantage anyway, the gloss is taken off a bit. But I think having a premature first baby must be much, much worse than the second one, because you've got nothing to compare the experience with; at least with the second one you can realize at some stage why it is that you feel the way you do.

'I just remember that there was this strange odd feeling that there was no baby anywhere and that there's been no pregnancy and you'd just spent a week in hospital, and you know what it's like anyway when you're in hospital with your first baby, it's so absolutely divorced from real life.'

Anxieties, conscious or unconscious, are at their height in the earliest postnatal period. This was the atmosphere on the post-natal ward when I was there with my baby daughter. Sally, whose baby is three days old, is asked to keep him in her room because he has an infection. She is overwhelmed with anxiety by this baby, who was unplanned. He seems to feed continually and defecate just as continually. She describes spending the night mopping up the milk oozing out of her breasts and 'the shit' oozing out of the baby's bottom. In the morning she begs the doctor to move him away from her, and asks the paediatrician to make a thorough examination, because she fears her baby to be abnormal. Sally is Canadian, and the birth puts an end to her stay in England and to her freedom; the couple have decided to return and settle in Canada. When she was pregnant her mother wrote to say she must get a nanny to do the feeding, and change the nappies. Like her mother, Sally feels unable to cope with an infant; unable to contain his or her own feelings. She cannot face the thought of leaving hospital, and begs to stay some extra days.

Meanwhile Jo's baby has to lie under a special lamp because she has jaundice. She looks tiny and pitiful lying naked with a white band around her eyes. Jo was in hospital with high blood pressure on a number of occasions during pregnancy; after the birth there were complications with the placenta for which she had to be rushed to the operating theatre and given total anaesthesia. She feels a special attachment to this baby, her second child, who has given her a difficult pregnancy and difficult delivery and now needs special attention and care. Jo is herself a midwife and the other women in the ward come to her for advice. She becomes the expert, yet one of them.

A baby has just died on the ward, a 'cot death', and the atmosphere is tense. The staff seem particularly brusque and the women's anxiety is at its height. Several women are sobbing. The young mother whose baby died stays in hospital a few days and the father visits frequently. They talk to the other mothers and establish a relationship with the babies. They seem reluctant to leave the hospital, where they feel they are leaving a part of themselves. The rumour spreads that a second baby has died. Panic spreads. Each woman fears for her baby. Trust in the hospital falters. Conversation around the dinner table remains innocuous: one woman wonders if she will fit into her old clothes, another complains about her aches and pains, a third complains about the food. A few jokes are cracked about the staff and there is now a feeling of solidarity. At the next table everyone is eating in silence. One woman asks the woman bringing the food if she can have a spoon. She is told to get it herself. A few women smile. All the time there is ambiguity as to how much a woman will be served in the ward and how much she is expected to do things for herself. A woman who has recently delivered sits down at the table. She is asked about the birth by a woman she met at the antenatal classes. The other women eat their stewed prunes and custard in silence. A baby is heard crying. A few women look up. One woman offers to go and see which room the crying is coming from.

The anxiety in this first week is basic, concerning life and death, and relating to the real physical and mental fragility of the infant and the power of the mother over life and death. She has just given life and she can take it away again. She has to keep the baby alive through appropriate care and feeding, and to keep destructive forces at bay.

In the hospital setting the strict routine and the presence of competent nurses regulate much of this anxiety. Rather than containment, however, there is often avoidance. Instead of helping mothers to confront anxieties there is a tendency for the nursing staff to take over the care of babies. Although this may relieve some of the anxiety temporarily, it bursts forth intermittently as I have just described. And many mothers, on leaving the structured setting of the hospital, and experiencing responsibility for the baby for the first time, feel overwhelmed by the previously unexpressed anxiety. Erica said: 'I can remember, the first time, looking out of the window and seeing a red bus, and suddenly it had a terrific impact on me: My God! there's all that lot to cope with as well!' It is only by actually dealing with her baby and getting to know her or him through continuous contact and care that a woman can gain confidence and contain her own and her baby's anxieties about life and death.

Help, emotional and practical, is essential for a mother – but it must be help which gives psychological space and time to both the mother and her baby.

For the woman who is in touch with these early anxieties and able to tolerate them, the first week in hospital can be painful. Responsibility is removed from her hands: she is told what to do and when to do it, regardless of the needs of her particular baby. More often than not the baby is removed from her after she has given birth, a time when she most wants to hold and explore and feel at one with her or him again after the traumatic separation of birth. Instead of being left to get to know her child, understand her or his needs and learn to feel less frightened of her ability to deal adequately with them, a woman is given standard instructions and assailed with contradictory advice.

Cecily described how her problem was that she had too much milk during the first days before the production of milk became regulated by the baby's intake – so that she was in great pain and the baby couldn't get hold of the nipple. The nurses in hospital assumed, in spite of what she repeatedly told them, that her problem was the usual one of not having enough milk, and she was given advice which only increased the difficulty. Only on her return home did she learn from her mother, who had had the same problem, that the way to deal with this was to wrap a cloth tightly round her chest and to express as much milk as possible before the feed, so that her breasts became softer and the baby could get hold of the nipple.

Tara felt disappointed when her baby didn't seem interested in taking the breast just after she was born. She had always imagined that was something which happened naturally and easily. The baby's lack of interest lasted for some time, and even when she tried to suck she soon gave up. Tara was upset and worried about this, as she wanted to breast feed. She had reluctantly given the baby some glucose water because she was crying with – Tara presumed – hunger. This is what she wrote in her diary on the third day: 'Today I tried the breast which she wouldn't touch at all, wouldn't attempt to suck and just cried. A nurse came in and started telling me that everything I was doing was wrong. First of all why had I not given Sofia the morning's glucose drink. She than grabbed her and gave her a bottle, leaving me in tears. She then asked scoldingly why I hadn't written down anything on the chart of feeds and proceeded to *make up* a chart for the last few days. She asked me if I put cream on my nipples, and I showed her the cream Sheila (the antenatal class teacher) had

123

recommended, but she said she didn't know what that was and I must put on Massé cream which she brought in. She felt my breasts and said: "They are still soft, nothing will happen for some days" . . . (Another nurse five minutes earlier had said: "Your breasts are hard, they will get engorged if you are not careful".) Same with the temperature. One nurse says the room is much too hot and the next nurse says the baby is going to die of cold.'

Tara's bursting into tears when the nurse took over would be called the 'blues' and ascribed to hormonal changes in the days after the birth. But in fact there were very clear reasons why she was crying at this point, to do with her anxieties about breast feeding, which wasn't progressing satisfactorily and to which was added direct criticism of her efforts at mothering (though at a less emotional time this would not have resulted in crying). It would have been less devaluing to her and more constructive if the nurse had discussed with her the pros and cons of giving glucose and, if it seemed a good idea, had encouraged *her* to give the bottle, rather than taken over in this way leaving her feeling hopeless and useless. Another problem intimately linked with the hospital setting is the lack of continuing relationship between the mother and one particular nurse. In the incident described Tara had never seen this particular nurse before, and felt bombarded with contradictory advice from a number of different nurses whom she did not know, and even from the 'tea lady'. It was only later that she spoke to the Sister, who gave her practical and constructive advice without criticism or the need to take over, and breast feeding became well established.

Her experience also illustrates the problems attendant on the hierarchical structure in the hospital, where the people at the bottom of the edifice are concerned with enforcing rules and accounting to their superiors – like the nurse who had to make up a chart, and a 'perfect chart', because the paediatrician would be coming around. (Needless to say, he never asked to see the chart.)

Lesley had to insist in order to keep her baby with her all the time: 'I couldn't bear to part with her, I didn't want anyone to take her away from me; I wanted to be there if she woke up and comfort her if she cried. I had a vague feeling that she might get lost – or something might happen to her if she went to the nursery, which was quite far from my room.' For the woman who feels this way, a home birth is the best solution. Even the more 'liberal' hospitals impose constraints on the relationship. For example, if the woman is tired and needs a rest the only solution in hospital is for the baby to go to the nursery, whereas at home the husband or friend or grandmother can help at night without necessarily creating a similar barrier. Mother and baby can rest together. In hospital the two possibilities seem to be that either the mother gets a rest without her baby or she can be with her baby but must cope singlehanded.

Of course not all women can find a helpful environment at home, and this is a problem for more than the first week. And some women adapt well to the hospital routine.

Sometimes acceptance only indicates fatigue, however:

Barbara . . . She cried as soon as her head was born, she cried and she was still screaming when the rest of her was born and they put her in her little cot and cleaned her up and she was still yelling, and she was quiet for about an hour after I'd fed her that first day, but she just screamed after that.

Dana What happened the first night – was she with you?

Barbara No, I said not, I would like to sleep that night, because I thought: She's only getting colostrum from me anyway, so I said would they give her water and if she really yelled would they bring her. Well, they didn't, so I don't know whether she yelled or not. The next day she was very good and she slept all night. I couldn't believe that. I put her to bed after a feed at about ten I suppose, and she didn't wake up until half past five or six. That was too good to be true. She's been waking up about every three or four hours. The first night I was in hospital they said she slept quite well and that she didn't scream much so they didn't come and bring her; I didn't sleep too badly the first night and they get you up at five anyway to feed the babies then.

Barbara was pleased to have a good night's sleep. She doesn't believe that the baby can need her – only her milk, and since her breasts have 'only colostrum' she does not feel necessary to her baby. Such an attitude is encouraged by hospital practices.

Feeding forms a central part of the earliest relationship with the baby. Each woman must decide for herself if she wants to breast feed or bottle feed; a decision to breast feed because she feels she ought to or because her doctor or her husband thinks she ought to is fraught with problems. To say that breast feeding is better physiologically or psychologically for the baby would be to assume that it always goes well and is enjoyed by both parties; this is not the case. Similarly one cannot talk about the merits of breast feeding versus bottle feeding without considering each particular feeding relationship, including the way in which weaning was carried out. As we can see from the following description by Mahler, breast feeding does not automatically involve greater intimacy and contact for instance: 'One mother . . . proudly breast-fed her babies, but only because it was convenient (she did not have to sterilize bottles); it made her feel successful and efficient. While breast feeding her child, she supported her on her lap with the breast reaching into the baby's mouth. She did not support or cradle the baby with her arms because she wanted her arms free to do as she pleased, independent of the nursling's activity . . . Another mother breast-fed her little girl, but her puritanical upbringing prevented her from feeling comfortable with a nursing infant, and she did not like to be seen nursing. On the other hand, there was a mother who thoroughly enjoyed her children when they were infants but did not breast feed them. During feeding she held them close, supporting them well. She smiled and talked to them.'[59]

Charlotte describes the pressures to breast feed which she experienced in hospital: 'I had my traumas with breast feeding. I found the nursery-nurses were the ones who helped us and unfortunately there weren't enough of them. I had about twenty questions to ask every time and you just couldn't find anybody to ask and I didn't seem to be getting anywhere. He seemed to be permanently hungry even when he'd had his feed. So they put me on the breast pump because they thought perhaps I didn't have enough, but that proved the opposite, it proved that I had quite sufficient. So they said "Go on to part breast feeding and part bottle feeding" and that *did* work, but I found that I was absolutely exhausted, to the point of falling asleep while I was feeding him in the middle of the night, and I could feel I was already tempted to drop the breast-feeding idea altogether, for my own benefit, otherwise I wouldn't survive. But then there was awful pressure against bottle feeding, you felt terribly guilty. One day I went down to the nursery and one girl said "That's it, I'm stopping, I just can't carry on" – the baby wasn't cooperating and all this – and I remember thinking: Oh, perhaps if she's done it I could mention it to somebody, but I didn't have the nerve, they all thought it was so terrible. I carried on once I got home, but in all for about four weeks, and he just seemed to be so happy when on the bottle; I mean it made me think perhaps I should have said something earlier on, but I think I was trying very hard to do the right thing, because I still know now, despite my experience, that it's a lot better, and you see he was big: up until about nine months he was much, much too big; now he's started to slim off, but I was recommended by a GP to put him on mixed feeding at four weeks, which I did because he was just so hungry and used to feed every two and a half hours.

'I'd convinced myself, while I was still in the hospital, that there was something lacking in me, that I didn't have the milk, and then they put me on this breast pump and I remember that day thinking: Oh, it's not me, it's him.'

A frequent reason given for unsuccessful breast feeding is the 'insufficiency' of the milk. Given proper advice and care, however, most mothers should be able to breast feed their infant. One researcher, by reducing feeds from six to five a day, caused the 'not enough milk' syndrome in about a third of the first-time mothers he studied.[60] Another has reported that babies fed on demand ate more frequently, gained more weight by the ninth day, caused only half as much nipple soreness in the mothers, and were more likely to be breast feeding at one month, than those who followed a rigid schedule.[61] He also writes that 'wide variations in the incidence of breast feeding can hardly be explained by the oft-repeated suggestion that women are now unable to produce sufficient milk to feed their babies . . . It is almost certainly the case that differences are due to differences in management of lactation.' And: 'Any diagnosis that breast milk does not suit a baby is always wrong.* Exceptions to this rule are so rare that I have never yet seen one.'[62]

---

*This view would not be held by everybody.

Some women have no wish to breast feed and in some cases even feel disgusted by the idea; this, no doubt, goes back to their own childhood feelings about their mother's breasts, influenced by, for instance, the anger they felt at being weaned. Some women fear for their figure or fear sexual excitement in breast feeding. To other women breast feeding seems undignified or embarrassing and is just 'not done' amongst the people they know.

The most appropriate choice of method depends on each particular mother and baby. What it is possible to say, however, is that breast and bottle feeding are qualitatively different experiences for the baby. The fact that the breast is a real part of the mother, as opposed to the bottle which can be replaced by another bottle, cannot but colour the experience. Winnicott, paediatrician and psychologist, talks about the difference of quality in relation to the aggressive element in the act of feeding: '. . . the human infant has ideas. Every function is elaborated in the psyche, and even at the beginning there is fantasy belonging to the excitement and the experience of feeding. The fantasy, such as it is, is of a ruthless attack on the breast, and eventually on the mother, as the infant becomes able to perceive that it is the mother whose breast is attacked. There is a very strong aggressive element in the primitive love impulse which is the feeding impulse. In terms of the fantasy of a slightly later date the mother is ruthlessly attacked, and although but little aggression may be observable it is not possible to ignore the destructive element in the aim of the infant. Satisfactory feeding finishes off the orgy physically, and also rounds off the fantasy experience; nevertheless there develops a considerable degree of concern on account of the aggressive ideas as soon as the infant begins to put two and two together, and to find that the breast that was attacked and emptied is part of the mother.'

Winnicott goes on: 'The infant who has had a thousand goes at the breast is evidently in a very different condition from the infant who has been fed an equal number of times by the bottle; the survival of the mother is more of a miracle in the first case than in the second. I am not suggesting that there is nothing that the mother who is feeding by bottle can do to meet the situation. Undoubtedly she gets played with by her infant, and she gets the playful bite, and it can be seen that when things are going well the infant almost feels the same as if there is breast feeding. Nevertheless there is a difference. In psychoanalysis, where there is time for a gathering together of all the early roots of the full-blown sexual experience of adults, the analyst gets very good evidence that in a satisfactory breast-feed the actual fact of taking from part of the mother's body provides a "blue-print" for all types of experience in which instinct is involved.' Winnicott then describes how the greater difficulties of the breast feeding situation go side by side with its richness: '. . . success in breast feeding does not mean that all problems are thereby smoothed out; success means that a very much more intense and rich experience of relationships is embarked upon, and along with this goes a greater rather than a lesser chance for the infant to produce symptoms which indicate that the really important inherent difficulties that belong to life, and to human relationships, are being met. When bottle feeding has to be sub-stituted there is often an easing in all respects, and, in terms of easy management, a doctor may feel that by easing matters all round he is obviously doing something good. But this is looking at life in terms of ill-health and health. Those who care for infants must be able to think in terms of poverty and richness of the personality, which is quite another thing . . . Difficulties can arise in the mother and the infant as a result of the richness of the experience of breast feeding, but this can hardly be taken as an argument against it, since the aim in infant care is not simply the avoidance of symptoms. The aim in infant care is not limited to the establishment of health, but includes the provision of con-ditions for the richest possible experience, with long-term results in increased depth and value in the character and personality of the individual.'[63]

For Barbara breast feeding progressed fairly smoothly.

Barbara It was just the same as four years ago, except this time I was wide awake when they came and said 'Breast or bottle' and I said: 'I'm feeding her and leave her alone' and that was the only time I was asked. After that there were just no bottles brought, that was it. The bottles arrived (for the other babies) and it was up to me to get on and feed her myself. They said

'Feed her three minutes each side, she won't get much yet', and I thought: Well I know that . . . that's how I felt – very cocky is the only word – I've done it this far . . . but they weren't a lot of help. She cried an awful lot the first day. All the books say they should go to sleep. Well, she wouldn't have any of that and the nursing auxiliary came and said feed her for longer, and I didn't see the point, but she said 'Do as you're told' and I did – and I finished up being so sore that they were writing on all the reports 'creams' and all the rest of it, and I thought: That's enough to put anybody off.

She was able to breast feed because she could adapt to her baby.

Barbara She tried to suck just the nipple, she wouldn't open her mouth very wide, so I had to try and compress more of all the surrounding area; it was three or four days before she could open her mouth more. So it was a question of threading inside so she could start, then she was OK. When my milk started coming it was very fast, and it always has been, it comes out in fountains in the morning . . . she sucks very gently now because it's so fast, you see, she doesn't need to suck very hard or she'd choke, and she's a very ladylike feeder really because it's so fast. At the beginning she sucked harder because there was nothing coming.

I felt she didn't really know how we'd be most comfortable and nor did I, but I felt: I will jolly well find out.

I did worry for the first six weeks almost, because she seemed so hungry; I thought: Oh heavens, and I tried supplementary bottles but I didn't get on with them – probably because I hated the sight of the bottles – but I was determined one way or the other that it wouldn't fail, so I suppose that's why it didn't.

For many women breast feeding can, in the beginning be extremely painful, either because the nipples get very sore or because the breasts get engorged – which, on top of the 'after-pains' in the lower abdomen,* may all feel too much.

*Contractions of the uterus which are important in restoring the uterus to its former size are increased when the breasts are stimulated and can be quite painful. Sensual feelings may also increase these contractions.

Abigail Lewis describes in her diary her initial feelings: 'I hadn't realized a natural process could be so painful. It is as if blinding light was poured into the eyes, or a deafening noise into the ears . . . The nurse said lovingly that the baby was "a good little nurser," meaning, I suppose, the way she rose to the breast with a snap of a hungry trout. After the first bite, however, it was not so bad; rather pleasant, in fact. I could feel my uterus contract and a purely physiological peace and warmth ran through me.'[64]

For other women the pain can last for weeks, particularly if the nipples become cracked.

Problems can come from the baby. Some babies are very sleepy and poor at sucking. They never seem to take a proper feed but want to suck every time they wake up, or in some cases don't seem interested in feeding at all. Other babies are too fussy to settle down to a feed, while others enjoy biting or chewing the nipple.

A mother who feels unsure about what she can give from herself to her baby and who worries about the quality or quantity of her milk may feel that the baby is refusing to suck because her milk is not good enough; is going to starve because he/she is not sucking for long enough; is 'attacking' her for not providing proper milk. If she feels too unsure of herself or not certain that she really wants to breast feed, she is more likely to give up if the baby is one who doesn't respond by immediate and full sucking followed by a long peaceful sleep.

Helen's comments about breast feeding illustrate how fears can interfere with long-term breast feeding: 'I felt just a little bit squeamish. I remember thinking: Oh my goodness if all goes well and I'm still feeding him at, say seven months, with great big teeth . . . When I put it this way, I must say that when I stopped at three weeks I was quite pleased. It was painful most of the time, but I thought it was good I managed it for three weeks in terms of mothers' antibodies and things like that.'

Like Helen, a doctor's wife, many mothers feel driven to breast feed when they really would rather not. Sometimes they discover a pleasure they had not anticipated, but often they give up with a sense of failure. Although there may be nothing more positive and rewarding than a successful breast-feeding relationship, equally there may be nothing more harmful than an unsuccessful one where one or both partners become tense, anxious, resentful or guilt-ridden. In any case, it is on the whole the women who are wholeheartedly intent on breast feeding who manage it. Indeed: one study showed[65] that women who expressed a clear wish to breast feed actually gave their babies more milk at an average fourth-day feed than the women who were half-hearted about breast feeding or those who preferred artificial feeding but were nevertheless trying to breast feed.

This study found that women who needed to give their babies supplementary bottles actually kept almost half their milk in their breasts, and the milk could not be removed by the sucking baby or the breast pump. It could, however, be removed by setting off the let-down reflex artificially by injection of a certain hormone. (The let-down reflex is the mechanism which leads to the expulsion of the milk, and is known to be very sensitive to emotions.) The study also found that women who had expressed a preference for artificial feeding during their pregnancy were more likely to report that the baby refused the breast or had difficulty in sucking, whereas the women who had expressed a preference for breast feeding were more likely to say that the baby refused to take the bottle. These findings give some idea of how a woman's feelings (especially her less conscious feelings) affect the course of breast feeding through both physiological reactions and handling of the baby. For example, one way of presenting the bottle or the breast to a baby is more likely to lead to rejection than another.

Another author, Merell Middlemore,[66] studied forty-six 'nursing couples'; she emphasized the importance of the behaviour of the baby, and in particular 'the strength or weakness of the child's inherent impulse to suck'. Difficulties arise when the baby sucks poorly. 'His failure soon affects the mother, although she may be eager to suckle and well equipped for it, and events may follow a course something like that described below. The child is weakly, perhaps, and inert. For a week or more he draws no more than a dozen times at the nipple before falling asleep; within a few days the mother suffers from his persistent refusal to suck. For want of a strong pull on the breasts her yield of milk is likely to be slow and scanty, and worry over the child's loss of weight will further decrease the flow. As things go badly, her concern about the slow establishment of suckling puts her in much the same position as that of women who start by doubting their ability to feed the child; nervousness makes her almost as clumsy and diffident as they.' There are two phases of suckling, 'the period of mutual adaptation followed by the period of equilibrium', and 'The mother's original attitude towards breast feeding is always modified by the behaviour of the baby, so that after a few days of suckling some women come to enjoy it more than they expect, while others dislike it more.' Middlemore also points out how some women may be able to deal with one type of baby and not with another. 'For instance, the feeding of inert babies involves the mother in difficulties quite different from those she meets when the baby is constitutionally fussy and excited, and she may be able to manage one kind of baby but not the other . . . Thus, the mothers of some of the inert babies under observation actually feared that their babies would die at the breast during sleep, and this worried them from time to time; but they cannot have feared to be hurt while giving the breast, for the babies made no attempt to bite them.'

Middlemore mentions that in some cases refusal to suck at the breast may originate in the baby alone, and gives the example of a baby who was later to have psychoanalytic treatment for her feeding difficulties. 'A girl of two years and nine months was treated for feeding difficulties. She ate very little – never without being persuaded by her parents – but in her games and fantasies during analysis and at home she was continually biting. Among other things she pretended to be a biting dog, a crocodile, a lion, a pair of scissors that could cut up cups, a mincing machine and a machine for grinding cement. The history of her feeding was peculiar. She was weaned during the first fortnight because she showed no interest in the breast and would not feed. She slept during sucking and refused the nipple repeatedly, not with much ado, but by quietly turning the head away. The difficulty in feeding seemed to have originated entirely in the child, for the mother secreted a fair amount of milk to begin with; moreover, she had suckled an elder child successfully and wanted to feed this one . . . What was clear was that the baby was unwilling to suck, while difficulties which began at the breast continued steadily through all kinds of feeding from bottle, spoon and cup. Until she came for treatment she had never put a spoonful of food into her own mouth. The point is that although she had never sucked the breast properly, still less "attacked it", she entertained very fierce fantasies of biting.' The author connects these fantasies with the feelings during hunger, the 'biting' sensations in the stomach.

Other difficulties are more directly linked with the mother: mechanical difficulties such as the shape of the breast or the mother's fear of giving the breast, her clumsiness, her fear of the pain or the sensations connected with breast feeding. Also, sedation during labour can affect the baby's ability to suck effectively for up to four days after birth.[67] In the cases of unsuccessful feeding there is often a vicious circle. The mother becomes more anxious or unhappy or exasperated when the baby is irritable or inert or having difficulties in sucking, which in turn increases the baby's problems.

It is important, though, to realize that even in cases which Middlemore calls 'satisfied sucklings' there can be problems during the initial period. For example, 'in spite of their enjoyment of the breast some of the active babies refused a few of their earlier feeds with some screaming protest. Some seemed to enjoy biting.' In addition, most mothers have at least some doubts about the quality of the substance which comes out of their body. As another psychoanalyst puts it: 'Such an intimate, close relationship is greatly affected and determined by the mother's unconscious feelings about what she contains inside her own body; what is the nature of this watery fluid which so many women are doubtful about at first, bearing as it does a slight resemblance to the real stuff that comes out of the bottle, for that can be measured and scientifically treated to be germ-free. The best help in allaying these anxieties is a baby who sucks firmly, becomes contented and is seen to thrive. But not many babies are able to reach this happy state without a little help.'[68]

In view of the difficulties involved in establishing a successful feeding relationship, the setting can be crucial.

Barbara wanted to get on with it on her own:

Barbara The nurse said 'How are you getting on?' I said 'Oh,

I'm not very clever yet but we'll learn.' I said 'I find it more awkward on this side (the left)', so when I finished the right side and I was changing her over, she got hold of her head and pulled my breast up and went clunk . . . she put the two together with great force . . . Beatrice didn't . . . I mean she could suck very well right from the beginning but to start off with she'd lose the nipple perhaps once, but as it slid sideways out of her mouth she'd push her back on to me, and I didn't like it and I was jolly glad when she'd gone. I never saw her again after that, I came home, but I thought: Supposing you had that three or four days, you'd say 'Oh no, leave me alone', wouldn't you; at least that's how I'd feel. It wasn't nice.

This is very different from the setting Winnicott[69] describes in the following passage. '. . . sometimes a baby will show a need to establish the right to the personal way by refusing food, turning the head away, or going to sleep. This is very disappointing for a mother who is longing to get on with being generous. Sometimes she cannot stand the tension in the breasts . . . If mothers knew, however, that the turning away of the baby from the breast or from the bottle had a value, they might be able to manage these difficult phases. They would take the turning away, or the sleepiness, as an indication for special care. This means that everything must be done in the way of providing the right setting for the feed. The mother must be comfortable. The baby must be comfortable. Then there must be time to spare. And the baby's arms must be free. The baby must be able to have skin free with which to feel the skin of the mother. It may even be that the baby needs to be put naked on the mother's naked body. If there is difficulty, the one thing that is absolutely no use at all is the attempt to force the feeding. If there is a difficulty, it is only by giving the baby the setting to find the breast that there is any hope of establishing the right feeding experience.'

It takes a most sensitive nurse to help a mother in such an endeavour. Even unintrusive and gentle help can be experienced as criticism during this early postnatal period. At home too, of course, a woman may not find the necessary unintrusive help from husband, mother or friends which she requires in these first weeks, or may experience them as critical and intrusive. But in hospital the continual change-over of staff makes it particularly difficult for a trusting relationship to develop.

CHAPTER ELEVEN

Yesterday I burst into tears and I don't know why

A GREAT many women, like Barbara, experience feelings of depression at some point after the birth of their baby. Some get very depressed and a few have severe enough reactions to require hospitalization. The term 'postnatal blues' is sometimes used to refer to crying which occurs in the first week after the birth. 'Postnatal depression' is often used indiscriminately to refer to all these different states, but I would say that this term should be reserved for a state in which depression is lasting and involves the relentless feelings of guilt and self-admonition characteristic of depression in general.* Postnatal depression is the expression of a postnatal disturbance.

The experience of having a baby, even when it is not disturbed, involves psychological processes of change and integration, and working through these changes inevitably involves some feelings of depression. They relate to the loss of the baby inside the body, and later to the loss of the mother and baby union of the first weeks and months, the loss of the 'old self' in the case of a first birth, and the loss of a fantasy baby and a fantasy mother in favour of the real baby and the real mother/self.

Feelings of depression also relate to a woman's struggle with her feelings about separation from her mother and with her feelings about good and bad mothering in terms of her view of her mother and her view of herself now. One woman may have feelings of depression and depletion because she has lost the baby inside her, but will then be able to regain a sense of union through breast feeding which makes her feel good about herself and her baby. The same problems and conflicts are there for the women who suffer from postnatal depression in the strict sense;

* What is called 'clinical depression' in the psychiatric literature.

such women get stuck in the experience of bad mothering and the need to attack themselves for being inadequate as they feel their mother was.

A woman in this state may feel unconsciously deserted by her baby whom she in turn rejects, then attack herself for being such a bad mother, reproducing her early feelings of desertion by and anger with her own mother. Any good experience from the past can no longer be called upon.

As for the 'postnatal blues' that occur straight after the birth, the feelings there can be part of a postnatal depression or can be the normal accompaniment to the changes referred to above. The term also refers to something different from depression and relates to a state of mind surrounding a physically and emotionally taxing major event, an atmosphere of emergency, leading to feelings of relief, exhaustion, heightened sensitivity to circumstances and people, disorientation, and so on.

Examples of women who suffered from a postnatal depression are Helen, whose depression was triggered off by the death of her mother during pregnancy, and Jane, who became depressed soon after the birth of her baby.

Helen's mother died when she was five months pregnant with her second child:

'I forgot all about the baby, in a sense; I neglected my appetite, I didn't eat much and at the same time I put on just the same amount of weight. And the whole thing also from five months to the birth is a bit of a blank because I was so tired the whole time, so tired because of all those late nights we were supporting my Dad, so really the unborn baby was . . . well, more than neglected in my thoughts. I didn't think much about it at all: occasionally panicky attacks when I'd think Oh good heavens, or it used to kick me or something like that, or I'd feel a movement and I'd think Oh yes, gosh, this baby's due . . . it's horrible really. I openly said to people I know well, I'm sure something's going to go wrong, and when it did, when he was born and didn't breathe, I remember sitting there most coolly and thinking: Oh yes, this is the next thing, I was right – almost patting myself on the back. (I had thought that I would have a handicapped child, or that something would go wrong with the actual birth.) I also remember thinking a lot because of these upsets I had had, emotional upsets after my mother's death, that that would cause something to go wrong with the baby. I was very conscious that my despondent attitude over those last months – throughout it really, except for the month and a half I had off (free from depression) – would affect him or her, that he or she would be born depressed or miserable.

'I remember after Bernard was born (her first child) I found that he was quite a cheerful, outgoing little soul, and I said to my husband "Well, thank goodness, after those three months of depression (at the beginning of pregnancy)" . . . because it was the first time I really experienced what I would call depression. I wasn't communicating, I was losing weight and just feeling no energy, feeling sick – I was sick so often, everything I ate – but it didn't seem to affect Bernard in any way, he was really quite happy. When Martin was born it was very dramatic because he didn't breathe and he looked – because of being born so quickly – he looked really peculiar; he looked really awful. He was all puffed up, and this thing about his eyes not opening for the first four days – I didn't really see him as a person because he didn't look at me, whereas Bernard had right from the start opened his eyes and looked straight up, but Martin looked a peculiar little thing.

'It wasn't just me who thought that, the nurses had a look at him and said "Oh yes, he's had a rough time"; he was all puffed up and bruised and his eyes didn't open at all till about the fourth or fifth day, and also of course he was very sleepy with the pethidine. I can remember being very grateful to the doctor who said: "That baby's had such a rough birth; you try and imagine yourself with a splitting headache, that's probably what that baby is experiencing." I was in ten days or two weeks . . . It took me a long time to warm to him and it was only when I left the hospital, travelling home in the car, that I had any what I'd call maternal feelings towards him at all; in fact I positively disliked him a few times, not because he was ugly – no, it wasn't just that – there was just something about him that I couldn't put my finger on. I think it was his sleepiness, because he wasn't interested in feeding particularly, he took ages over his bottle. He had hair and everything . . . Looking back at the photographs, he wasn't grossly ugly in that he had big blotchy patches or that his skull was misshapen or anything. It was just not opening his eyes and the feeding, and also I felt something was going to happen and I was carrying on this mood.

'I can remember going up to visit after about a week and that was the climax – I remember insisting to the nurse and to my sister that there was something wrong and I withdrew from him. It was me, because my sister said, "Oh I think he's sweet"; she couldn't see anything, she said "It's probably you're being a bit emotional after having the baby." But I wasn't like that, I was completely the other way around with Bernard, absolutely delighted. It just didn't occur to me to think anything else but that he was lovely. I was so excited after Bernard's birth I didn't sleep the whole week practically, but with Martin I withdrew from him, I slept well – mind you they dish out sleeping tablets. I slept well except for the first two nights, and that was only because there was a noisy woman in the next bed and I withdrew a little, and each time Robert came to visit I said "He's not like Bernard" and I kept questioning him. I tried to find excuses: I thought maybe it's because my mother isn't here, because I missed her at this stage, she'd visit every day when I'd had Bernard. So I missed that, though I didn't think about it a lot; I probably blocked a little. No, I just had this feeling that I didn't like him particularly, I was really withdrawn. I wasn't particularly concerned about changing him. I had to be reminded a few times: "Do you think you ought to change him?" I would feel awfully guilty about that. They obviously thought: "Well, she's had one baby, she should be doing a little better." And I was terribly tired in spite of sleeping so well. As I said, I first started liking him when we got into the car and on the way home. It must have been something to do with looks too because by then he was beginning to look quite sweet, and looking at me, feeding better, and by the time he was three weeks old, he was just like any other healthy baby.

'I wasn't really involved after my mother's death: I had to remind myself to go to check-ups, I let myself go, I didn't pay any attention to my appearance. When my mother died when I was five months pregnant my first reaction was to be flooded here (her breasts) – I was quite full by five months: the colostrum, that was my first reaction, and from then on the pregnancy was out of my mind; indifferent and too tired to cope with it all. Now that I've used the word indifference for the pregnancy I wonder if it isn't a little bit of indifference to Martin: yes, I think it would be a very good word to describe the way I sometimes feel. Sometimes lately I look at Martin, just an expression and I think – the face he's pulling – "Oh that looks like Bernard", and I feel nice then; or else when he's being particularly charming I feel warm towards him, but it doesn't last long. Maybe I can relate that to tiredness or the way I've been feeling lately, or the stresses of having two children, a hard-working husband, and being a little bit isolated living here, buying a home and things like that.'

Helen's tiredness and indifference are a form of depression. With the loss of her mother she describes a loss of her own capacity to mother (she has to be reminded to look after her infant). Her fears during the pregnancy that the baby will be handicapped perhaps refer to the handicap of starting life without a mother. 'Perhaps,' she says, 'it's because my mother isn't here', the baby becoming herself without a mother. When he is born, she experiences dislike because she finds the baby completely unresponsive and even believes that, as she had feared, he is mentally handicapped. Probably she dislikes in her child that aspect of herself which is unresponsive and rejecting of Mother at a time when her anger with her own mother for 'not being there' and letting her down at this crucial moment is aroused yet painful to accept. If her mother had not died just then, Helen would still have had to struggle with her images of good and bad mothering, but the time at which the death took place led her to become overwhelmed by and identified with the negative view of her mother.

It also comes out clearly how this particular baby fits in with Helen's fears that he will be abnormal or unhappy. His lack of responsiveness to her in the first week accentuates her own lack of responsiveness and interest in him. It is the responsive baby who feeds well and thrives and expresses demands unambiguously who makes the mother feel gratified and motherly and consequently more able to respond.

*

Jane – the woman mentioned earlier (p. 113) who felt that her first baby was the son her mother wanted her to be and the boy her husband's family wanted, to the extent that she felt the baby was not hers at all – became very depressed after the birth of her first child, John.

'I had a super pregnancy, I went to National Childbirth Trust classes. It was great, a great big build-up; the actual birth was all right. It was very painful in the end and they gave me pethidine and it knocked me out. I was out for two hours and I came to in time for the actual birth, I could push. For the first two days I don't think John murmured and I thought: Heavens! and then he started and I don't think he stopped. I gave birth and they put him in the cot without checking him. Jack got him out and said, "He's not breathing" and nobody had done anything about it. They said "Oh no, he's not." They took him to the special care unit and had him syphoned out. But I wasn't at all worried, I knew he was going to be all right. It's funny: I feel more for Jill (her second child); I know it's a terrible thing to say, but maybe I just felt like that about John; I never seemed to worry about him, he seemed so resilient, everything he does he comes out of all right. I don't understand it myself, there's a barrier between us. I don't feel like his mother – I never felt like his mother – it's really weird. I've always felt he was a third member of my marriage, he was just John.

'I cried solidly for nine days in hospital. I hated it: they were very unkind, terribly, terribly officious – I mustn't do this, I mustn't do that – and John cried and cried and cried and he used to wake all the other babies up; as soon as he opened his eyes he cried. At night all the babies would wake up and be fed and he'd scream; every night I had to go to the nursery, and every night they had to give me a sleeping tablet because I got in such a state, and it went on from there really. Breast feeding made it worse because he was always crying and he was quite satisfied – he was putting on masses of weight, he was huge – and everybody said "Oh, it's because you're breast feeding" or because of this or because of that. I felt very rejected because he cried all the time, and in the end very resentful; I never seemed to be able to do anything right, ever, and I still can't. He's a very discontented little boy. I should think that a good part of it was my reaction, but he definitely is a difficult person to get on with. When we came home, we were living in a flat, which wasn't very good anyway: everybody could hear every single sound – and he used to cry all day and all night; he used to go to sleep at ten o'clock at night and wake up at four in the morning, and Jack used to have to come and take over because I'd be frightened I'd kill him. Also I was breast feeding, and that was so awful to have to sit and breast feed a baby that you really didn't like – I really didn't – by the time he was six months old I didn't like him. Breast feeding was easier than bottles (I'm very idle), and during the day it was all right but it was at night that I really felt antagonistic.

'I really loved him, it was a love–hate relationship, I loved him so desperately as well as all these antagonistic feelings, and I wanted to breast feed him; I wanted to cuddle him and I wanted him to respond to me lovingly, but he never did. In the daytime he did, and he'd follow me around and he still does; and also I didn't know very many people – that's the other thing, it's the isolation when you've had a baby. I had the added thing of the girl downstairs, who'd had a baby at the same time as me; she knew it all, she was younger than me and yet she used to come and say, "Oh, you're not doing this, you're not doing that", and be very, very crude about the fact that I was breast feeding. I don't think I've ever been so unhappy.

'I didn't know that other women felt murderous at two o'clock in the morning: I honestly thought that I was the most evil mother in the world, because my mother – I couldn't tell her, she wasn't very much help; she's dead now – and Jack's family thought John was. . . . Oh they had him on a pedestal: that was one of the reasons I had another baby, to take the spotlight off him, because he really was a god, and Jack was too before we had John. I had all this to live up to; it was quite unbearable, and our marriage was a bit rocky anyway. Having a baby made me feel totally asexual. I just felt fat and old, a middle-aged mother; it was quite horrifying to look in the mirror and think I was somebody's mother; I lost myself, I lost my personality for a long time. Also I'd had an episiotomy and I felt pretty sore, and it put me off sex for months and months; Jack couldn't understand how I was feeling. I didn't like the idea that I was expected to do everything, and then I became difficult to live with anyway and Jack would do anything

143

for John. When he was there at the birth, as John came away from me literally, Jack looked at me and said "Are you all right?" I said "Yes" and he'd gone, and I didn't see him for about three hours because he went with John to the special-care unit and I was left there on the table for hours. He was so overwhelmed with John: he fell in love with him, and he used to change his nappy and get up in the night; he used to do anything for him. Where do I fit in all this? I just felt as though my life had gone, as if that was it, and it took a long time to realize I was still a person.

'In fact our marriage did break up for a while. I had a nervous breakdown. I lived on my own with John and that was the only time John and I ever got on really well for a length of time, I was happy with him then. I suppose I find it difficult to love them both together or something: they're terribly alike. John is very demanding and Jack is very demanding, and just having them one at a time was all right. I was trying to prove to myself that I was still young and sexy and I started having men. Oh, I went to pieces completely and Jack just came back and took me away. It still wasn't right when we got back together; I finally took an overdose and I went to be pumped out and they were so unkind. They said, "How can you do such a thing? . . . You've got such a lovely husband and such a lovely baby" – and I took the overdose because of Jack. At nine months old John had his own plate, his own cup, his own spoon and I wasn't allowed near him. And I used to say to Jack, "I feel superfluous." I felt very left out of the whole thing. I felt stuck at home. People used to come and before they'd say "How are you?" they'd look straight past you to the baby. John would never laugh, he was always grumpy. Also he was always ill as a baby; he had every allergy under the sun. I think that was worse than anything, the continual illness. I felt very much under criticism. There was nobody who approved of me: I think that was a lot of why I was depressed; also the loss of freedom. I still feel guilty at how angry John can make me feel. I don't know how much was the fact that he was a difficult baby or how much that I was a difficult mother, I really don't know – or how much I resented him – maybe I just resented how having him made me feel. But I think at the beginning I didn't feel antagonistic; I did feel that he really wasn't mine but that I loved him very much and I was very thrilled with him.'

In this poignant description Jane makes it clear how her depression revolved around her inability to live up to the image she created for herself of what she should be like as a mother. She felt criticized by her husband's family, by the nurses in hospital, and by the baby himself, whom she felt she could not please or get any appreciative response from. She felt she couldn't take pride in this baby as coming from herself: that he was 'the most beautiful child ever born' and the apple of his father's eye, but somehow he had nothing to do with her; she could not feel he was her child. At the same time his presence seemed to negate her as a person; she felt excluded from the baby–father relationship, and years later she still thinks of him as an intruder. It was as if his presence negated her own. Within the family context she felt she had produced the goods they had ordered and was now redundant. She also felt that no one was there to help and mother her; only the baby was getting care and attention.

In my research on first-time mothers[70] I found that the women who experienced difficulties of various kinds at this time (in particular postnatal depression) tended to have a more idealized notion of what a good mother should be like (perfect, selfless, all-sacrificing) and a greater depreciation of their own performances as mothers than did other women. In other words, they had a strict picture of how they felt they ought to be, and found that they could not possibly live up to this image. Very often the ideal picture was one which was also at odds with their experience of their own mothers, so that they were depreciating themselves in their identification with their mothers.

Jane gives evidence for a dichotomy of this kind (between how she sees herself and how she ought to be) as well as for the conflicting way in which she views the baby, who is both perfect and awful at the same time. For Jane the baby comes to represent the people in her life (from whom she feels she received no love). 'My mother and I didn't get on; she used to bash me. She adored Jack and when we got engaged she tried to talk him out of it because I wasn't good enough for him . . . 'There's eight years between my sister and me; she hated me and I adored her.' The baby's crying she experiences as a similar rejection of her, and this increases her self-deprecation. A vicious circle is set up.

With her second child, Jane reacts differently. First the baby is a girl, second she seems to be a different sort of child.

'She just is so placid. John would open his eyes and scream; Jill would think before she let rip, and even when she did, it wasn't this terrible pitch. John used to have this pitch which used to really jar; hers is rather apologetic, and she's been fabulous. She was very ugly, Jack and I both noticed. First thing we said was "My God she's ugly", whereas we thought John was the most beautiful child ever born; and she grew on us, she's so loving. Everything I do is right. I did like having a girl and I felt that she was my baby because I knew that the family liked boys. It's funny because I was prepared for anything except for such an ugly baby. I couldn't believe it. I suppose she seemed more ugly because she was a girl and an ugly boy isn't so bad. I think she looked like my mother.'

But even with this child Jane's feeling of being able to mother is precarious and one wonders if it isn't the baby who is depressed this time.

'I fed her until she was seven months, but I think there was a stage when I was starving her. I did try with a bottle, but she wouldn't have it, so I started to spoon feed her milk and I gave her powdered food, and then the milk would come back and I thought she wouldn't die for want of food. The awful thing is that I could have starved her to death. She got very thin and her motions were green. But she hardly ever cries for food. It was the woman next door, who is a midwife, who said "I think she's not getting enough food." She cries for her breakfast, but that's the only meal she makes a fuss about. During the day if she doesn't have another thing she won't mind; she'll just go to bed. It's quite frightening actually – I tend to think she's not hungry because John would yell and be absolutely indignant if his meal was three minutes late.'

But Jane finds it easier to cope with this very placid, un-demanding baby, who doesn't make her feel so criticized by constant demands and so rejected by constant crying. (For another woman it could be the placid, undemanding child she could 'starve to death' who would be the most difficult to bear.)

Depression after the birth of a baby can take different forms:

lack of interest as in Helen's case or violent feelings as in Jane's case. It can be short-lived or very long lasting. It can be fairly benign or devastating. It can be restricted to a feeling of inadequacy or it can actually affect the capacity to mother.

Depressed feelings can occur at different times. Soon after the birth, concerns can relate to the birth: to the loss of the foetus and a consequent sense of inner deadness. Later, concerns centre on the ability to care for the baby, and on resentment towards the baby.[71]

Here three women describe their feelings. The first became depressed in hospital: 'Immediately after the birth of my first baby I felt high and exhilarated. But that night I got sad. I cried all night long. During the next few days I lay on my bed thinking of how I would kill myself. I looked at how the windows opened and I concentrated on figuring out times when no nurses were on duty. I couldn't sleep at all. I tried to tell them I was depressed, and all they gave me were sleeping pills. I felt as if I'd never feel anything again but this incredible despair – that it would never end. I had nightmares. The one I remember best is where I would be feeding the baby. I would fall asleep and the baby would fall off the bed and be killed. I don't know why I had these dreams and impulses. I have a happy marriage and it was a wanted pregnancy.'[72]

The depression of another increased on returning home: 'My depression deepened into a profound inertia. I found it impossible to start any project, knowing that I would be interrupted by the baby's feeding schedule. Except for meeting the baby's needs I let everything else go. My image of myself as a responsible, competent adult was utterly destroyed. I hated myself for feeling depressed. A good mother should be serene and happy. This of course intensified the depression in a vicious cycle. In therapy I began to learn that I had a right to my feelings whether they were acceptable to others or not. Every few months, some of the depression would lift and I could feel more able to relate to people and to things.

'I was lucky that my baby was responsive to my attempts at play and this set me on the road to recovery. By the time my child was a year old I could hardly remember why I had felt so hopeless, even to the point of contemplating suicide. When I felt that way I thought my life would never change – that I would always feel that way – but my life was changing. Though I continued to find it hard, I was learning how to make being a mother a part of my life without being so overwhelmed by it that I couldn't meet my own needs as a person.'[73]

The third woman became depressed later: 'When my baby was about five weeks old I quite suddenly started getting these panics and I felt depressed and tense and exhausted and completely cut off from people and reality. And, above all, feelings of terrible inadequacy started coming over me in great waves, as though I'd never be able to manage anything. I couldn't understand it: I'd felt so marvellous for the first few weeks, and that's the hardest time.'[74]

Some women get depressed after an initial phase of excitement at having a new baby. The total involvement of the early phase dissipates when they fully realize the major changes brought to their lives. Other women are prepared for a difficult beginning and become depressed when after six months or a year their child is still waking up at night; or later when they discover that a toddler is more time-consuming than a baby or that having a child interferes with the pursuit of their own interests.

Adrienne Rich describes poignantly the difference between the stages: 'I envy the sensuality of having an infant of two weeks curled against one's breast; I do not envy the turmoil of the elevator full of small children, babies howling in the laundromat, the apartment in winter where pent-up seven- and eight-year-olds have one adult to look to for their frustrations, reassurances, the grounding of their lives.'[75]

Psychological explanations of postnatal depression have concentrated in particular on the woman's relationship with her own mother. One author[76] found that 'conflict over mothering' was the greatest difficulty for the majority of postnatally depressed women, and was rooted in an 'ambivalent identification with a controlling–rejecting mother'. Another author[77] mentions the particular difficulty of women 'whose relationship with their own mother was especially conflicted'. This comes out in Jane's earlier description of her relationship with her mother and her hatred of her son for being the favoured fantasized brother.

Postnatal depression has also been seen in terms of other

family relationships. For instance a woman may experience competition with the baby for the love of the other partner[78]; guilt connected with hostility against the baby,[79] or guilt about her parents when the baby is felt to be something stolen from the parent.[80] One study stresses the fact that husbands of women suffering from severe postnatal disturbances often increase their wives' feelings of inadequacy by competing with them for the mothering role rather than supporting them.[81]

Becoming a mother requires a change of roles. Most often, if it is their first child, women have to face the fact that work outside the home is no longer possible. Rewarding part-time work and good child-minding facilities are rarely available. Even when they are, many women feel qualms at handing over the care of their child. One study claims that 'present day role conflict' was more important in producing continuing difficulties in the women interviewed than 'personal insecurity related to past experiences'.[82] Ann Oakley also found that depressed moods after birth were related to current circumstances such as housing problems, segregation of roles between husband and wife, and lack of employment outside the home.[83]

In my own study of first-time mothers,[84] I looked on a first pregnancy as a crisis requiring a great deal of change in the mother, with similar conflicts to those experienced by all mothers, coped with in different ways. I interviewed sixty women twice during pregnancy and once three months after the birth of the baby. I found that the women who expressed considerable anxiety during pregnancy were less likely to become depressed after the birth of the baby. I saw this as reflecting the importance of working through and preparing for the coming major change. Confirmation was also provided that the women who were best able to deal with a child were those who did not have an idealized notion of the mother role as all-perfect and self-sacrificing – a model which they found they could not match up to – but saw it as involving a lot of hard work. Indeed some women feel guilty if they do not enjoy being with their children all the time.

A sense of helplessness and passivity is prominent in women suffering from postnatal depression. Obstetrical procedures, as with Barbara's first experience of childbirth ('I couldn't even

149

manage *that* on my own') are only one possible precipitant to the
sense of passivity and depression. In Jane's case the feeling is that
her body is the vehicle for her family's wishes and expectations
('I've never felt he was mine, he was everybody else's baby; I
never felt he was anything to do with me (p. 114) . . . Where do I
fit in all this? I just felt as though my life had gone, as if that was it,
and it took a long time to realize I was still a person.') Her
passivity expressed itself concretely when, one night, she found
she couldn't get up from her bed any more. 'I had hallucinations:
it was just like another world going on, and I was like a bystan-
der.' Jane felt obliterated by everything she could not be: this
baby was what she should have been for her own mother who
had so wished for a boy, and it made her superfluous at once as a
mother and as a child.

I found that the women who were able to deal well with having
a baby were those who could feel themselves to be, on the
contrary, active and creative – not only were they confident that
what they had produced was good but that it was *they* who had
produced it: they were able to care for and provide for their baby.
This fits in with Ann Oakley's finding that 'it was those women
who were able to conduct their labours with least intervention
who were least "depressed".'[85]

A good experience of childbirth is fundamental if a woman's
trust in her ability to bring her child into the world is to be
enhanced, and therefore her trust in herself as a mother who can
hold and then let go as and when she chooses; who can give birth
to her child safely for herself and the baby. A technological
childbirth where the baby is 'taken from' her will arouse a sense
of being proven inadequate as a mother, feelings about having
her baby stolen, about being too destructive to be able to give
birth naturally, about being punished.

It is not chance alone which will result in one sort of birth or
another. A woman's ability to value herself, to value her body, to
believe in her right to have a baby, and her positive feelings about
her mother (all of which have their roots in her past but also are
selectively reinforced by her present circumstances) will
influence what childbirth she wants and will have. This in turn
will selectively reinforce her feelings about herself and will affect
her relationship with her baby. We saw how Barbara was in quite

a different frame of mind during her first and her second pregnancy and the effect this had on childbirth and her feelings about herself. The second time she was prepared to stand up for herself at all costs, not least perhaps because she felt she had found in me a good mother figure who believed in her ability to actively give birth.

CHAPTER TWELVE

Some sort of routine

April

Barbara I'm trying to get some sort of routine at the moment; it's chaos, isn't it, to start off with. Because I don't feed her just every four hours, I feed her whenever she feels like it. We didn't realize that breast-fed babies were dirty quite so often – the washing! It's not too bad now; it's easier than adjusting to a first baby: you haven't so much to give up: all your social life tends to stop with the first one. Breast feeding is easier, because when you're bottle feeding you've got to come down and get the bottles. I don't get so tired as I did. The only thing is if you want to go out, simple things like popping down to the shops because you've forgotten something . . . it involves – well, if she's asleep I don't like to wake her up to get her dressed, and it's too cold to just pop her in the pram and go out; there's such a lot involved that for the last four weeks I've thought I must get Peter's hair cut but I can't make an appointment because I just don't know what time she'll be having her feed. She's good, she's not a model baby but she's good to us: we've only Peter to compare her with, and we hardly know we've got her most of the time. I rather thought that her routine seems to be the same as it was before she was born; when I used to be busy then she would sleep, when I used to sit down she always used to get up. When I used to sit down in the afternoon she used to wiggle – well, now it's the same, she doesn't sleep in the afternoon. When she cries I feel dreadful, absolutely dreadful, but she doesn't cry as much as Peter used to. I can't just leave her and let her cry. When I feel at my absolute wits' end is when I have a toddler who argues and then she cries because it's tea time or something; then I really feel desperate, I just don't know what to do. Mostly I feel happy about her and I'm more worried about Peter, because with Beatrice I know she either needs feeding or changing or she wants to be cuddled: I know where I am; but I'm not sure how to handle Peter. The first few days we were very happy and we were on top of the world still, then the following week Patrick gave up smoking, and gloom descended on the whole house – oh, he was dreadful, he's just getting over it now, getting irritable. If he was irritable, I got depressed. When he's irritable I have to think it's not because he's irritable with me; I have to say: 'Look, don't take it out on us just because you're not having a cigarette, go and kick the car or something', otherwise it's going to start a whole chain of us being angry.

Dana   You don't think it has anything to do with how he was after Peter was born?

Barbara   No, I told him that yesterday, if he starts another three years of that I'll do something drastic. I don't think so, no; but I can't tell for another few weeks. It's similar but after I say 'Hey, come on', he's all right again, and after he's done what he's going to do, kick the car or whatever.

She goes on to describe how breast feeding makes a difference to her relationship with the baby and her feelings about herself:

Barbara   I found that I'm anti bottles, I cannot give her a bottle; I feel dreadfully guilty giving her . . . she won't take it anyway. The first thing that happened was that she got a cold and I had the doctor in because she couldn't feed at all. The health visitor said I should give her a bottle, but she wouldn't have it. When I told the health visitor that, she said had I tried an extra bit of sugar, so I said 'I tried everything and she just doesn't want to know' and it was: 'How are you going to give her orange juice, dear?' and all the rest of it. She takes quite well from a spoon because we've given her gripe water from a spoon for hiccups. After that the health visitor gave up with me and didn't come back any more.

Barbara wants to feel totally responsible for the feeding. The wish to be the only one able to satisfy her baby is often expressed in this competitiveness with the bottle, this need to prove that the bottle cannot possibly replace the breast. The wish to be indispensable is expressed slightly differently by Ginette, who feels put out by the fact that her baby is already sucking his thumb at one week and sleeping through the night at two weeks. She regards this as a rejection of herself – a rejection which she always anticipates will come and confirm her sense of inadequacy.

Barbara also feels freer not knowing how much milk she is giving her baby:

Barbara   I find it's easier with breast feeding. With Peter if he cried I thought: He can't possibly be hungry because he's just had eight ounces out of the bottle; whereas if she cries I think: I'll give her a few minutes and see if she wants any more – whether she's getting anything or not – and quite often I found she started to cry in the evenings and it was more or less directly after a feed; it wasn't that she was hungry: she just wants to suck, she just wants the cuddle and the sucking, whereas with a bottle-fed baby you wouldn't know what to do, you can't just give them an empty bottle. Breast feeding does make a terrific difference.

I wanted to breast feed because I didn't breast feed Peter and I felt bad about it afterwards but . . . I didn't feel 'I will and I must', it was just something I did after I had her; to do anything else now would feel positively criminal. I felt just as close to Peter bottle feeding, but I knew how much he'd had and he should have; it's quite worrying when you've got a set of rules laid down . . .

For some other women, however, not knowing how much the baby is getting while breast feeding is distressing. Because milk never seemed to gush out of her breasts, because her breasts never leaked and because milk never overflowed and dribbled out of the baby's mouth, Lesley continually feared she had very little milk, and she assumed that whenever her baby cried it was a sign of hunger; only the baby's steady weight-gain enabled her to feel secure enough to carry on. Also, unlike Barbara, Lesley became anxious if her baby sucked when there was no more milk: anxious because she feared the baby's disappointment or rage, and her own inadequacy.

Babies often play at the breast with their mouth, tongue and hands before, during or after a feed, sometimes so much so that they seem little interested in actually taking milk. Some women are made anxious by such non-purposeful sucking because it is purely for pleasure, and they find their own sensual feelings aroused by breast feeding so disturbing that they prefer to use a bottle. The sexual interplay between mother and baby in the breast-feeding relationship is not least responsible for the notion that bottle feeding can more easily be controlled and regulated.

Barbara describes how her feelings about her breasts are intimately related to her ability to breast feed:

Barbara Because I felt guilty that I didn't feed Peter I turned off breasts from sex altogether almost until now – not as a definite thought, but I've always, from the time I had Peter, discounted them as if they didn't exist. It's because I felt so bad about it, so guilty about it. Perhaps I felt I'd failed that way and so I just dismissed them: they were useless, especially since once you don't feed you can't change your mind. And he got so big on the bottle and everyone was criticizing me, 'you're giving him too much to eat,' and then the health visitor came and said 'Don't give him so much milk, put him on solids, perhaps he won't gain so quickly, reduce the milk' and do this and do that, it all made him a lot worse. If I'd been feeding him myself nobody could have said anything.

Breast feeding changes the concept of your anatomy altogether, doesn't it? I said to Patrick, 'You're worried about people seeing me feeding because I think of my breasts as feeding mechanisms now and you see them as sexual objects, and it embarrasses you and it doesn't embarrass me.' When you're in hospital, for feeding, you always draw the curtains around and feel sort of: Oh, don't let's be undressed. After you've been feeding a while, gradually you think: Oh crumbs, I can't keep on going locking myself away. What's the point?

Lesley, when her baby is about three months, has the following dream, pointing to her awareness of a parallel between the feeding intercourse and sexual intercourse. 'I was chosen to demonstrate a dance by an attractive man. He chose me because last time I had danced in a very sexy way. But this time the dance had to do with feeding. It involved moving the bust forward spasmodically. The spurts of milk were a bit like an ejaculation. It was a fertility dance with milk/sperm.'

The experience of breast feeding as sexual, as well as the intimacy of the situation, may even influence the ability or desire to breast feed a child of one or the other sex. One study in Israel found that nearly twice as many mothers of boys as mothers of girls expressed extreme enjoyment of breast feeding. The author concludes: 'I think that it is the first time that it has been documented that mothers regard their infant boys of only three days old as a sexual entity.'[86] However, Ann Oakley found in her English study that girls were more likely to be breast fed than boys, and she sees the reason as being the sense of greater identification by mothers with their baby girls.

Women experience breast feeding differently in other ways too. Kate feels 'absolutely drained after breast feeding, especially in the evening – in the end I gave it up because I felt so tired.' For Lesley 'it was a totally relaxing experience; I would just sit there after she had finished feeding, totally relaxed in a dreamy state, unable and unwilling to get up. When I finally did get up and put her in her cot I felt quite refreshed, though I felt in a different world and it took time to get back into things. This was particularly so with the evening feed.' These two women experience the similar sensations in opposite ways. What one woman feels as a draining sensation, the other one experiences as relaxation and almost revitalization; she is able to let herself be carried by the experience into time off from the practical world, from which she can re-emerge with renewed vivacity. The dreamy state she describes (and it may be significant that it happens at the evening feed) is almost akin to taking a nap from which it takes a while to reawaken.

One study of fantasy during breast feeding[87] compared the stories told in response to pictorial cards by women while they were breast feeding with stories told by women who had breast fed but had now completed the weaning of their baby. One difference between the groups was that the themes of the stories told by the women still breast feeding did not concern interpersonal situations. The author suggests that 'the nursing relationship is so close that it is not experienced by the breast-feeding mother as a "relationship" at all. Rather, nursing may be felt by the mother as a fusion or unconscious union of self and infant, too immediate to be adequately conceptualized as a "relationship" between separate "individuals".' And this gives some understanding of why for some mothers (those who – like Lesley – can enjoy this union) giving to the baby is not contrasted with fulfilling a personal need and therefore not felt as depleting (as it was for Kate, who soon gave it up). The author also found evidence in her study of a 'relaxation of secondary-process thinking' (that is, the type of thinking most adaptive to reality characterized for instance by chronology and purposefulness) in the mothers during breast feeding. The dreamy state described by Lesley would be an example of such loosening.

However gratifying they may find breast feeding, most mothers experience at one time or other a sense of being drained, pumped out or even eaten up during it.

Barbara (*while feeding*) . . . Surely you haven't finished that already! . . . Honestly it's just like a vacuum pump. Shuu . . . one second (*while she changes breast*). I'd better have my afternoon gallon of tea to keep up with her.

Lesley has the following dream when her baby is two months old: 'I was in a "home" for children and all the little babies had gone into Vivien's basket, like a litter of kittens. On Sunday morning as a special treat the women working there ate cooked whole pigs, one pig each, for breakfast – on waking up I thought of my husband saying about Vivien feeding greedily: "She looks like a pig".' The dream is expressing feelings about a cannibalistic interchange between mother and baby.

In those early weeks the question of feeding is also intimately related to the more general aspect of communication. From the mother's point of view learning to understand and adapt to her infant may not be easy. Books on baby care say that mothers will soon recognize one cry from another. That is a rather idealized view of motherhood, and many women feel guilty or inadequate when they discover that they cannot do this.

Barbara (*to her baby*) So that's what it was, you were hungry. Here I am, experienced Mum, and I don't know one cry from another, a hungry cry from a tired cry or any other sort of cry. You can tell if something really hurts them; not much else. (*Later, to me*) Sometimes she keeps crying while she's being fed; she'll feed for a little while and then all of a sudden she'll get cross and scream and then she'll feed again and get cross and I don't know if she's got wind, tummy ache or what. They say sometimes they're getting too much milk too quickly, but I can't tell – neither of us is transparent: I don't know what's going on. She does that and then I don't know what to do, and of course that starts a vicious circle because if I start getting . . . she gets crosser than ever.

Even judging whether the baby is hungry or not is no easy matter. Some mothers resolve the uncertainty by feeding purely on schedule or, if bottle feeding, by sticking to the standard amount. For the mother who is eager to feed on demand, distinguishing between cries becomes vital.

I visited Ginette when her second child was one week old. The baby started to cry two hours after a feed, and both parents thought he was probably hungry but could not decide whether to try to make him wait before giving him another feed. They were torn between an eagerness to make sure the baby would go on to some sort of schedule and an anxiety lest he was not getting enough; and, beyond this, between a fear of his demandingness and a fear of depriving him – a fairly common conflict. How parents react and deal with their baby will reflect their feelings about their own greedy, demanding, or deprived self. When I spoke to her during her pregnancy Ginette had said she would rather not have a girl because 'girls are clinging', and although she had a boy it is still this fear of her own clinging nature that she is apprehensive of in her baby. At the meeting described above Ginette's baby did not strike me as being particularly hungry; whether or not he was, I was surprised by the fact that she did not consider that he might just want to be picked up and held. On coming to know Ginette and her baby better I came to understand how my observation at one week reflected a more general pattern, Ginette's anxiety that she wasn't providing enough for her baby but also that she wasn't very good at 'getting babies to stop crying', was 'not very good with little tiny ones.' Feeding seemed easier to her than comforting in a less concrete way; when feeding she felt she was actually doing something, that ingesting milk would help her baby, whereas she feared that anything which

involved her mothering capacity more directly, such as just holding, would not be enough.

An infant has few ways of communicating, and crying is the
main one. The baby who hardly cries may in some cases be more
worrying than the one who cries a lot, because for some reason
he/she is making very few direct communications and demands.
The baby who cries very little may also in consequence receive
much less attention from the parents because he/she seems
apparently contented.

Although crying is a potent form of communication which
impels a response, some mothers avoid listening by putting the
baby out of hearing or turning on the wireless, or gritting their
teeth, or 'switching off' rather than responding. Sometimes this
is done in the name of 'not spoiling the baby'.

Ginette, after putting her baby in his crib, explained: 'I have to
go downstairs immediately because I can't stand it when he
cries.' Other mothers feel so anxious when their baby cries that
they must respond immediately to every cry (sometimes with a
set response like feeding).

But the crying is useful as a signal, and its counterpart, anxiety
in the mother, unless it is disproportionate, is a useful response if
the mother can act on it appropriately and thereby make the baby
feel comforted and understood. The mother has been described
as a 'container' for the infant's intense feelings, feelings which at
this stage are intimately linked with his physiological state. She
provides the 'thinking' for the baby and in this way reflects to him
his fears and fantasies in a more realistic version.[88] Some women
wish for a 'good baby' because they are unable to tolerate such
intense feelings of fear, anger or distress in their baby and also in
themselves.

Although it may not always be possible to distinguish between
cries, mothers do come to some reasonable understanding of
their baby as the weeks and months go by. In particular they
come to distinguish a distressed cry from a cry which does not
require immediate attention. Trial and error can also resolve a
troublesome situation, and general concern may bring relief
whatever the cause.

Reva talks about her three-week-old daughter: 'She sometimes
takes a long, long, long time over her feeding. She'll feed and

then she'll have some wind and then she'll be awake, then she'll rest and I think she's gone to sleep, and then she wants some more; and this will go on for quite a long time, maybe a couple of hours, but then she'll have another stage where she'll sleep for four hours . . . I'm just learning really. I'm beginning to discover that it's been unnecessarily long sometimes because I'd put her down and she'd cry and I'd think she's not all right, she needs some more or she's windy, and in fact I'm beginning to discover that some of these cries – if I leave her alone she goes to sleep and so that's what I didn't know at first. I don't think I'm always right yet. I usually know if she's really hungry or if she's not hungry but wanting a bit more sucking all the same, but with the kind of thing where she's a bit uncomfortable . . . I think she's also just beginning to be sociable, to be awake . . .'

Other things are learnt too: for example, which position is best for putting the baby to sleep, or what the baby is most responsive to and soothed by: the mother's voice, being able to see her, being wrapped up securely or being held.

Mothers and babies adapt to each other, as a mother's way of handling will influence her baby's preferences and patterns: her ability to understand and bring relief to her baby helps the baby's self-understanding. The experience of satisfaction and relief from distress is the basis of the development of communication between mother and baby and of the baby's motivation to communicate with the outside world. The ability to tolerate frustration (waiting for meals, for instance), which is minimal at the beginning, also grows through the experience of needs being met. A person's identity and sense of identity originates in this early interchange between parent and infant.

That individual differences exist from the start in babies is now widely recognized by psychologists,[89] and mothers are generally better able to cope and respond to one type of baby than another. There can be a good or a bad 'fit' between mother and baby. Very soon, individual characteristics are enhanced or modified through the interaction between the baby and the environment (in particular the mother).

One woman described how important her child's responsiveness was in enabling her to overcome the initial difficulties: 'The first month was awful. I loved my baby, but felt terrifically apprehensive about my ability to satisfy this totally dependent tiny creature. Every time she cried I could feel myself tense up and panic. What should I do? Can I make her stop – can I help her?. . . After the first month I got the hang of it, partly because I had such an easy child. She rarely cried. She slept a lot, and when she was awake she was responsive – she'd look at me alertly and smile. Gradually my love feelings for her overcame my panic feelings, and I relaxed, stopped thinking so much of my inadequacies, and was just myself. It was pretty clear from her responses that I was doing something right.'[90]

The following conversation I had with Serah, whose first child was born at the same time as mine, illustrates the intimate connection between a woman's feelings about herself, and her baby's behaviour:

Serah In seeing Mark so awake and feeling so drowsy, I'm thinking: You're so asleep, you *want* to sleep . . . in fact there is no sign of it, it's because *I* want to sleep, because I'm so drowsy and I look and think it must be so nice being rocked and think how nice it would be if someone did that to *me* and I would go to sleep so quickly. I would *feel* when to change the rhythm of the rocking.

Dana One can really invent things.

Serah I would say 'Shu-shu-shu'.

Dana Sounds like 'Bom-bom-bom', probably like a heart-beat.

Serah Yes, rhythmical sounds. If he's getting really tense, really violent swinging works, and usually it's because you think: Oh for heavens' sake go to sleep.

Dana The violent swinging is a way of getting one's anger out.

Serah I felt that there were certain things that *I* would like if it were done to me. I thought if someone sings to me it would wake me up so I wouldn't sing to him, just 'Mum-mum'.

Dana Like babies do.

Serah When I've finally put him to sleep, I just want to dive into bed but in fact I just stand and look at him. He looks so sweet and I feel as if I'm rested.

Dana Yes, I find I just want to hold her.

Serah If I've had him in my arms I feel all I want to do is put him down, and I feel he's so heavy, but when he's asleep I just want to hold him. I think he must feel so nice and warm. Then I know he'll stay asleep.

Dana They seem lighter when asleep. They make you feel you're such a good mother.

Serah When I put him down and he wakes up it's like a rejection. I feel he's saying 'You're no good, you're not doing it properly, pick me up and do it properly.' I used to think: How can people hit babies?, but now I can understand. It makes you feel you're not good enough. Sometimes I get so angry with him.

We saw earlier how Jane felt criticized and unloved by her baby, who cried incessantly and who, at a later age too, made her feel rejected and superfluous. In an article on parental abuse of infants,[91] Steele reports the following statement, by a mother who put such feelings into action and battered her baby: 'I have never felt really loved all my life. When the baby was born, I thought he would love me, but when he cried all the time, it meant he didn't love me so I hit him.' He goes on to explain: 'Probably all parents have a need for the infant to respond in rewarding fashion . . . The abusing parent differs from the "normal" in the excessive intensity of expectations that are expressed too early in the infant's life. Further, such parents are deficient in true empathy and disregard the infant's lack of ability to understand commands and its limited repertoire of responses. Difficulty inevitably arises because of the discrepancy between the premature, excessive demand of the parent and the inability of the infant to respond properly. The parent feels that the infant is failing to do what he should, and solves the problem by scolding and criticizing the child and punishing him physically in order to get him to behave better.' Such parents were often themselves criticized and battered when they were infants. 'Commonly noted are misperceptions of the baby as being "bad". Abusing parents in various ways describe their infants as too dependent, too fussy, uncooperative, stubborn, disobedient, inconsiderate, unloving, worthless, and bothersome. To an outside observer the baby looks helpless, little, sometimes content, sometimes fussy, crying, and hard to comfort. He is not a bad baby, he is just a normal baby, busy being a baby. A clue to the meaning of such misperceptions are statements made by abusing parents, such as "the baby gets his stubbornness from me", "she's as bad as me when I was a kid. I was always doing the wrong things when I was little, too, and had to be punished". In short, the abusing parent sees the offspring as another edition of his bad childhood self.' The sex of the baby may come into this: Marion hopes her second child will be a boy like the first one because, she says, she was so dreadful when *she* was a child. Barbara, however, on the contrary, fears the harm that could befall her infant from an external source:

Barbara I'm still quite frightened that something's going to happen to her, I'm frightened somebody is going to walk off with her when I'm in a shop. I took her out of the carry cot, I was so afraid she was going to suffocate. I've got this . . . not exactly preoccupation, because it's not on my mind all the time . . . but what worries me a lot is that she's going to die. That's why I took her out of the carry cot: I was sure she was going to suffocate and there's absolutely no reason for it . . . not just her but people dying in general. I seem to have got a thing about it – no one in our family has died or is ill. When I hear sad songs on the radio I get terribly upset, I don't know why.

I rather felt with Peter . . . when you don't feed them, all the milks just fills your breasts up and then it just goes away, and I thought it must be awful for a mother who's had a child and it's died and then all the milk comes in all ready for it and there's nothing there, and that's when I felt terribly upset with Peter because I hadn't fed him, so I sort of told my body that the baby I'd just had had died and it hadn't at all so I felt I'd cheated myself. It's very involved . . . So now I think, I would hate for her to die now because the same thing would happen.

Dana At the time you felt it was as if he had died.

Barbara Yes, that's how I feel about breast feeding, that's my hang-up about breast feeding.

Dana What exactly?

Barbara That I didn't with him, so the baby which I'd had which was him might as well have died, because I didn't feed him. I felt it was so wrong, and yet with this one I didn't have any set ideas, but now that she is OK and she's feeding so well and everything – I think it must be terribly sad if a baby dies, I don't want it to happen to me. I don't think it will or even feel it might, it's just that it must be awful for anyone it happens to, and the whole idea I can't, I don't like to think about, it frightens me so much – I'm so worried that something's going to happen to her. I used to listen to him breathe and everything, but I suppose I knew he was there all the time because he used to wake up so often; but she goes so long and is so quiet that I have to keep going to look – I can't believe she's so good. I shouldn't grumble.

Dana Does it make you feel guilty that you didn't feed him?

Barbara Now, no; until now, yes perhaps. I think so, yes. I was upset at the time that I didn't feed him, but it was too late then. I don't feel that feeding her has wiped out all the guilt or anything. When all the milk arrives, it is as if the baby had died, because that's what would happen, it would just go out again. It seems criminal to me; there must be somewhere some woman whose baby dies; it seems dreadful that all these other women's babies are OK and they don't do anything about it, they don't feed their babies when they can. It's a very mixed-up emotion, I don't even know where it comes from. And yet when I was expecting her I didn't think: I *must* breast feed, come hell or high water; I'm glad I did, though.

Dana You remember when we talked about why you didn't have fears about the baby when you were pregnant, I said maybe you were *too* frightened to think about it, too frightened to have conscious fears? Maybe it is the same, that now because you can feed her you can feel how terrible it would be if you didn't. It's only when you do it that you can feel how terrible if you didn't, or when you've had her you can feel how terrible if she wasn't the way she is.

Barbara We were visiting Patrick's mother and father and I got more and more miserable on the way home; by the time we got home the baby was crying, Peter wanted something or other and I was thoroughly fed-up and I just burst into tears. That didn't make sense to me at all. My little nephew, who they just discovered is deaf, was there. I don't think it was that: I didn't specifically feel upset because he was there or because of anything that happened. It's becoming more and more obvious. When they're Beatrice's age it doesn't show, but then it becomes more and more obvious.

Dana Are you worried that something might show with her later?

Barbara Perhaps, but I did worry with Peter that something might show later too. I know she can hear . . .

Barbara feels it was 'criminal' not to breast feed Peter, that she was doing something deliberately harmful to him and that the milk 'going away' was like a death itself. Now she seems to fear she will be punished by something happening to Beatrice.

Each child in a family has a particular meaning for the parents, depending on its sex, position in the family, or other characteristics and circumstances. Barbara describes how her second child is quite special to her:

Barbara I found I was much more possessive with this one. I didn't want – now I can do it – to give her to other people to hold: I didn't want to do that, I wanted her for myself. I haven't wanted to hand her around to visitors, and with Peter we went to everybody. I'd much rather have her at home. I couldn't believe it. I still have periods where I can't believe that she's here. I think I must have been quite worried that something was going to go wrong or something was going to be wrong with her without knowing, perhaps something like that. It started I think when I had Peter, because I was so finished with having children then, I thought I'd never have any more; then I decided to have another one, but even when I was nine months pregnant I couldn't imagine having two children, I was so frightened about it; once she got here all in one piece and was all right I just couldn't get over it. Perhaps I was worried about her without acknowledging it. I remember you asked me if I thought there was anything wrong with her and I used to say no, but perhaps I did, because afterwards the relief that she was all right was pretty terrific.

Dana You were so scared you couldn't even think about it.

Barbara Yes. I still get periods of that. Yesterday we had my mother-in-law and my brother-in-law there with his little boy who is deaf. I started worrying about her . . . well, I know she can hear.

At the antenatal classes, one couple particularly asked what they did with badly deformed children – if the abnormalities were so bad that the child wouldn't live very long anyway would they leave it at birth – and I didn't join in that conversation either.

It could have started when my father said: 'You'll never have another one', and 'Come back and tell me when you're a few months', and Patrick later said 'Well, he can't say you're not pregnant now' and I would say: 'Let's wait till afterwards, till it's here and everything is all right.' I thought either I'd lose it or there would be something wrong with it . . . he seemed to think I'd never have another child. He hasn't said anything now. He's seen her but he hasn't said anything.

Barbara points out the influence of having had one child already on her handling of the second baby:

Barbara I just didn't know what I was doing with Peter. When I first had Peter I didn't even know how to change a nappy. I wish I could have another one, or rather it's not that I wish I could have another one but I wish it wasn't the last one, because I never want her to grow up. She's five weeks on Friday and I feel that's tragic, the five weeks have gone so quickly; I wish the last five weeks of pregnancy flew by like that. I couldn't wait for Peter to grow up, I was dying for him to do things, have teeth and talk . . . but this one I just want her to stay little.

I don't feel so frightened of handling her as I did with Peter. If she's tired I'll put her down in her pram and even if she cries I'll leave her there, and she won't cry for more than four or five minutes. It won't be terrible screaming. I know she cries because she's tired and I didn't know that with Peter.

At the first cry in the night I feel: Oh no, oh crumbs, and I don't move for a couple of minutes because she doesn't wake up with a terrific yell. Peter used to wake up very quickly, he used to be screaming, but she wakes up slowly and I kid myself for two or three seconds that maybe she'll go back to sleep, then I get up; I don't feel so cross: I used to be really resentful of getting up, I used to hate it – it used to be terrible, I used to lose my temper getting up with him – I don't now, perhaps it's because it's easier to breast feed because you only have to undress, change a nappy and that's it. She's so good, she's just so good, I was expecting another one like Peter. Peter would cry all the time. If he slept, he would sleep for about eight hours but he'd do it from seven in the morning until two or three in the afternoon, and that would be it; then he would cry, he'd want cuddling and walking about all the rest of the time. I used to be up all night for months and months and months; he still wakes up at night now more than the baby does. I don't know why they're so different. I was at my wits' end, I didn't know what to do. A lot of people say it's because you're more confident with a second one, they say it's that.

I feel quite guilty when she's asleep all the time. Because Peter was up, I would talk to him and play with him; he developed very quickly, he seemed quite bright very quickly; and because she's asleep all the time, I'm worried that she's not being stimulated enough. It's quite a relief to me when she wakes up and I can talk to her. I wish I had more time with her. It's probably my own fault: if I'm at home I'll always find something to do, so I don't spend much time with her, she's always asleep anyway. Peter was with me all the time. If I was doing the washing the pram was right alongside the sink, he was with me all over the house, wherever I was. She generally wakes up around three and then is up and down until eight. In the afternoon I cuddle her a bit and she falls asleep on me. In the evenings she generally screams: she won't just sit quietly, she just cries then, I don't know why. I've tried feeding her the last few nights every couple of hours to see if it's that but it's not, she just carries on crying. She finishes a feed and then just carries on crying. We left her in her pram and let her cry for about ten minutes: when we picked her up she was quite cooperative after that; before that she really screamed. It broke my heart, I don't like them crying. That seemed to be enough then, she'd had a good yell. I don't know why they do that: perhaps that's how they get their exercise, I just don't know.

Peter had a dummy, the ones that are like a small bottle; I used to hate seeing him with it. We first tried it one night when he was about four weeks and neither of us had had one night's sleep since he'd come home from hospital and we gave up . . .

We gave it to him, he went to sleep almost straight away and all he woke up for then for a few nights was if he dropped it; he wanted it put back in his mouth. I kept trying to take it away. I gave it up for him when he was about fifteen months because by then he could talk and walk, and I suddenly 'lost' it and we kept looking for it and we couldn't find it and so Peter had to go to sleep without it, and the next night we couldn't find it either and the next night we forgot to look. I don't think the crying I get from Beatrice warrants anything like that. If she screamed all day, then perhaps I would. She's generally not miserable for more than three or four, at the most five hours a day, not twenty-four. Peter would wake up and have a bottle and he'd lie awake and cry if he couldn't see me. He cried when there was no one talking to him or picking him up, so we would pick him up all the time. He would go to sleep some time during the day from exhaustion. He wanted your attention all the time. Almost as soon as we'd go to bed he'd start crying. All he wanted was for me to go to the cot, pick him up and stick the dummy into his mouth. He wanted the security of company. But Beatrice isn't like that. When she wakes up, if I've changed her and fed her and put her back in her cot, I think she'd just stay up there all day, but I couldn't do that: I have to bring her down and put her in her pram even if it's just downstairs with me; I don't like to just leave them on their own all the time, it seems wrong to me to shut them away in another room. I don't think she should be so cut off from the rest of the family, she should be with us even if she's asleep.

I could never envisage loving another one as I loved him even while I was pregnant; I couldn't imagine how I could possibly, and the thought of me being in hospital while Peter was at home really upset me, and when the second one actually arrives you feel just the same about them all over again.

I was really impatient with Peter to start off with. When I came home from hospital and I was trying to rest upstairs and I wasn't very mobile I was impatient with him then, and I knew I should be extra patient, that's what made it so hard.

Barbara finds her second baby much easier to cope with, partly because she is more experienced and partly because she feels the baby responds better to her mothering. She feels she can gratify and soothe this baby more easily; breast feeding makes her feel more able to provide for and satisfy her child.

Having a second baby is often quite different, not just because a woman is more experienced in child care but also because her life style, which may have required great adjustments with her first baby, especially if she had a job, is now ready to incorporate the second baby often without further change. If, for instance, she carried on with her job full time or part time, she will have child-caring facilities already organized and will have explored the different possibilities available to her. Similarly she will have found some babysitting arrangement enabling her to get out in the evenings. The domestic work which was greatly increased with having one baby will be little more with two children.

Helen compares her handling of her two children: 'Bernard had a completely different start – probably being a new Mum, and because I was working part time, I was very conscious that I might not be giving enough to him, so I tried to over-compensate. I had a friend who used to look after him: she used to come up to the house. I used to plan it so well that he used to be sleeping when she actually arrived, and if he wasn't asleep I was a bit upset, which now seems ridiculous to me. I'm much more realistic now, because I know I've changed my views – babies should get used to mother substitutes from quite an early age, as long as they know their mother is going to return. If the situation is repeated fairly often, it's a good thing. It was a shame really that I felt guilty about teaching.'

Susan describes the differences with her third child, after a gap of about six years: 'I think I see him more as a person and not just a baby: I think this happens when you've had one or two children. I don't see exactly what he's going to be like or anything like that at all, but I see a shadowy image of Jim as a toddler and Jim starting school and Jim as a seven-year-old and a nine-year-old, because my children are up to that age. With the first one, with the two really because they were so close together, they were something static. They were up to where you were with them now in the present and that was that . . . and lack of experience of other children as well – I didn't really have even a vague idea of them as a toddler when they were babies, or them

169

as a school child when they were toddlers, and so on, whereas I have a shadowy experience of Jim older even now which I think makes me more aware of him as a person in development . . . and therefore you see things that are going to come and go, and stages, and you're more tolerant and easy with them.

'I'm a bit more flippant, I don't take his crying or upset so seriously unless it really does get bad; and maybe this helps him to be more casual, not so intense about things. I think it will be easier to be firm with him, because I'll feel I know more what to be firm about; you're experimenting with the others and you feel sorry for them when you first have to start saying no, whereas I don't think I will be sorry for him because I feel it's good for children to have a very firm background, which they can be fairly free within, and to accept no; and the firmer and more casual one is about it the easier they accept it. I think they sense if you're not quite sure yourself or you dither or you don't really want to say no because you feel that it's obstructing. You're worried with the first that it's going to affect your relationship: they'll resent making limits to their environment; and when they're toddlers you accept this and they have a tantrum and it soon disappears, but later on they start talking and they sulk, or they start saying that they don't like you and so on; although you accept it it's difficult, whereas now I expect it with him and it just won't be such emotional involvement for me. You start off – certainly I did – with a baby and toddler, by using distraction as a main way of coping if they're doing something they shouldn't; very soon they turn to something else, or talking, but it gets to a certain stage where you can't use that and they say "I'm going somewhere" and you say "You're not", and they say "Yes I am", and you've got to say "No" and stick to it and it produces a tenseness, an anxiety, and also a kind of resentfulness, because you think: Well I really am a very reasonable parent, I don't say no very often and when I do say no they really are unreasonable. You think that, but of course they can't see it, all they can see is that at that moment you say no to what they want, and you really feel a bit resentful.' Susan also thinks of herself differently: 'I think I see myself as a mother now, whereas I don't think I could before. My whole role in the family is different. Before it was just me and I happened to have children and I couldn't really see myself as a mother. I don't know if it takes time or what. Maybe it was a long time because of the difficulties between Simon and me, and I didn't feel a family unit. Now I feel a family unit with Paul and really happy with him in that way.'

Marion also describes her greater confidence and lesser anxiety with her second child: 'I wasn't so worried with Derek . . . just allowing him to be without worrying: that he cries for a little while, or he'd do this or he'd do that – much calmer because it's the second one and because they'll live, they'll cope . . . you can see beyond tomorrow, you know that eventually this stage will pass, and you know what's to come: the next thing he'll do is turn over or he'll be crawling or he'll have a couple of teeth. You have some idea of what to expect; I suppose it makes you more secure, therefore you are more relaxed.'

It is not just a question of being more matter-of-fact with a second child; nor of knowing that however fraught things are today it will be easier when the baby can crawl, or make use of a teddy bear, or sleep through the night; nor of having a set routine which makes it reassuring for baby and mother – but also simply that it is not possible to devote the same sort of attention to a second or subsequent baby.

Paula felt that she changed more after the birth of her second child. With the first she tried her best to meet his every need. 'It was a sort of omnipotent feeling, a feeling that if I did everything right, did everything I could for him, he would be all right, free from suffering and psychological problems. But with the second, you just can't because there's the first one there too with his needs. That was a shock.' And Paula has to come to terms with a sense of inadequacy, with the feeling that she is not as good a mother as she was to her first child, with her sadness at this inevitable imperfection. But with this, she also feels, comes the realization that perhaps the perfection she aspired to earlier was not as crucial as she had thought. 'With the first one I wanted to breast feed all the time, no one was to come near the baby; with the second I was very tired and the nurse gave him a bottle at night in hospital; it just didn't seem that important.'

One can understand how it will be those women who try the hardest to be very good mothers, and who need to feel good in their child's eyes who will find it hardest with a second baby when their care is necessarily divided, and also when they have to face the first child's anger with them.

This sense of inevitable imperfection is of course not confined to second and subsequent children. Lesley experienced this in relation to her professional occupation. 'I felt I had to go on with my work, even on a very part-time basis, but I always felt torn – I always felt it was taking something away from her, that I ought to be there all the time, that it was my own needs versus perfect mothering. And yet at the same time I knew that in the long run it would be better for both of us if I didn't give up my professional interests.' The psychoanalyst Frieda Fromm-Reichman puts it like this: 'We know from psychoanalysis that there are few sacrifices made without resentment. Therefore we do not think that a mother should give up her own happiness for the sake of her child. The happier the mother can be, the more she will be able to secure happiness and freedom of growth for her child; the more happiness she sacrifices for the sake of her child, the more she will resent the child for whom she did so, thus diminishing her capability to deal with him without hostility and resentment.'[92]

The guilt about being an imperfect mother we have seen in terms of a woman feeling she is not doing as much as she ought to be doing, or that she is looking after her own needs at the expense of her child's needs. Another frequent source of guilt relates to the mother's anger with the baby for her or his relentless demands or incessant crying which cannot be soothed, particularly at night. Such guilt can contribute to postnatal depression when a woman feels she really is a totally bad, depriving mother, reproached by her infant for being so inadequate.

Her own experience of being mothered will influence a woman's ability to sustain an image of good mothering inside her in spite of the inevitable ups and downs of the early relationship with her infant.

The partner's faith in the woman as a mother, or on the contrary his disparaging attitude, will have a contributing influence. Some women find the help of their own mother in the first week invaluable. If she is supportive rather than critical it helps sustain their faith in themselves. Sometimes the rivalry between the woman and her mother (whether mutual or one-sided) over mothering abilities and ideas can make the presence of the mother more of a strain than a help. The resentment relates to feelings about how her mother dealt with her when *she* was a baby. Before the first visit to her mother, when her baby is two months old, Lesley expresses this tension: 'I dreamt my mother was giving solid food to the baby and I was furious about this, about her taking over. I told her it's not good so young and it makes babies get fat.'

Charlotte finds the presence of her parents on return from hospital unbearable: 'I'm normally very independent. I felt so pleased to get home. I thought I was going to be very worried that I'd never cope, but I found I got myself organized quite well in a very short time. But the day I came out – my parents live up north and they were going to come down within a couple of days of me coming out of hospital. My mother was coming down and I thought: That seems a good idea, everybody says you need your mother. The day I came out I remember the phone ringing and it was my father saying he was coming as well and he was bringing his great alsatian dog, and that absolutely . . . I burst into tears, uncontrollable crying fit I had. I then felt I don't want that, I've now decided I want to be on my own, but there seemed to be no way of putting them off. It was a mistake to have them there. They stayed a week, and then my in-laws came for a week, and I cracked up several times in that fortnight because I felt everything at that stage revolves around your baby, you can't be bothered even making people a cup of tea and yet you feel you've got to make this effort – you know, saying "Can I get you something?" – and yet it wasn't sincere because I wasn't interested. So I found that a terrific strain. Also I wanted to do everything for Leo myself, I wouldn't let my mother do anything for him. She was allocated things like making up feeds, and even with that I can remember saying "You aren't putting too much sugar in, are you?" (she's the type who'd think, Oh he'd like a bit more sugar, babies like sweet things, let's give him a great heap of sugar, so I was always a bit wary of that). But once they were all out of the way I seemed to manage quite well. In fact I think I was more tolerant then than I am now. It must be because I expect more of him now than I did then.'

One of the problems Charlotte touches upon is the more general one which faces the new mother: how to be independent and separate from her mother (that is, a parent in her own right) while at the same time identifying with her mother in this new situation.

This leads us to the question of self definition and identity which is at the centre of many difficulties at the time of having a baby, both during pregnancy and after the birth.

Women differ greatly in the extent to which the baby is important to their self-definition or to their purpose in life, and the extent to which it is a hindrance to their sense of identity. Susan gets easily depressed, feeling life is pointless; when she is pregnant, however, and when her children are young, she feels she has a purpose: 'I feel much less analytical about myself when I'm pregnant than at any other time, because to me you just exist, you *are* and there's a purpose in being, you don't have to justify anything. It still continues when you're looking after a young baby; you don't have to think: Am I making the best of my time, and what kind of life do I really want, or what is the purpose of it all? and you just . . . you have to fit yourself in. You know you need food, a certain amount of rest, and it takes over in a way I find, and I feel very happy and contented. In this sense I am less introspective during pregnancy and I am more in tune with nature.' If her existence is justified by having children this is a problem for a woman when her children start school and, later on, leave home, when she is in a sense robbed of this purpose. This can contribute to the depression so common at the time of the menopause, which also marks the end to the possibility of childbearing.

Susan also feels that she can only look after herself when she is pregnant, when her body belongs to her baby: 'I can look after myself without feeling guilty. Normally I eat things that are no good for me, I have no control in this way – but when pregnant I eat things that are good for me and I look after myself.'

During pregnancy in a sense what is good for the baby is good for the mother: they are in tune, there is a common aim. If a woman rejects her pregnancy and feels invaded by the presence inside her, she attacks her own body and the baby inside at one and the same time.

Patricia describes her first pregnancy, before she met her husband: 'I felt very lonely, I'd go through the whole story of it to myself, I'd repeat the whole thing over and over again; I must have done it hundreds and hundreds of times as though I was talking to somebody else and telling them about it. I did this every night standing in front of the mirror until eventually by Christmas I'd worn myself off; by the time I had the baby I felt completely free of the whole thing, I just talked it out of my system. When I was pregnant I was very unhappy, I was hysterical a lot of the time, I drank quite a lot, I smoked quite a lot, meaning to *obliterate* myself from everything . . .' The baby was stillborn.

Many women go on experiencing, after the birth, a congruence between their needs and the baby's needs. Winnicott uses the term 'primary maternal preoccupation' to describe the total absorption with the baby which most women experience in the first weeks. Lesley describes her great pleasure in being the centre of the world to her infant, and she feels gratified to be needed so intensely by her baby for whom she wants to be available on demand. 'When I was feeding her I loved the feeling that my breasts in a sense belonged to her. She would latch on avidly as if she really could do what she wanted with my breast and it was nice to feel she enjoyed it so much.' With breast feeding the timetable is joint for mother and baby and it is a relief for the mother to feed when her breasts are starting to get too full and painful.

Other women describe the conflict they feel between their own needs and the baby's needs: 'One afternoon the baby was asleep in the other room. I fell into a deep sleep and after about ten minutes he began to cry. I went to the cot and shook him and shouted "Shut up for God's sake!" I felt I *had* to sleep and sleep. That was the most important thing, he yelled so much and I was shattered.' 'The day I came home from hospital, I realised that I'd never be able to follow my own line again.'[93]

Ann Oakley in her study of first-time mothers found that a mother's feelings for her baby tended to be more negative if (amongst other things) she obtained little help from her partner with the housework, if the baby didn't sleep much, and if she felt tied down by the baby and missing outside employment.[94] In other words, that her 'work' condition in the house will have an influence on her feelings about the baby. As the child gets older, the needs of mother and child may grow increasingly apart: 'The child might be absorbed in busyness, in his own dreamworld; but as soon as he felt me gliding into a world which did not include him, he would come to pull at my hand, ask for help, punch at the typewriter keys. And I would feel his wants at such a moment as fraudulent, as an attempt moreover to defraud me of living even for fifteen minutes as myself. My anger would rise; I would feel the futility of any attempt to salvage myself, and also the inequality between us: my needs always balanced against those of a child, and always losing. I could love so much better, I told myself, after even a quarter-hour of selfishness, of peace, of detachment from my children. A few minutes! But it was as if an invisible thread would pull taut between us and break, to the child's sense of inconsolable abandonment, if I moved – not even physically, but in spirit – into a realm beyond our tightly circumscribed life together. It was as if my placenta had begun to refuse him oxygen.'[95]

Barbara (*describing this conflict*) If I did a drawing of myself in the mornings I would draw myself in a prison: the washing piles up everywhere, there is so much to do. There would also be a sea of faces in the background that need attention. Oh dear, there's so much to do and I'm so tired. When I had Peter I felt I couldn't cope; this time I can cope but I have to have a laugh about it sometimes otherwise I go nuts.

This morning I said to Patrick, 'Let me rush down to get some cheese before you go to work so that I don't have to dress the children and take the pram just for one thing', so off I went down the road and it was such a beautiful morning and I said to Patrick when I came back: 'I nearly went out for a piece of cheese and never came back again' (*she laughs*). It's not fair, because she was asleep and Peter wasn't being naughty.

Dana You never get a chance to be on your own.

Barbara Sometimes in the evening they're both asleep – it's bliss. Patrick rarely·goes out. Wednesday evening Patrick's going out; if they're both asleep I shall be on my own. I shan't get much of my identity back until about September – Christmas-time I suppose, because all the time I'm feeding Beatrice I can't leave her very long. I shall go back to night school in September, to do yoga or something, something that takes my mind off children and babies and housework.

With Peter I was very depressed, I'd sit and cry for an hour or two; sometimes I'll have a little grizzle for five minutes but it doesn't last for very long. I don't mind; I think: Well, that's what I expected anyway. When I was pregnant with Peter I didn't know what to expect; because I'd been an only child I didn't even know what it was like with another baby in the house; but this time when I got pregnant I rather knew what to expect so now that it's arrived I don't feel too resentful. Anyway I think we shall go out one evening even if it's only for an hour or two.

I'll tell you when I get cross and depressed; it's not during the week when Patrick's at work, it's at the weekend; if he says he's going to the football match and I think 'I've had the children for so many days a week and for heavens' sake why can't he take them out just one afternoon?' – that's when I get depressed.

Dana   Does he ever take them out?

Barbara   No. He'd never taken Peter out until I was in hospital. The only time Patrick has Peter is Sunday morning when he's tinkering about with the car or doing the garden and Peter goes outside with him, but otherwise he's always been in bed when I've gone out and Patrick babysat.

The sense of loss of identity is sometimes experienced acutely. Erica relates it to the cessation of her professional activity: 'I felt isolated not working, and very much not me any more. I was just a Mum with a pram, I just found that very very hard and I hadn't realized that I would resent so much not being seen as me but being seen as somebody else's Mum.' She started work again soon with a slight change in career. 'At the same time as having the kids I probably felt that I wanted – or rather because of having the kids I wanted – to make more of a mark as a professional person than I had ever felt before. Maybe I wanted to make more of an impact because I had kids and was then being seen as the mother of children and I didn't particularly want to, because I've never wanted to be a career person before. Perhaps having babies doesn't have this effect on most women but it certainly did on me, a depersonalizing thing. I've now got to be quite a career person and in order to make the process a bit quicker I've got to take a full-time job. It's good for the kids because they have an almost totally equal relationship with both of us: at the moment we're almost interchangeable. He does the cooking, the washing, the ironing; the only thing he doesn't do is the cleaning. I don't think he notices the dirt. We had a big row about that last night, but things work out very evenly. Actually I find I like my children better when I don't see them too often – it's like a marriage: if you see your husband all the time you get pretty fed up.'

From her interviews with first-time mothers Ann Oakley suggests that: 'What is characteristic of childbirth and becoming a mother today is the tendency for women to feel they have lost something, rather than simply gained a child. What is lost may be one's job, one's life-style, an intact "couple" relation, control over one's body or a sense of self, but the feeling of bereavement cannot be cured or immediately balanced by the rewards of motherhood – just as the bereaved person will not cease to feel anguished if offered alternative relationships and occupations.'[96] I would add that the lack of availability of an extended family nowadays to help in a 'natural' and easy way with child care is in no small way responsible for this.

But I think it is also true to say that any change, even desired, inevitably involves loss as well as gain. In the case of motherhood I should add to Oakley's list the loss of the childhood self and of the hope of being cared for as a baby oneself.

CHAPTER THIRTEEN

More the way I was

May and June

BARBARA The other day I slung a plate of dinner along the kitchen top, which is the nearest I've ever got to throwing anything. We never used to row at all because if Patrick used to get mad about something or start being rude about something I would avoid a row at all cost. After I had Peter the whole atmosphere in our house changed and I was just trying to keep the peace all the time. Now I don't, and if I feel angry I jolly well say it and I find it helps. One day, I just hit the roof. I said if he could make the effort to be pleasant during the last four or five months, well, make the effort now or else I was going, kids and all. He said he was sorry, he didn't know he was doing it, or else he knew it but he couldn't do anything about it, it was just a mood he got in. I said 'I get in moods but I don't take it out on you. The children might have driven me mad all day but I don't say "Oh here's your tea, get out of my sight." ' He tends to pick on things that I do. If I haven't washed up and I feed Beatrice first . . . what's an hour . . . he'll go and do it and I feel he's criticizing me for not doing it. I would do it given half an hour. But he is better to Peter now. Peter isn't being smacked or pushed around like he was before.

One lunch-time he started criticizing the way I budget; I do all the budgeting in our house and I said 'I'm going to keep a list of all the things I buy for a week and see what isn't necessary because I can't see where it's going', so he said I couldn't possibly have spent so much money in so little time and I started giving a list of the things I had to buy, and I thought: Why should I account for absolutely every action? And that finished it – oh, I was . . . I don't think I've ever gone up in the air like that about anything. I made a noise for about ten minutes, and he apologized and he's never said 'I'm sorry' before, and ever since then, having found it worked, I've been quite aggressive. It helps.

I thought I'm normally, before we were married, quite a forthright person, I say what I'm thinking; whereas after we were married I became quite reticent, quite quiet, 'Don't let's row about it'; and I'm more the way I was now, so perhaps I changed to keep the peace, but I said was he more friendly because when we were first married he knew I was dependent on him and he was sure that I loved him – perhaps he thought that I was growing more independent and so he thought I didn't love him so much or something.

I said 'Do you like it . . . because between six and nine months pregnant I don't do quite so much so I'm more dependent because you can do more for me and I'm more obviously dependent on you', and he said that was a lot of rubbish . . . he didn't think about it, he just didn't want to talk about it.

Her sense of being more 'forthright', as she used to be before she got pregnant with Peter, seems linked with her determination and successful childbirth.

Barbara   I was thinking of the difference after I had Peter: I felt a complete failure, I couldn't even have a child on my own, let alone . . . you know, I couldn't do anything. As I was coming down, a doctor . . . I said to her, 'Well, I couldn't even manage that on my own, could I?' And she said 'Not this time but perhaps next time' – that even makes you feel worse. Perhaps that's why I want another one, because I said I wanted two, you see, and I don't want to prove that it was a fluke, I want to do it again, perhaps . . .

The experience of having a baby is one which involves a woman's feelings about her femaleness and her sexuality and, as we clearly see with Barbara, touches on her self-confidence and valuing of herself. We saw how it precipitated her inability to breast feed Peter, adding to her self-deprecation and feeling of guilt – it was to her as if this child had not really come from her. 'Your body thinks you've lost one', she says, talking about the milk drying up and menstruation starting again. We can speculate that her feelings of having failed had an influence on the way in which she handled her baby. It is also possible that some of the difficulties she experienced with her first child originated, partly at least, in this initial sense of failure. It is not until she can regain confidence in herself through a positive experience in childbirth that she is able to feel 'forthright', 'more the way I was'. And this is not without effect on her relationship with her child:

Barbara Peter always seemed to cry; there's no joy in playing with Peter or cuddling Peter. It's true, she isn't any trouble and you love her all the more for it – oh, she's so good. Peter is still more miserable than Beatrice, he grumbles a lot and cries a lot, and it seems to be part of people's make-up to turn away from people who are miserable.

The psychoanalyst Therese Benedek emphasizes the vicious circle which is created when the infant is unsatisfied and the mother feels unable to satisfy her baby. Under good circumstances the mother, through the experience of being able to satisfy her infant, establishes her self-confidence and trust in her own motherliness and a similar confidence develops in the infant. In a sense, one comes to reinforce the other. In the case where the infant's needs are not met the experience is one of frustration and can lead to more frequent crying; if the crying brings no gratification then the infant gives up crying altogether, and this can be the sign of a more serious disturbance. But here we are talking of neglect. There is also the case of the infant who is difficult to satisfy: 'The development of confidence does not depend solely upon the mother's ability and willingness to give, but also upon the child's innate or acquired ability to receive, to suck, to assimilate and thrive. If the infant, because of congenital or acquired disability, cannot be satisfied, he remains frustrated and in turn frustrates the mother. The frustration of the mother manifests itself in her anger and discouragement, in the fear of her inefficiency and probably in (more or less) conscious guilt feelings.'[97]

Some mothers have higher standards than others. The mother who always wants to see her baby content and satisfied and finds it hard to tolerate her baby's crying is more likely to feel she isn't doing well. Guilt has to do with resentment, but also to do with wanting to perform so well. When the gap between what the woman feels she is doing and what she would like to do for her child is too big she becomes depressed – or angry with this child who makes her feel so inadequate; this in turn increases her guilt. Other circumstances also come into play. It is easier to be a good mother to one child than to two or more children. It is easier to be a good mother when there is help and support from a partner or other people.

A lot is expected of mothers, and mothers expect a lot of themselves. They expect to be able to be devoted and attentive all day long (not to speak of the nights) to their children, even-tempered and understanding twenty-four hours a day while coping with the house, the shopping, the laundry and the meals single-handed. Anything less than this is accompanied by guilt. And for many women there are still very few possibilities of handing over some of these tasks to another person, or getting help with the children. The emotional strain of coping with the children's anxieties and frustrations and carrying some of these feelings for them can be enormous for the woman who is isolated in her house for hours or even days on end.

One of Barbara's difficulties is in tolerating her older child's incessant demands:

Barbara With the second I quite expected a lot of crying. Well, I just haven't got it, she's so good. I get really cross with Peter because he cries more than Beatrice does. It's all right if I'm with him and we're doing something together but he won't occupy himself. It's a good job I didn't have them the other way around. If I'd had a baby like this first and then had a horror . . . I don't know what would happen.

Although Barbara feels much more confident in herself and more like she was before, the marital harmony is still disturbed. Barbara tries to understand her husband's moodiness. Perhaps it has to do with her lesser dependence on him, on his being less confident of her love for him. And in this way she hints at the question of rivalry with the baby. Making room for a new person in the family does not go without difficulty in most cases, and many couples experience some measure of disharmony at least for a time, after the birth of a baby. For the man it means accepting the woman's involvement and preoccupation with the infant while he feels, in many cases, relegated to the background. Contrary to the common belief that having a baby can 'patch up a marriage', in many cases having a baby will disrupt a marriage – sometimes irreparably. And most couples feel that 'it just isn't like before', when they could more easily gratify each other's needs.

One study of first-time parents found that 'the general level of sex desire reported by husbands and wives was somewhat lower after the birth of the child as compared to before the pregnancy'. On the whole, though, they found that couples who had a good sexual adjustment before pregnancy had also a good sexual adjustment during pregnancy and after the birth, though in a minority of cases there was a change for the better or for the worse.[98]

In Barbara's case the marital disharmony is also reflected on the sexual level:

Barbara I went to the FPA to get a cap. Well, I thought I must try this thing out so I did and it was most uncomfortable. There's me trying to think 'Is it psychological or isn't it?' but by the morning . . . I left this thing in over night, I didn't test it out, I just left it in and by the morning . . . in bed I thought: 'No it's in the mind', but in the morning I thought I jolly well can feel it. Anyway, when I took it out I really had tummy ache deep down and I thought 'What am I doing?' and I had a discharge for about a day and a half and I thought: Oh I got an infection or something. I was so upset. I thought, 'What do I do now, I don't like the thing, it's uncomfortable.' It seems too big, it hurt, it really hurt. I was trying to think was it me because . . . I've been spoilt while I was pregnant, we haven't used anything, and used the pill before that. I don't like the thing, I'll admit that to myself but it isn't just that, it is uncomfortable and I don't want to go back again. I thought, 'Well, I could try a smaller size', but it's uncomfortable putting it in and out, I don't like that either. I definitely don't want to take the pill until I finish feeding Beatrice; then I will, I think. I don't want to make excuses to Patrick, they all sound a bit feeble, don't they? It's just the same, I don't know what to do and then I felt quite angry and I thought, 'Well, it's not for my benefit anyway because I don't feel like it.' In the end I thought: I don't know how I'm going to say this to Patrick, because it sounds like excuses, excuses. Patrick isn't insisting that we do or anything, in fact he's hardly mentioned it, but it sounds as if I'm trying to get out of it all the time. In the end I picked an appropriate moment, I said I was worried, I didn't know what to do, to go back again or not, and he said 'Oh well, don't worry about it for a little while and we'll think about it later.' All the sexual athletes would think that's dreadful I suppose, but I don't (*she laughs*). So it's just been left in the air. The problem isn't solved, it's just pending. With Peter there was hardly any gap between having him and getting back to normal, but with this one . . . perhaps it's because I'm not on the pill: I'm worried about getting pregnant, because I went straight on to the pill with Peter.

Barbara's reluctance to have intercourse is not as clearly located as it is for Mrs O., who feels that she cannot belong to both husband and baby, and needs to delineate carefully her role as mother and as sexual woman: 'Mrs O. was plagued by a dream: she was in an auditorium; a girl in a very sexy black dress sat there and Mrs O.'s husband got up to sit with that girl. The dream reminded Mrs O. that she was self-conscious about her figure and afraid of losing what had been most precious in her life: to be a woman, loved and in love. Her own feelings had become less passionate and intercourse had become a duty for her. She found some comfort in her husband's objection to breast feeding: he said her breasts belonged to him. She agreed with him although she had heard that nursing a baby was the most blissful sensation. But keeping a part of herself and her beauty reserved for her husband gave her some confidence that she might be a mother and an attractive woman as well.'[99]

Conversely Barbara feels that the rest of the family interferes with her relationship with the new baby:

Barbara I feel frustrated that I don't have time to sit and hold her all day. The best time of day is the five o'clock feed or six o'clock when everybody else is asleep and I can sit and cuddle her and talk to her all on my own, it's so peaceful. I haven't got to get up and do anything afterwards. Mind you, four o'clock

in the morning isn't such fun! which I thought this morning –
that will teach you, I thought . . . Saturday afternoon Patrick
and Peter went out and we were alone then and it's so nice and
quiet and peaceful and calm, you know, and the house is
empty and you can just feed and cuddle.

At the same time as the difficulties inherent in becoming a
family Barbara feels that there has been a positive change in her
relationship with her husband. Her commitment to the relationship only became firm with a second child and with the realization that although she felt it might have been possible for her to
leave with one child, with two it could no longer be envisaged.
Deciding to have a second child became for her the decision to
become committed:

Barbara I remember thinking: If I leave because I don't feel very
happy, Peter is going to go through the same sort of feelings
that I had as a child, with divorced parents, so I decided I'd
commit myself and stay, and I thought I must be doing something wrong that is making Patrick act so different. Having got
that far, knowing I was going to have to stay I had no choice
but to have a second child because Patrick wouldn't have left
me alone and life would have been unbearable. I was frightened of having another baby, but then every one of my
friends became pregnant and I thought, 'Well the odds of my
having another forty-eight-hour labour aren't that high, so I
will.' All my life has been temporary phases and I found it very
difficult to make a permanent commitment even though I got
married. I found it difficult to think of it in terms of years and
years and the rest of my life; I still do. I felt quite relieved really,
having decided that this is it, I'm staying. Having had her I feel
more confident. That's probably why I can be more argumentative with Patrick, because now I feel I'm somebody, I can do
it, in a way.

It may also be that within the context of a more committed
relationship Barbara feels less frightened of expressing anger or
demands, or being 'argumentative'.

Being tied down by the birth of a child is relevant not only to the
marital relationship but to the more general question of an inde-

pendent life. The loss of personal freedom, whether in terms of a career or more generally of a life outside the confines of the home, can be experienced acutely. Finding a solution or a compromise will depend on personal circumstances and on feelings and ideas about being a mother.

Charlotte finds herself very uncertain about what solution to adopt: 'I seem to be so up and down, it's unbelievable: the slightest thing will bring depression, and yet sometimes I can't even pinpoint what it is, I just get up and feel "My God, not another day like this!" My latest theory is that what I resent the most about my situation is not having any time to myself. I did think at one time that I had this great craving to get back to work. I thought about it and went as far as going to agencies to get a job, and I was going to let Leo go to a registered child-minder, and then I really sat down and thought, "Do I really want to go out to work or do I just want to be away from Leo for a while: which is it?" And I've got this very strong feeling now that I just would like time to be myself, not to be somebody's mother, not necessarily to be anybody's wife, just for half a day. Having moved down here, not really knowing anybody, made it that much more difficult because I did have some quite close girl-friends I'd met in hospital, and I'd envisaged that we'd look after each other's children, we'd have days out in town and just time for things, and that of course hasn't materialized because of the move. We decided to move because we felt we were getting in a bit of a rut. And the idea was to set up a business. And the nature of the business has changed so many times. Now, it's almost ready to be launched. I hope this will solve my depression or get rid of it, because not only will it be something to do but also it will be money which will give me my independence, which is what I also miss terribly. It will be interesting to see if once I'm doing something like that, and also gain a bit of independence through having some extra cash, whether I will then not feel so resentful.

'But also whenever I think about a child-minder and I resolve to do it, the next day I have such terrible guilt feelings, I think: "*You* decided to have him, you're supposed to be an intelligent reasonable person, you should have expected this, you should cope with it and if you can't cope with it you can't be an adequate person, an adequate mother"; so it goes on . . .

186

'Some days I've felt so desperate, terribly imprisoned here, and thought "If I don't get out and do a job or do something I'll go out of my mind", and I've said "In the morning I'll ring up my health visitor to arrange it" and that morning comes and I've slept on it and I thought, "Oh Christ, I shouldn't have had a child if that's how I'm going to carry on." I've always said you should give your child all your time. If I were sitting down and discussing it and didn't have a child I know I would say what books say, that a happy mother makes for a happy child, so that if you're terribly depressed being at home, yes you should go out and have a change and then you'll be better for your child. But then when you've got one it's very different, isn't it, you just can't be so rational.

'I was going to go back to work when Leo was three months old – I don't know why three months, it's just one of those things you work out, and everybody said "You might change your mind." I was adamant: in no way would I change my mind, and I remember being invited up to town to lunch one day and big carrots being dangled in front of me and I couldn't even have contemplated going back. And then there are times when I don't know what I'm missing the most, whether I'm missing work or whether I'm missing the money and what that brings basically in a sense of independence. I've never ever been in a position where I've had to once a week stand there and say "Give me my housekeeping money, and oh dear you'll never believe this but I'm two pounds short, I need some more", and I positively hate it, I really do hate it. In many ways I long for the day when that's no longer necessary. But I really still can't decide whether it's the stimulation of the job that I miss or the rewards that it brings, financial rewards. Then when I started to look for a job down here it really is a different world from London, the jobs that they were offering, albeit they were part-time and you don't expect to get terribly involved and people are using you for convenience and you're going there for convenience, but they were clerical or shorthand-typing jobs and they said, "Well, don't expect challenging jobs if you only want to work part time" and also with what I've done in the past everything seems a bit . . . just a real come-down.

'I did write to the university, first I thought I'd apply to go to university and then that died a death; I can't remember why it did: they sent me the prospectus and everything and I read through it; I was quite strongly motivated because I knew they had a crèche as well and then I dropped the academic idea of it. I decided it would be too much of a strain and I applied for a couple of jobs there, secretarial jobs, and nothing came of those and that depressed me . . . I thought, "Marvellous isn't it, I can't even get a job, nobody even wants to employ me any more." I even have a big thing about going into agencies and having to put "Occupation: housewife". I can remember the first time it happened, I went to the FPA when we moved down here and I had to fill in a brand new form because I was a transfer patient, and she was filling it in for me and she said "What do you do?" and I said "Pardon?" – it didn't even register – and she said "What's your job?" and I said "Oh I'm a mother" and I didn't even think of the word housewife. One definitely gets an image once one is a parent and there are times when it doesn't bother me and there are other times when it bothers me a great deal. I think "Goodness, I can't be the same person." I was regarded by all my friends and people I worked with as being incredibly ambitious. I'm sure I don't give that impression any more, it's quite frightening.

'We're going to start this small business with a girl-friend who's just moved down here. Say I make a little money, I then hope I could afford to have somebody just for half days or even three half days a week when they would look after Leo and I would feel that all the pressures weren't on me.

'There are days when things work out beautifully for me and he doesn't sit there whining . . . yesterday he literally drove me mad; I was standing here screaming and yelling because all he was doing was pulling at me the whole day; I just kept saying "Leave me alone." If I had parents or family down here, it would be a completely different story.'

Three months later (with Leo one and a half): 'I was getting progressively more and more depressed and couldn't snap out of it and my best girl-friend started dropping big hints. She said the only thing that would get me out of it would be to work. I took quite a bit of notice of that and started buying the newspaper, and meanwhile I went to the doctor feeling suicidal at the time. He just couldn't give me anything. I went with Leo for some reason, maybe the innoculation, because I never go to the doctor. That was my way in, and I said "Actually while I'm here, I want to say, I'm feeling terribly low and Leo isn't sleeping", which he wasn't at the time. And I asked could he give Leo something to help him sleep. He said "You realize I'm treating you, snap, snap, but here you are" and literally gave me a prescription, walked across to the door and showed me out. And I came out of there thinking "Well, he's not going to help me, that's that out", though I don't know really what I expected him to do, and I seriously started looking for jobs.

It was a pinnacle of depression that I reached. I have a feeling that was what started it – Leo would just not go to bed at night any more and I've been used to having no problems putting him to bed at seven o'clock and then for over a week it was half past ten, eleven o'clock, half past eleven, and up at five, and there was no way I could carry on; and I thought "Oh my God, I thought things got better as they went on" – but he went backwards. I'm pretty sure that's what it was that made me a lot, lot worse. I was saying "I don't even have my evenings now, I've got nothing left", and that drove me to looking. I looked in the newspaper a bit half-heartedly at first because I thought . . . I didn't know what to do first, whether to look for someone to look after Leo or find a job. I had the feeling that jobs were more scarce than the baby-minders. I only went for one interview and when I was there, I was incredibly nervous; compared with places I have worked it's very slow tempo but they were very friendly. I went to the interview and they said "Yes we're very impressed but we gave the job yesterday to someone but don't . . . I hope you don't think we've wasted your time." I just couldn't react, I was so astonished because I had the feeling they were going to offer me the job and I was very excited just sitting there, and I was thinking it's quite nice to be here, just from nine to one, a pound an hour, which down here I realized was good money, so I tried to be a bit philosophic about it and said "Oh no." As I left the managing director said "I have a feeling that this girl may not turn up" and about a fortnight later they phoned me up one morning: the girl hadn't turned up and there hadn't been another part-time job advertised and I said "Fine, lovely", straight away. For the first week to ten days this girl-friend looked after Leo; she knows him very well and she came around here every morning, but I realized that couldn't go on, and meanwhile I phoned up all the baby-minders on the list given to me by the social services – and it's the most ridiculous list, either they were disconnected numbers, or the women left years ago. I decided to put an ad. for a part-time nanny five days a week and the phone never stopped ringing. I tended to talk quite a long time on the telephone to get some impression even before asking them to come over. I wanted definitely to get someone in their thirties who'd had a child, but strangly enough this girl Tina, when she came, Leo took a real liking to her, and she just seemed a very capable but quiet person so she started then straight away. First of all we had screams that lasted ten minutes after I'd gone, then it got less and less; he always cried for a few minutes and looked a bit pitiful when I left, but this week as I've picked my bag up he's gone to hold Tina's hand and he shouts bye-bye.

'He became completely different, he was manageable. I realize that I had a different attitude obviously but I think apart from that, of the people that have known Leo all along, all said he's . . . he just . . . he doesn't niggle. That's what was driving me mad before, the whining, not really knowing what he wanted but demanding it from you and he didn't know what it was he was demanding and that dropped. I still get a great reception when I get back from work and we go out for a walk, go shopping and he's incredibly contented: just so much easier to handle that it makes me wonder why I didn't do it before. He's not as strange with people generally either now. I've got a feeling he mixes now. The great thing is that I do not think he's suffered in any way, which is what I dreaded. If I'd felt that I definitely . . . I would have made another effort.

'He's just more manageable generally. In the mornings he used to wake up crying and I'd bring him into our bedroom and he'd kick around and fight – not in a playing sense – and now he wakes up and he'll say hello and I bring him into our bed and he just lies there; he likes to lie on top of me on my stomach: he's not asleep but he relaxes there.

'I appreciate him so much more in the afternoons. I'm much more relaxed, much happier. Life's more hectic but I prefer it that way, in fact there's more incentive to get things done.

I appreciate him much more now; I can't really lose my temper with him, which I was quite capable of doing before. I find it difficult to get cross with him, I tend to laugh at situations now whereas before it took very little and I'd get it all out of proportion.

'I'm just not made to stay home all day, I've decided. Because I'm able to go out in the morning on my own, the first week just catching a bus on my own was thrilling: it was nice just being out on my own, and also silly things like having blokes around you, messing around or chatting you up; or being able to talk to people – I just thought it was good for me.

'My theory is that it's very nice being somebody's wife and somebody's mother but it's important being yourself for some part of the day. I certainly couldn't go to work full time, I couldn't live with myself. If I wanted to do that I should never have had Leo.'

Charlotte's tribulations illustrate the difficulties some women encounter in their search to realize their own needs and potential while at the same time providing what they feel is right for their child. This varies tremendously from woman to woman, but the conflict occurs when she feels she ought to be providing more than she is or than she wants to provide. Before she began her part-time job, Charlotte found herself in a situation with her child where she became exasperated by his demands, unable to satisfy him, and a cycle of increasing resentment built up between them which was only broken when she decided to work in the mornings and could experience pleasure in being with him again.

For Beryl there is apparently no such conflict and guilt. From the start she employed a full-time nanny to look after her children while she carried on with her work. 'It's very important that I do my work, for me. I don't see why I should feel guilty; I'm a separate person. I do other things besides being a mother. I wouldn't feel complete if I wasn't doing my work. This is so much part of me, my identity, my personality, it's the way I express myself best. I'd be useless . . . I mean I wouldn't be a good mother, I wouldn't be a good anything. When I wasn't working those last few weeks I was just very, very aggressive and I was absolutely tearing my hair out, out of frustrated energies.' But Beryl does draw a line, and that has to do with physical distance and what can be seen as the idea that the house is an extension of herself: 'I couldn't actually leave the house and go to the office, that would be out of the question; but I'm just so lucky with the job that I'm doing. Being here I can keep an ear and an eye on the children. It's completely unnatural to leave one's children, physically . . . physically leave them and go out and not see them, or perhaps see them an hour a day; I'm listening and chatting and I have lunch with them: in actual fact out of the day I spend a reasonable amount of time with them and then I come down at, say, five o'clock and if Eva goes to bed at eight or half past, I've devoted that much time to her.'

CHAPTER FOURTEEN

She is going to grow up

July

HER CHILD's growing independence is a central preoccupation
for Barbara at this stage. Her conflicting feelings about this are
reflected and concentrated in her concern and anxieties about
weaning:

Barbara I've been reading everything on mixed feeding but I
don't think I will yet. I was going to start last week and then I
put it off because I don't want to start feeding her anything else
really, she's putting on so much weight already, she's about
eighteen pounds and a bit now and she's so happy I don't
think she needs anything else yet. Really I think she ought to
start around now, because she sleeps through the night; she's
been doing it for about a fortnight regularly: she sometimes
wakes up for a snack around nine, but normally it's seven to
seven or seven to eight. Well, when she gets up in the
morning, you see, obviously I'm absolutely bursting, there's
pints of it and she can take as much of it as she wants then and
so she's full, but a full tummy's worth doesn't last her four
hours any more, so perhaps she does need something else –
until it gets a bit more urgent, perhaps I'll put it off for a little
bit. I've got a sentence from Sheila Kitzinger's book stuck in
my head: the introduction of any solid food decreases the
breast milk, and it strikes fear in my very soul, believe me; I
don't want to start mixed feeding for that reason. I'm quite
attached to breast feeding, I enjoy it.

It's not sexual satisfaction, it's because she's so dependent
on me and I feel 'Oh, she's lovely', that I do something for her,
that's what I like really. If I introduce solids I feel I lose her
then. I shouldn't really, I shouldn't be like that, I know it's
wrong. A friend of mine fed her baby for six months and after

193

that she said she'd had enough, and I thought, 'Well, perhaps that feeling will start coming over me' but it doesn't. A lot of it is because I'm compensating, I think, for not feeding Peter and it's making up all my lost days.

I'm just wondering if she's the one who will give it up. I told you that I'd made up my mind to wean her but I didn't feel like it yet, and I find it easier. Once I've made the decision, it will gradually come, the feeling.

(*One month later*) Beatrice is growing up . . . she's growing up. I've actually started her on solids. I was reluctant at first. She was always having a feed about half past five irrespective of what the previous one was: it was generally about two or three; she always wanted a feed about half past five and then again at seven when she goes to bed; so I thought, 'Well, that's the one, I'll give her something at half past five to take her from three to seven' (that way I didn't feel I was cutting out one of my regular feeds), so that's what I did and she's very happy with that and so am I. She has just a teaspoonful and a bit of orange juice and then a breast feed before going to bed.

Dana So you haven't really given up anything.

Barbara No, I didn't feel I was giving up anything really. She just started waking up early in the morning and I was wondering which other feed to start introducing solids if she goes through another hungry phase or to feed her every three hours and step up the supply again. I was trying to see if there was one feed she wasn't particularly interested in, but there isn't.

I suppose the time will come when she will seem desperately hungry, and then I'll have to put her on to something else. It seems silly just as a matter of principle – just because she's a certain number of weeks old.

I don't feel quite so intensely about breast feeding, het up about it: when I fed her, boy! . . . now it's more a matter of routine. Oh, it's difficult to explain . . . but I felt very tender towards her when I fed her; now I don't feel so much, because she's awake more now, so she's part of our everday life. I can pick her up and cuddle her and make her happy any time, not just feed times.

Dana So feed times are not so important now, just part of a whole.

Barbara   That's how I feel anyway. If you analyse it in terms of
minutes I probably don't spend much more time with her, it
just seems like it. Perhaps I'm getting more used to her. She
acknowledges me now, she'll laugh and smile. She adores
Peter. She doesn't seem very dependent on me, she's quite an
independent baby . . . Peter at that age was happiest when he
was being cuddled, actually physically with you. She's happy
so long as you're paying her attention, she doesn't need to be
physically held or anything. Sometimes she does, she has a
period of the day starting mid-afternoon when she's always
been a bit restless, but even when she is fidgety, you can still
get away with it: you can still put her down, she won't really
scream.

For both mother and baby the question of dependence and
independence and the balance between the two is central. From
the total involvement and need of the beginning gradually
emerges a situation of looser dependence of mother on baby and
baby on mother. Barbara's preoccupation and ambivalence over
weaning is a reflection of her concern about her child's growing
independence from her. In this sense the word weaning does not
refer purely to the mode of feeding.

Winnicott points out that at the very beginning the baby is not
even aware of the dependence and only learns to make his or her
needs known when such an awareness develops: 'The great
change that is noticed in the first year of life is in the direction of
independence. Independence is something that is achieved out
of dependence, but it is necessary to add that dependence is
achieved out of what might be called double dependence. At the
very beginning there is an absolute dependence on the physical
and emotional environment. In the earliest stage there is no
vestige of an awareness of this dependence, and for this reason
the dependence is absolute. Gradually dependence becomes to
some extent known to the infant who, in consequence, acquires
the capacity for letting the environment know when attention is
needed.'[100]

It has been suggested that problems can develop when babies
are forced too early to become aware of this dependence, as when
their needs are not met soon enough. Problems can also occur

when, on the contrary, a mother is never able to separate from her baby.

Winnicott uses the term 'primary maternal preoccupation' to describe the state of involvement of most newly delivered mothers with their baby. Weaning, in its widest sense, involves for the mother the ability first to give herself over and then disengage herself from this state of total involvement. Barbara hints at this when she describes not being so 'het up' any more. Lesley describes it in these terms: 'When the time came to go back to work as I had planned, I just couldn't do it. I hadn't realized how much time a baby took up. I thought they slept for long periods of time, which she never did. And also I felt I couldn't bear to leave her with anyone except her father. I felt I needed to be with her. Again I was surprised when I found that at six months, and even more so at one year, I began to feel that she needed me much less. Weaning wasn't a problem: when the time came it went very smoothly. By the time she was one and a half or two, though, I came to realize that she could understand about staying with someone else, and I felt I could work in the mornings without feeling guilty. By then it was with surprise that I began to feel that it wasn't so restricting after all having a child, that one really was only totally tied down for one, at most two, years.'

Sometimes a woman's fear of losing her identity, of being 'swallowed up', makes her unable to become totally involved with her baby.

In my research on pregnancy and the postnatal period[101] I found that women who experienced various difficulties (such as postnatal depression) became totally preoccupied with mothering. But in contrast with Winnicott's 'primary maternal preoccupation' (deep involvement with the baby) they succumbed to a morbid preoccupation with their own capacity to mother, and generally experienced a discrepancy between an idealized notion of what a good mother should be like and their own imperfect self, blaming themselves for it.

Mary Kelly in her 'Post-partum Document'[102] describes, based on her own experience, three 'moments of loss' for mother and baby. The first is the weaning from the breast: 'Weaning from the breast is a significant discovery of absence not only for the child but also for the mother', which ruptures 'the symbiosis of the biologically determined mother–child unit'. And she adds: 'Weaning from the breast did not imply, literally, the termination of breast feeding (as it can go on for over a year, or never be initiated at all) but more specifically, the inevitable end of an exclusively liquid diet and the introduction of solid food. This transition has usually taken place by the infant's sixth month.'

Second is 'weaning from the holophrase'. The holophrase is the child's single-word utterance which is understood by the mother as a complete sentence. Weaning from the holophrase therefore refers to the moment when the child develops beyond single-word utterances, around eighteen months, when there is a loss for the mother in the sense that she is no longer the interpreter of the child's single utterances.

The third moment of loss is the 'weaning from the dyad'. This refers to the end of an exclusively two-person relationship and the entry of the third person, symbolized by the growing impor-tance of the father* and reinforced by the child's entry into an environment outside the home, when he goes to school. I would add to this the arrival of another baby, which precipitates this third type of weaning.

Mary Kelly's conceptualization highlights the sense of loss which accompanies the growing independence, for both mother and baby. The first years are characterized by a fluctuation be-tween dependence and independence, with many regressive moves to dependence before a new spurt towards independence. For the mother it is a question of re-experiencing her own sense of loss which accompanied the growing independence in her own childhood, and she may deal with the pain of loss by either precipitating or delaying the weaning of her child (in the general and the specific sense of the word).

Joan Raphael Leff points to the parallel between the growing differentiation of mother and baby during pregnancy and the growing separation of mother and baby after the birth so that 'pregnancy may be regarded as a condensed rehearsal of the mother's intense relationship with her baby in the two years following birth.'[103]

It is no easy task for a mother to adapt to her infant's changing

---

* I would say that the importance of the father (or the third person) occurs much earlier than Mary Kelly seems to imply.

needs as they arrive, because of the strength of her own needs. Margaret Mahler contrasts mothers who find more difficulties with the initial stages with mothers who find it hardest to let their children separate from them: 'Those mothers who had been most anxious because they could not relieve their infant's distress during the symbiotic and differentiation phases were now greatly relieved when their children became less fragile and vulnerable and somewhat more independent. Those mothers and their children had been unable to take undisturbed pleasure in close physical contact, but they were able to enjoy each other now from a somewhat greater distance. These same children became more relaxed and better able to use their mothers to find comfort and safety.

'By contrast, another mother–child interaction pattern was observed in those children . . . whose mothers had the greatest difficulty in relating to them during the process of active distancing. These mothers liked the closeness of the symbiotic phase but once this phase was over, they would have liked their children to be "grown up" already. Interestingly, these children found it relatively difficult to grow up; they were unable to enjoy the beginning ability to distance and very actively demanded closeness.'[104]

The third moment of loss which Mary Kelly talked about brings other problems to do with allowing another person in and the conflicts relating to a three-person relationship.

August

Barbara has problems with the 'third person':

Barbara Last week I had a dreadful week – I felt the worst I've ever felt: since I had her, anyway. I really felt awful, I didn't know what to do any more; I was in such a muddle, I wrote a list of all the jobs I'd got to do and it was a couple of foolscap pages, and I got so depressed. I don't know how to describe this . . . I felt more than anything that I wanted to be on my own with Beatrice and nothing else, and everything that came between me and the ultimate ambition, which was everything, got on top of me; I can't explain it any other way. I was so tense, as soon as Patrick came in I'd start moaning at him and

I'd get cross and have temper tantrums. Sunday I was OK. Patrick took Peter out Sunday mornings. I said 'Please, please take him out', and then in the afternoon I didn't have to do anything very much, and in the evening we went out and had a drink and after that I was fine.

I've never been in such a muddle. I didn't know what I was doing, I couldn't even think properly. I don't know how it started, I couldn't tell you. A lot of it was that Peter kept getting up all night and I got so cross. What makes it worse is having a baby who sleeps all night and then a four-year-old . . . but I'm not alone, which is comforting. A lot of mothers say that they get really cross if their older child wakes up, and it's not fair and you know it's not fair but you do get cross. Older children just seem to be particularly frustrating: perhaps you expect it from a baby but you expect rather more from the older one and they're not that much older. One night I could . . . Oh I literally could . . . have done him injury . . . Also I have an awful job getting back to sleep after I've been woken, and as soon as I went to sleep he'd get up. In fact at one o'clock in the morning I decided to have a bath because it didn't seem worth going to bed and that's how the whole thing started.

Someone suggested to me that I put Beatrice in with him because she still sleeps in our room, and I said 'Well, it's partly I don't want her to sleep in there because, you know how I don't want to give her up, I like her sleeping with . . . I can't even see her but I like her there, but I am afraid that if he keeps waking up two or three times a night she will wake up . . .' I'm still possessive about her. Well, I'm jealous of her if you like. I don't like sharing her with Patrick and Peter, I just like to be alone with her. I'd like some peace and quiet to enjoy her.

Over the last couple of months or so I've had occasions when I reject everything male and everything concerned with men. I've no time for Peter, I've no time for Patrick. I don't even want to see them in a way. I felt almost hatred, I didn't want anything to do with them at all. Just go away. I didn't want to see Patrick, I didn't want to know. The sooner I got Peter to bed the better. I can't explain, just a feeling. I didn't want anything to do with the male sex.

This specific antagonism to the male sex seems to reflect Barbara's feelings about the father who comes in and disrupts the close relationship between mother and daughter, a reproduction of a resented childhood experience.

We can also see how her older child, Peter, more specifically comes to represent the one who intrudes and disrupts the would-be perfect relationship between Barbara and the new baby, who breaks into the close dyad with his jealousy and demandingness. We can speculate that Barbara's difficulty in coping with Peter relates to her own difficulty with feelings of envy and jealousy in relation to couple relationships. Her intolerance of such feelings adds to her wish to go on feeding Beatrice for ever and devoting her exclusive attention to her. In this way she feels that the baby, with whom she is identified, need not experience jealousy, loss, frustration and the intrusion of a third party.

It is probably significant that before her second child was born, Barbara had a similarly exclusive relationship with Peter so that he could never be left without his parents and only started going to a play group after the second child was born.

The difficulty Barbara experiences with Peter is accentuated by her polarization of her two children. All along Beatrice has been the baby who made Barbara feel that she was a good and successful mother. She gave birth to this baby easily and naturally, she was able to breast feed her, and the baby was a responsive and calm baby. 'She's a lovely little girl; when she wakes up she doesn't scream blue murder like Peter. Peter still does when he wakes up; she lies in her cot and goes mmmm like this.'

A similar difficulty to Barbara's can lead to early weaning when a woman cannot bear the *elder* child's jealousy and envy of the new baby. Anna weaned her baby at three weeks because she felt that breast feeding prevented her sharing the baby with her older children, whereas they could help her with bottle feeding.

Early weaning from the dyad can also take place when a woman cannot bear extreme dependency. 'I don't think babies get interesting until they're one, really,' says Linda, who mainly values her own rational rather than bodily and emotional self. Total reliance on one person seems terrifying and weaning from the dyad is precipitated.

September

Barbara's baby is now six months old and she is struck by a difference in her child:

Barbara After I saw you, I left Beatrice with my mother-in-law. When I returned she was crying a lot and she didn't stop until I fed her. It wasn't that she was hungry, because I fed her before I left, but she didn't realize it was me until I fed her, she was so upset. I'd left her previously but she'd never been worried before. She calmed down after I fed her. I felt quite gratified really that she'd missed me. She'd always been quite independent before . . . I used to leave her Sunday morning to play tennis but after she had a cry that evening I haven't left her since. I thought she was going to be so . . . she didn't like to be held, you couldn't sit and hold her like this[hug], she hated it, she still does; I felt quite rejected by that and so having found that she cried when I was away I thought 'Well, *she does* need me then!' She's a lot more suspicious of people now. If she hadn't missed me like that I would have carried on. I didn't know what to do. I was talking to her and she didn't take any notice, she just kept crying and I thought 'If I feed her she's bound to know it's me.' I held her to the breast and she didn't even react, she didn't even realize who it was, she wouldn't look, she was so upset, so . . . I haven't left her since. It happened on the Wednesday, she became ill on the Saturday. If you could have seen me that day – I was sure she was going to die. You know I worried about this since she's arrived. Well, I was convinced that that was what was going to happen, I really was. She was white and she just lay there. When I went to the hospital . . . the doctor at the hospital said that she was a remarkably strong baby and he said that when she had a cold in the future he didn't recommend that she had antibiotics straight away. It reassured me a lot that he said she's really a strong baby. I must have very deeply ingrained fears about her dying. Perhaps it's linked with all my fears about when I was pregnant, although I would never have admitted it then.

Then I was ill and I couldn't feed her – that was a crisis. I lost all my milk for about a day. I couldn't feed her very much and I had my mind made up for me. When I fed her there wouldn't be much so she'd cry. So I said to Patrick to try a bit of food before her feeds and, hey presto, Beatrice became a three-meals-a-day baby. I was ill and I didn't mind at all, I was just grateful that she'd stopped crying. She seemed to enjoy the food. I recovered in a few days and continued to give her a spoonful or so at each feed. She fed OK after that and my milk came back. I kept on the solids. I started making less milk, I'd wake up with less in the morning; I was disturbed about that. I thought the milk supply was going to stop very easily, and I still hadn't got over the feeling of not feeding Peter, and all the milk disappeared within two or three days – this shook me at that time.

Barbara is finding it difficult to wean her baby, a problem linked with her wish to remain the centre of her little girl's world. The fear of harming Beatrice, and the idea that her baby could die suddenly, is ever present in her mind, and in her conversation she links the fact of having left her for a few hours with the onset of the baby's illness and maybe even her own later. Separating and weaning arouse feelings of deprivation, abandonment and anger. The fear of dying is the most primitive reaction to separation. Barbara identifies with her little girl ('my mother says Beatrice is like I was'), and we can only speculate that this was a problem-area in her relationship with her own mother.

Winnicott writes about weaning: 'In the baby's dreams the breasts are no longer good, they have been hated, and so now they are felt to be bad, even dangerous. That is why there is a place for the wicked woman in the fairy stories who gives poisoned apples. For the newly weaned infant it is the really good mother whose breasts have become bad, and so there has to be time allowed for recovery and readjustment . . . Eventually the child grows up and gets to know her just as she really is, neither ideal nor indeed a witch. So, there is a wider aspect of weaning – weaning is not only getting a baby to take other foods, or to use a cup, or to feed actively using the hands. It includes the gradual process of disillusionment, which is part of the parents' task.'[105]

And the mother too can become acutely aware of the sadness involved in this process of disillusionment and growing up which inevitably involves a loss. In the case of weaning from the breast, it is the feeling of it being 'gone for ever'.

Women have various ways of coping with the introduction of solid food. Lesley describes how she had to keep the breast feed and the solid feed quite separate. 'I found that I couldn't breast feed her just after giving her some food with a spoon . . . something about her mouth full of food on my breast . . . a feeling that I was stuffing her if I gave both at once. I would breast feed and give solid food at different times and that was no problem. She also seemed to want it that way. After having had solids she didn't seem interested in the breast.'

We can speculate that for both mother and baby, after the solid food, 'the breasts are no longer good' to use Winnicott's terms, and gradual weaning could only take place (without refusal of either breast or solids) when the two were kept apart.

Anna, when her baby refuses food, sieves it 'to get rid of the lumps' – the lumps coming to represent the bad food which is least like milk.

The psychoanalyst Melanie Klein describes a similar reaction to Lesley's baby in a six-week-old baby who had to be given a bottle following the evening feed because the breast milk was insufficient. At first the bottle was accepted but later she became reluctant to drink from the bottle. The mother did not force the baby and just put her in the cot. The child cried with hunger and the mother gave her a bottle which she emptied eagerly. Next evening the same thing happened. The baby refused the bottle while on the mother's lap but took it at once when in her cot. Melanie Klein[106] concludes that 'when lying in her cot A. accepted the bottle because, as I would suggest, in this situation the new food was kept apart from the desired breast which, at that moment, had turned into the frustrating and injured breast. In this way she may have found it easier to keep the relation to the mother unimpaired by the hatred stirred up by frustration, that is to say, to keep the good mother (the good breast) intact.'

The two situations are very similar, only with Lesley's infant the separation is done in terms of time, whereas with infant A. the separation is a physical one. It is interesting to note how Lesley describes in herself the need to keep the situations apart, paralleling such feelings in her baby, pointing again to the way in which early childhood feelings are reawakened in women in their relationship with their infants. Such feelings and the way a woman deals with them will have a major influence on how weaning is instituted.

Some babies are more able to tolerate the introduction of a bottle than others and to transfer their feelings from the breast to the bottle. Ginette's baby Tony, normally very placid, cried for two days when he was weaned from the breast at six weeks. Tony and his mother seemed less in contact with each other for some time but after a few weeks he could take the bottle with enjoyment. Tony held his hands around the teat of the bottle, against his mouth, reproducing the skin-to-skin contact of the earlier situation. Reactions to the breast and to the bottle were similar. At five weeks Tony's mother had to interrupt a breast feed and put Tony in his cot while she attended to her older child. When she picked Tony up again, she noticed that he wouldn't take the breast for a while. A similar refusal took place when at eleven weeks Ginette lifted her hands off the bottle and it fell and Tony then wanted to suck his fingers instead of the teat when the bottle was presented to him again. In both cases, the breast or bottle were refused, we can surmise, in anger, for a while after they had 'gone away'. In the latter case, sucking the fingers is also a way of dealing with the loss, by replacing the bottle with something which the baby is in control of.

After a very sudden and brief illness Barbara incurs permanent damage which leaves her deaf in one ear. Her condition is physically debilitating and she naturally becomes psychologically preoccupied with coming to terms with this bodily change. But now again she relates this to the idea that she should not have had a second child, as if the awaited punishment has finally arrived. In her mind there is a link between the new child and her present disability:

Barbara I always expected something terrible might happen to Beatrice, but I didn't expect it would happen to me. I had the feeling that something awful was going to happen and this is it. Things will never ever be the same. I'll never be able to hear Peter on one side and Beatrice on the other. Yes, I did think the two were related, that I was so worried about Beatrice and that this has happened to me. I thought that was because my father said you won't ever have another one.

And again she reacts by feeling she is no good as a mother.

Barbara This is difficult to explain: I started to stop feeding Beatrice. I don't mean I was weaning her, I mean I started to work out ways of substituting other . . . I thought, if I give her a drink now I won't need to feed her, and if I do this I won't need to feed her; now this was mostly subconscious. At the same time I told you I was getting her on to three meals a day but that was nothing to do with it, I was thinking of stopping feeding her all within a few weeks. I wouldn't have admitted that, but that's what I was doing, and I thought 'I'm not feeding her any more', it wasn't because . . . yes, it *was* because of this indirectly – because I feel that I'm not good enough any more, because I'm not all in one piece any more, I'm not . . . you see when I was 'perfect' then I was fit to look after her, but because something went wrong I started thinking 'No, I'm not going to feed her, because I'm not perfect, it's not good enough for her, so I don't want to feed her any more.' Having sussed that out with myself I got over that; now I just feed her after I've given her her solids, but I found I *was* deliberately trying to give it up without even thinking about it. I thought that was similar to Peter, when I had Peter, this . . . oh-I-couldn't-have-him-on-my-own-so-I-couldn't-feed-him reaction. Now that I've thought it out, I shan't drop any more feeds for a while. I was so miserable. Peter wanted something and he was on the wrong side of me and I couldn't hear what he was asking me, and we took Beatrice to have her vaccination the same day, and there were all the other Mums all talking to their babies and I had her on the wrong side and I thought she was going 'Dadada' and she was this side so I had to change her over. With these two unrelated things I thought 'All these other Mums there, they don't have to shift their babies' and I felt sorry for myself and I got into a deeper and deeper depression. By the time I got home I felt almost suicidal: I thought the children would be better off without me altogether. I wasn't contemplating suicide, but I began to think how they would get along if I wasn't there. Then I had a good cry and I felt better and then I thought *'That's* what I've been doing, I've been feeling so miserable and I've been trying to think of a way of getting the children to do without me because I was feeling so depressed that I was honestly thinking of . . . not jumping off a cliff or whatever, just not being there' . . . that's what I thought. I was trying to get away from Beatrice so she wouldn't need me.

I don't know if it's because I'm on these drugs (for my illness) or not but it doesn't worry me now whether I wean her or not. Yesterday was her six-months birthday, and to celebrate we sat her up at the table, and she had her first grown-up dinner. I said to Patrick it really seems like a milestone having reached six months, sitting there so grown up.

As from yesterday I give her three breast-feeds. I've cut out the three o'clock one. It's seven, twelve-thirty and six-thirty. But she had a snack this morning, she had about two minutes on this side at eleven because she was nuzzling at me, when she starts making 'mummy' movements I don't say 'Oh no you can't, you can't,' I have to give it to her; I feel bad if I don't. If she starts nuzzling around I give her a little bit and surprisingly she doesn't seem to want any more, it's like a little drink. Another thing that made me decide is that she seems to have lost interest in large breast-feeds. She probably won't finish one breast and then start the other . . . it's not the way it used to be where she wouldn't look at anything or stop till both sides were completely empty, but she isn't so insistent now, and Patrick says 'Perhaps it's you who finds it difficult to give up breast feeding, not Beatrice' . . . it's quite likely. But I don't feel so strongly as I did about it.

And for the first time she looks upon weaning as the beginning of a greater freedom:

Barbara I'd like to become the drink after her dinner, or the drink after her meal, rather than her main source of supply that I used to so desperately want her not to be dependent on anything else. I came to accept her having solids. I found it awfully difficult to start her on solids and then once she seemed to be happy having them, then I became more pre-

pared to become the back seat. I don't know why. It does seem
a bit mad, doesn't it . . . no, perhaps the four-hourly feed was
getting a bit of a drag as well, so it's partly just being selfish.
For the first six months I was quite prepared to do everything
for her comfort and for every whim, and then after that I
started thinking more about me, and I thought she's got to . . .
now we'll have a bit more give and take. I used to have to get
home by three o'clock for her feed if I was out shopping and I
thought 'Well, it is inconvenient'. If it won't upset her greatly
then I'll try to get her on three meals. We're gradually growing
apart, I'm getting my individuality back and she is becoming a
personality. You see I'm starting to do my things again. I'm
starting to get back to *my* life at the same time as she is growing
up: as she becomes more aware and I feel less protective, in a
way.

Yet Barbara cannot enjoy the greater freedom and distancing
from her daughter without the niggling feeling of guilt about
what this might be doing to her baby:

Barbara I'll tell you what I do worry about. Supposing she
should be ill – and I know that breast milk is the most easily
absorbed, the ideal food – supposing she should be ill and I'd
finished feeding her . . . that worries me. I shall be a bit
worried for some time about her getting whooping cough now
that I've decided not to have the injection. It used to be
gastroenteritis that I was worried about.
  Patrick is getting fed up with me breast feeding. He doesn't
say so in so many words but he said: 'Goodness she looks
much too big to be breast fed now, it's as if you're feeding a
grown-up little girl.' It's partly probably because he wishes we
could get back to a normal sex life, and I told you I tend to link
the two things together: I expect he has too, we haven't discussed it. He still tends to feel that part of my body belongs to
the baby and he's had enough of it, nine months and seven
months feeding – he probably has just had about enough.

Tied up with her difficulty in weaning Beatice is the idea that
the close exclusive bond between them is being broken, in particular by her husband, and the feeling that to go on breast

feeding is a way of keeping the baby for herself, and almost of coming between Beatrice and her father. She links the baby's loss of interest in breast feeding with a growing interest in her father:

Barbara She seems to be really going off breast feeding, she's distracted so much. I've even tried going into the other room and shutting the door. All there needs to be is a flicker of sunshine across the room and she's distracted. I'm still full up this time because Patrick came in and she absolutely stopped.

CHAPTER FIFTEEN

I'm quite jealous

October and November

FOR the first time, Barbara expresses feelings of jealousy:

Barbara I found that yesterday I was quite jealous: quite jealous of the way Patrick fusses over her. The first few months have been very different with Peter and Beatrice. He's all over Beatrice and he was a little bit wary of Peter. I don't think it's just because he was the first, I think it's because she's a girl as well. He makes a fuss of her all the time and I thought I'm getting quite jealous really.

Dana Maybe that's why *he* found it quite difficult with Peter.

Barbara Yes probably, especially since she's the reverse of Peter. She says 'Dadadada' when he arrives and she'll put her arms up to him to be picked up and she won't to me. He walks through the door and she's beaming – Peter didn't really take much notice, it wasn't till later when he started looking delighted when Patrick arrived. Peter was the opposite, he was 'Mumumum', and he'd come to me if there was anything wrong whereas she'll go to her Dad. Yes, I think he was probably jealous of Peter. You wouldn't believe a man could make so much fuss of a baby. He ignores us and comes straight in and picks the baby up and he'll walk all around the room showing her anything and everything, then he'll have a laugh with her or tickle her, then he might come round to saying hello to me or he might say hello to Peter. It's quite brutal the way he talks to Peter, it's a shame; it certainly doesn't do Peter any good. He talks to her in a more . . . well, in a more romantic way I suppose. He sits with her on the settee and tickles her and tells her how beautiful she is. He can't leave her alone and yesterday I thought 'Oh my goodness, here we go again, another hour of it', and then I thought: 'For me to think that I must be quite jealous', and I said to him he should try and divide himself up a bit more equally, so, if he's listening, which he does once every six weeks or so, he might say hello to Peter. At meal times, if she starts fretting (she generally doesn't want anything in particular, she just grumbles), he'll finish his meal with her on his lap. He'd never do that with Peter. Peter had to stay there till we'd finished or I'd pick him up. You see the situation is completely reversed.

Jealousy, and the accompanying fear of being excluded or relegated to second place, contributes to many women's wish to give birth to a boy. As one woman says: 'I wanted to have a boy because deep down I wanted to be loved, I wanted to be the centre of his world, I wanted to be the most important one'; or, as another woman puts it: 'I've had a girl, now I want to have one *for me*'.

In my study of first-time mothers I found that the women who were depressed three months postnatally were more likely to have a girl than a boy. They were also more likely to feel that they lost their temper easily. Ann Oakley, in her research, did not find depression to be more likely among mothers of female children, but did find a tendency towards mothers feeling more irritability with girls.

These findings need to be interpreted in the context of the greater achievement linked with having a male baby and the greater preference for a male baby as firstborn in our society, and to the more ambivalent relationship which tends to exist between mother and daughter than between mother and son.

The baby's looks are sometimes relevant to the feeling of possession or, on the contrary, exclusion. Veronica says: 'Everybody says she looks like my husband. That and the fact that she is a girl makes me feel left out of their special bond. It's almost as if I'm superfluous to the whole business. The fact that they look alike makes me feel that they belong together.'

And Bridget: 'He looked incredibly like my husband. Oh yes, the minute I saw him he was . . . I really thought if I hadn't been here I would have thought I hadn't had anything to do with it. It would have been awful if it had been a caesarian, because he looked just like my husband and I couldn't see anything of me in him.'

Besides her jealousy of Beatrice, Barbara describes some rivalry between husband and wife:

Barbara   Patrick and I are going through a very peculiar phase. Instead of this tense relationship we've had before, we're going through a *teasing* sort of relationship. I can't think of an example. I think part of it is because Patrick goes out to night school. I've been at school or college for years and if I used to talk to my friends in front of Patrick or I used to make reference to something that happened when I was at school – he left school when he was about fifteen – he felt a bit excluded. There was always a barrier between us, not just over this but he used to speak of himself as if he was rather inferior to all these college people. All he's done is go for an evening class and it's given him so much more confidence it's not true. With the confidence he's got he doesn't need to bully us so much; I don't know if it is just that or something else, but he's very happy when he comes home from night school; it's something else to talk about too, and it's made our relationship much lighter. I can tease him about something and instead of him getting cross, he'll tease me back which makes it a lot easier.

Dana   You feel that he used to be threatened by feeling that you were somehow superior.

Barbara   Yes, so he used to bully me, perhaps as a result, and since Beatrice was born – well he was there when she was born, he was so different after that . . . he was so serious and stern about everything and this brought a lighter atmosphere.

Dana   Because he was there, he didn't feel inferior, he actually participated.

Barbara   I think he felt terribly bad about not being there the first time and it alleviated his feelings to be there this time and he really felt he'd done something. I said: 'It was really good to have you there', and he said 'All I did was to hold your hand' and I said that was just what I needed at the time and he felt good then, and gradually everything else that he's doing at the moment is on the up and up.

So gradually our relationship is changing, not directly because of Beatrice but it was a great help his being there at the birth, and other things now are carrying on from there and I'm

not under this awful strain all the time of being so worried
about having another baby.

Maybe it all goes back to Patrick not being there when Peter
was born. He felt he'd let me down then even though he
couldn't have been there because of the vacuum extraction. He
felt he'd failed in some way.

Barbara is hinting at the envy many men feel about a woman's
ability to be pregnant and give birth, and the way this envy can
become destructive to the relationship when the man is not able
or willing to participate in the experience. Barbara describes her
husband's sense of inadequacy and of exclusion after his first
child was born, and his consequent withdrawal.

But the rivalry works the other way too. We can speculate that
weaning is so difficult for Barbara partly because this is her
prerogative and the area where she can do something which her
husband cannot.

Barbara's and her husband's roles are quite strongly and traditionally delineated, with the woman assuming the total care of
the children. When there is rivalry between them, it is expressed
as rivalry over each other's special domain or over the bond with
the baby. In families where greater role-sharing takes place, the
burden of child care is greatly eased for the woman. In some
cases, though, sharing can turn into rivalry over mothering in a
destructive way. One study of eight women suffering from a
severe postnatal disturbance[107] found that the husbands tended
to compete with their wives in the female role, increasing the
wives' feelings of inadequacy as women. The authors conclude:
'Women who tend to destroy the masculinity of men are sometimes described as "castrating females". We suggest that there is a
male counterpart to this classification, and that the husbands of
women with postpartum psychoses fall into that group.'

CHAPTER SIXTEEN

I'm more worried about myself

December

THE final weaning from the breast takes place in December, not without considerable hesitation on Barbara's part:

Barbara I really wanted the baby to give up her own feeds; I didn't want to have to say 'Right, you're eight months old so now you've got to be on so many feeds a day.' Now she's showing signs of not being very interested in the midday feed, I thought I'll try stopping it. If she starts turning to me and searching all over I shall feed her again probably. I'm not so sure it's not me that is very keen on feeding and her not so much.

    (Nearly three weeks later) We're down to two feeds a day. Now she makes me feel guilty because she sucks her thumb all day. She never used to. She was losing interest in the feeds and I thought she's losing this sucking thing, but now she sucks her thumb all the time. It makes me feel dreadful. I feel I've deprived her – then on the other hand I can't go on feeding her until she's Peter's size. I had planned to cut out another feed by the end of this week if she was cooperative. I don't know now, and I don't know which one to drop, first thing in the morning or last thing at night, because she seems equally eager for both.

    I felt very bad because I had loads of milk, and so awful that I'd got it and I didn't give it to her. Patrick was right behind me saying: 'You've got to give it up somewhere . . . here she is eight months old . . .'

    I expected I would get a little further apart from Beatrice as she stopped feeding, but in fact it's the reverse. I thought she'd be more independent but she isn't now. She quite often likes to be held, she doesn't push away as she used to, so instead of getting further apart we're getting closer together. Perhaps it's not the sucking she needs, perhaps it's the physical comfort of being held. She'll be held more, whereas before she would wriggle and squirm. I don't know if it's because she isn't being held or feeding every three hours, or what. I like that but it's difficult to divorce one feeling from another. I still feel quite sad about stopping feeding. I feel a bit mixed-up. I have a muddle of feelings.

With separating herself from the baby, she becomes more aware of the other child:

Barbara Now I feel guilty about Peter. Sometimes he cries and I feel for him. I try to set aside some time, usually in the evening. I put Beatrice to bed and then I read a story or we just play cowboys or something. I think he does feel a bit isolated from the rest of us sometimes. She's sleeping in his bedroom now. He was starting to feel he was left out, the three of us all together against him. The first couple of nights she woke him up a few times but they don't seem to wake each other up now. When she woke him up I told Patrick I felt a malicious delight. All those nights after nights he's woken us up, now you know what it's like, the justice of it . . . [*she laughs*]. Patrick was worried, he said it wasn't fair to have him disturbed. I said, 'No it wouldn't be if he was going to school or if it seriously affected him, but it only happened for two nights and after that he slept OK.' It didn't worry me much, that's how I felt, serves you right!

What seems to happen, I see it with friends too, is that when you get frustrated with the baby, you tend to get angry with your older child, not angry with the baby. You think: Oh, what can I try next? and your other child will drop something and you get cross about that, when it's really the baby that's been frustrating you all day. It's pretty tough really on your first one, especially since he's had three and a half years with all my attention and then not only is he having to share the attention but he also gets all the frustration.

From the beginning Barbara has expressed some withdrawal of interest from her older child accompanying her involvement with the baby. This she expressed in a drawing which she made of herself soon after the birth of Beatrice. While drawing, she spontaneously remarked: 'Oh, Peter seems to be standing on a different floor to me' which can be taken metaphorically.

Janet expressed a similar idea concerning the switch in involvement with the new baby: 'When I was pregnant I said to a friend: "How can I love the second one as much as I love the first one?" and she said: "Don't worry, the problem will be more with loving the first one" ', and Janet commented that indeed when the new baby was born she found it difficult to feel loving towards her first child, who was expressing her jealousy by becoming as demanding and difficult as she could possibly be.

Some mothers find it difficult to get too involved with the second child. During her pregnancy Ginette expressed her fear that 'second children tend to get rather neglected'. When her baby was born she found it difficult to pay much attention to him and mainly played with him when her eighteen-month-old child was in bed. She breast-fed him for a very short while only, much shorter than with her first child; when he was a few weeks old she dropped all but one breast feed a day, the one she would give while her older child was asleep. At the time she repeatedly expressed her fear that the new baby was being rather neglected. It is most likely significant that Ginette was herself the eldest child in her family, which increased her identification with her first child in his jealousy of the second baby and her fear of harming him.

Both Barbara and Ginette in the above passages express their guilt. When we listen to mothers talking, the question of guilt is one which recurs time and again: guilt if there isn't 'love at first sight'. Janet put it like this: 'When my daughter was born I felt she was quite nice but nothing special – take-it-or-leave-it sort of thing – and preferably leave it. It took over three weeks before I started feeling differently, and then I went overboard; I became enthralled with her. You feel very guilty when you don't love the baby immediately; you feel everyone expects you to, doctors, friends, everybody, and yet you don't.'

Guilt then appears later on when a woman feels she does not do enough for her baby, or does not want to do more, or finds that he is different from the child she wished for, or feels incensed by the continuous crying and demands, or any number of other reasons.

We all carry inside us a notion of a bad, neglectful or rejecting mother, an image which stems from our own childhood and the feelings we had when our wishes were not immediately gratified. As Anna Freud points out,[108] even the most devoted mother will be felt to be rejecting at times by her child because his demands are limitless, because life outside the womb is by its very nature frustrating. And in his anger a child will in his mind transform his mother into a wicked harmful witch.

Each mother will have to deal with such images inside herself, images of the neglectful or rejecting mother. Identification with such images is at the heart of postnatal depression, and the woman now attacks herself as the neglectful mother.

January

Barbara I finished feeding Beatrice the second week in December and then I fed her off and on for the next week because I couldn't stand not feeding her. I kept cheating, I kept giving her a little feed at bedtime every couple of days, but eventually she got fed up, and I didn't mind so much when *she* got fed up with it, but to start off with I thought she was missing it. Patrick thought it was my imagination. I was terribly depressed afterwards for about three weeks. She'd only been having a two-minute feed from each side at bedtime, and she was very happy with a cup, so I thought 'Right I'll give her a cup tonight' and I did and I felt terrible, when she'd gone to bed I cried. I don't know why, I just felt bad, but the next night she woke up so I thought 'Aha, the perfect excuse', and I gave her a little bit then and it went on rather like that: every second or third day I'd feed her and she wasn't interested so then I didn't care, I didn't bother any more and that was that. But it was dreadful for me, I felt I was denying her something she ought to have, that I was being mean. I felt the depression went like magic as soon as the milk had gone. When there was still a little bit there and I felt I could feed her I felt dreadful, really dreadful: I used to think 'Oh it's all going to waste'; I had that same feeling just for those few days when

Peter was little and I didn't feed him, but as soon as it had gone I was OK. Now that it's finished I wouldn't want to go back to feeding her, I don't wish I could, and I thought I might regret it dreadfully. It's such a final thing, when the milk is gone it's gone and I thought I might feel dreadful about it but I don't.

When I was feeding her I wanted another baby and now I've finished feeding her I don't – isn't that weird? All of a sudden I thought I don't want any more, and yet for nine months I'd been positive I'd want another one eventually. Now I really don't want another one at all.

(*About the next to last feed*) Two days after I last saw you my periods returned – at last! I had expected to feel miserable or depressed since I wasn't looking forward to that, but I felt quite pleased – a return to femininity from motherhood. I was pleased to see a return to normal – from sterile, I presume – when, before this I didn't want to be fertile. A very complex mixture of feelings. Two days later I dropped the morning feed. The two events were not related . . .

And yet the fact that she talks about the two things at once makes me wonder if there is not some unconscious connection between the beginning of menstruation and the dropping of the feed, what she calls 'a return to femininity from motherhood'.

There is an old wives' tale which says that the milk of a menstruating woman is 'poisonous' for the baby, and some babies are taken off the breast deliberately at the onset of menstruation.[109]

Up until now Barbara had been almost exclusively preoccupied with the baby, and this preoccupation was in large part concentrated around the breast feeding relationship, with its implications for mutual dependency and exclusiveness. For Barbara the total dependency of her child was an important aspect of her desire to breast feed and her mixed feelings about weaning. We may suppose that this extreme dependency expressed an aspect of herself which she is unable to accept directly as is evidenced by what she said about the birth: 'What upset me most about the whole thing was feeling so dependent on Patrick.'

When she does finally feel able to wean her baby Barbara becomes once more aware and preoccupied with other areas of her life, her sexuality and her own fulfilment.

217

Barbara Stopping breast feeding has made me much more sexy, much more interested in sex altogether. Patrick says thank God – he'd given up. I told you I was using the feeding as an excuse but I thought that would be it, I thought when I stop feeding I shan't feel any different, it's just I shan't have an excuse; but it wasn't directly, it wasn't the day I finished feeding her I thought 'Oh well that's great', but later on . . . I don't attack Patrick as soon as he walks in the front door but I'm certainly a lot more interested than I was.

I have the odd phase when I feel I shouldn't be married at all, I can't be bothered with the children, I just think they're a lot of work. I don't love them any the less but I just can't be bothered with them. I find going out helps. I went out a couple of evenings last week and then I felt better. Once I can get out so that they can't scream and I have to go to them . . . I find them all a bit demanding at the moment and I just want to get away from them all. Patrick's making much more effort than he used to: he's more considerate than he used to be – and in return I ignore him, just cussedness.

I'm not quite so tolerant as I was. I think of Beatrice more as a child rather than my little baby, and if she keeps yelling, instead of picking her up and walking around and saying 'There, there', I tend to say 'Oh *do* be quiet'. You know the mothers that bash their babies around, perhaps that's something to do with it, because a young baby that screams and screams and screams, if you can feed it you feel you're *doing* something and it will stop crying for a while, and you're more emotionally involved, I think, when you're feeding a child.

I'm not quite sure what I'm going to do yet: I might do this adult literacy training, I'm going to see about that tomorrow. I want to do adult literacy, and I want to do some sports and I want to do something else, and I don't know what I'm doing yet because I've only got two evenings a week that I can do it in. But it's myself I'm wrapped up in, not the children. I don't feel just like a Mummy now. I'm more worried about myself. I used to be such a slave – particularly to Beatrice – to the children in general, and now I'm more concerned with what *I'm* going to do and what *I* feel and what *I* enjoy rather than the children.

When I started interviewing Barbara I decided that rather than set an artificial finishing-date I would go on seeing her until there was a natural finishing-point, a point which seemed to mark for her the end of a first phase with her baby. Since for her the breast-feeding relationship has been so central, it seemed natural to end with the end of breast feeding. This would probably often be the case with mothers who breast feed for a fairly long period of time, when both mother and baby have come to attach significance to this side of the relationship. Lesley puts it like this: 'I fed her for nine months, I stopped the day she turned ten months: maybe it had something to do with my mother telling me she had fed me for nine months and that gave me some sort of reason to set ten months as the limit. But anyway by then I felt we had both had enough. At first I thought I would never want to stop and I thought she would be miserable when I did. In fact I weaned her so gradually that by the end she didn't really seem to mind; it seemed very natural to stop. I felt incredibly sad when I put her to bed without that last feed the first night, but that was it. It certainly didn't seem to affect her although she had enjoyed it very much. I think by the end I had very little milk and she had found that more frustrating than anything else.'

Sometimes the end of this first period of intense involvement is experienced as the end of a biological unity. Lesley dreamt that she was seven months pregnant and bleeding, with the idea of a threatened miscarriage. Her baby was in reality seven months old and the dream was saying something about the end of a psychological pregnancy – in other words the baby's independence from her (with weaning) being experienced as a birth, a separation from her body and, in her mind, a premature one.

Such an experience is often accompanied either by thoughts about the next baby or, when this is the woman's 'last baby', a feeling that she must readjust to a new image of herself and her body. As one woman put it: 'What with having had two children and being involved for so many years now, it makes me feel hollow to think that I won't have any more children, that I've got this space inside which won't ever be filled again.'

*

219

Some time later Barbara writes to me: *'Beatrice is now two and a half. I'm not planning any more children – just waiting until Beatrice sleeps all night without waking so that we can have a decent night's sleep! I now have a job as a slimming club teacher – did the training and now have two classes . . . The job is interesting and involves dealing with people individually and in group therapy, so it will keep me occupied for a while.'*

She goes on to reminisce about her childbirths: *'Peter's birth, induced and a nightmare, gave me the feeling I couldn't do anything myself – my baby was born without my participation somehow. With Beatrice – my goodness I could do it – labour was under my supervision, I coped with contractions and I pushed Beatrice into the world and saw it happening, she wasn't pulled out for me. I also think that breast feeding is something I felt cheated of with Peter and highly satisfied with myself over with Beatrice. The experience gave me so much self-confidence I have a little job I could never have faced before, and I'm saving for a little car of my own now too.'*

Since then Barbara has taken her A levels, and she is now at university.

Notes

1. 'The Baby Book', ed. N.F. Morris, Charing Cross Obstetric Department, Newborne Publications.
2. Hanford, J.M. (1968), 'Pregnancy as a state of conflict', *Psychol. Rep.* 22 (3), pp. 1313–42.
3. Lewis, A,. *An interesting condition, the Diary of a Pregnant Woman*, Odhams, 1951.
4. Faraday, A., *Dream Power*, Pan Books, 1972.
5. Richards, M., 'Early Separation', in *Child Alive*, ed. Roger Lewin; Temple Smith, 1975.
6. Gillman, R.D., 'The Dreams of Pregnant Women and Maternal Adaptation' in *Psychological Aspects of a First Pregnancy and Early Postnatal Adaptation*, ed. Shereshefsky, P.M. and Yarrow, L.J., Raven Press, 1973.
7. Rich, A., 'Of Woman Born', Virago, 1977.
8. In 'Our Bodies, Ourselves', The Boston Women's Health Book Collective, Simon and Schuster, New York, 1971, p. 168. Page numbers in subsequent notes refer to U.S. edition. Also published by Penguin Books, 1978.
9. Rosberg, J. and Karon, B.P. (1959), 'A Direct Analytic Contribution to the Understanding of Postpartum Psychosis', *Psychiatric Quarterly* 33, pp. 296–304.
10. *Our Bodies, Ourselves*, p. 171.
11. Lewis, op. cit.
12. *Our Bodies, Ourselves*, p. 167.
13. Rich, op. cit.
14. By Sue Farrell.
15. Gillman, op. cit.
16. Van de Castle, R.L. (1968), 'Dream Content During Pregnancy', *Psycho-Physiology* 4 (3), pp. 374–5.
17. Lomas, P. (1966), 'Ritualistic Elements in the Management of Childbirth', *Br. J. Med. Psychol.* 39, pp. 207–13.
18. Demoriane, H. *Life Star, A Diary of Nine Months*, Alan Ross, 1969.
19. Paige, K. (1975), 'The Curse on Women', *Psychology Today*, No. 2.
20. Kitzinger, S., *The Experience of Childbirth*, Penguin Books, Harmondsworth, 1967.
21. Ballou, J., *The Psychology of Pregnancy, Reconciliation and Resolution*, Lexington Books, 1978.
22. Kitzinger, S., *The Experience of Childbirth*, ed. cit.
23. Deutsch, H., *The Psychology of Women*, Grune and Stratton, New York, 1945.

24. Kitzinger, *The Experience of Childbirth*, op. cit.
25. Rich, op. cit.
26. *Our Bodies, Ourselves*, p. 204.
27. Deutsch, op. cit.
28. *Our Bodies, Ourselves*, p. 170.
29. Demoriane, op. cit.
30. Richman, S., Goldthorp, W.O. and Simmons, C., *New Society*, October 1975.
31. Kumar, R., Robson, K., 'Previous Induced Abortion and Ante-Natal Depression in Primiparae', *Psychol. Med.* 10, 78, 8, pp. 711–15.
32. Tweedie, J., 'Polished Delivery', *Guardian*, 13 October, 1975.
33. Liebenberg, B., 'Expectant Fathers' in Shereshefsky and Yarrow, op. cit.
34. *Our Bodies, Ourselves*, page
35. ibid.
36. ibid.
37. Länger, M., 'Psychoprophylaxie, apport analytique', *Bulletin Officiel de la Société Internationalé de Psychoprophylaxie Obstetricale*, April–June 1964, Tome 6, No. 2.
38. *Our Bodies, Ourselves*, p. 171.
39. Rojas Bermudez, J., 'Imaginations et rêves dans les groupes de femmes enceintes', *Bulletin Officiel de la Société Internationale de Psychoprophylaxie Obstetricale*, April–June 1964, Tome 6, No. 2.
40. Blitzer, J.R. and Murray, N.J. (1964), 'On the Transformation of early narcissism during Pregnancy', *Int. J. Psychoanal.*, Vol. 45, pp. 89–97.
41. Liebenberg, B., 'Expectant Fathers' in Shereshefsky and Yarrow, op. cit.
42. Shereshefsky, P.M., Plotsky, H. and Lochman, R.F., 'Pregnancy adaptation' in Shereshefsky and Yarrow, op. cit. p. 89.
43. Quoted in S. Kitzinger, *Giving Birth*, Sphere Books, 1973, p. 194.
44. Lewis, E., 'The Management of Stillbirth, Coping with Unreality', *Lancet*, 18 September, 1976.
45. Bel Mooney, in the television interview 'A Birth of Hope', BBC 2.
46. *Our Bodies, Ourselves*, op. cit.
47. Lewis, E., op. cit.
48. *Our Bodies, Ourselves*, p. 171.
49. Milinaire, C., *Birth*, Omnibus Press, 1974, p. 137.
50. Rich, op. cit.
51. Milinaire, op. cit., p. 137.
52. Quoted in S. Kitzinger (1975), 'Childbirth by Appointment', *New Behaviour*, No. 7.
53. Milinaire, op. cit., p. 171.
54. Shereshefsky and Yarrow, op. cit.
55. Leboyer, F., 'Welcoming the Newborn' in Milinaire, op. cit.
56. Mahler, M., Pine, F. and Bergman, A., *The Psychological Birth of the Human Infant*, Hutchinson, 1975.
57. Macfarlane, A., 'The First Hours and the Smile' in *Child Alive*, Temple Smith, 1977.
58. Kennell, J.H. et al. (1974), 'Maternal Behaviour One Year After Early and

Notes

Extended Post-Partum Contact', *Develop. Med. Child. Neurol.* 16, pp. 172–9.
59. Mahler, Pine and Bergman, op. cit.
60. Egli, G.E. Quoted in Harfouche, op. cit.
61. Illingworth, R.S. and Stone, D.G.H. Quoted in Harfouche, op. cit.
62. Illingworth, R.S. Quoted in Harfouche, op. cit.
63. Winnicott, D., *The Child, The Family and The Outside World*, Penguin Books, 1964.
64. Lewis, op. cit.
65. Newton, N. and Newton, M. (1950), 'Relations of Ability to Breast Feed and Maternal Attitudes towards Breast Feeding', *Pediatrics* 5, pp. 869–75.
66. Middlemore, M., *The Nursing Couple*, Hamish Hamilton, 1941.
67. Harfouche, J., 'The Importance of Breast-Feeding', *J. of Tropical Pediatrics*, September 1970, pp. 135–75.
68. Harris, M., *Thinking about Infants and Young Children*, Clunie Press, 1975.
69. Winnicott, op. cit.
70. Breen, D., *The Birth of a First Child*, Tavistock Publications, 1974.
71. Rosenwald, G. (1972), 'Early and Late Postpartum Illnesses', *Psycho. Med.* Vol. 34, No. 2.
72. *Our Bodies, Ourselves*, p. 208.
73. *Our Bodies, Ourselves*, p. 209.
74. *Spare Rib*, No. 47, June 1976, p. 34.
75. Rich, op. cit.
76. Melges, F.T. (1968), 'Postpartum Psychiatric Syndromes', *Psychosom. Med.* 30 (1), pp. 95–108.
77. Yalom, I.D. et al. (1968), 'Postpartum Blues Syndrome', *Arch. Gen. Psychiat.* 18 (1), pp. 16–27.
78. Kline, C.L. (1955), 'Emotional Illness Associated with Childbirth', *J. Obstet. Gynaec.* 69 (4), p. 748.
79. Horney, K. (1933), 'Maternal Conflicts', *Am. J. Orthop. Psychiat.* 3, p. 455.
80. Lomas, P. *The Significance of Postpartum-Breakdown in the Predicament of the Family*, Hogarth Press, 1972.
81. Beach, S., et al. 'Husbands of Women with Postpartum Psychoses', *J. Psychiat. Social Work*, April 1955, p. 165.
82. Gordon, R. and Gordon, K. (1967), 'Factors in Postpartum Emotional Adjustment', *Am. J. Orthopsychiat.*, Vol. 37, No. 2.
83. Oakley, A. *Women Confined*, Martin Robertson, 1980.
84. Breen, op. cit.
85. Oakley, op. cit.
86. Rosenthal, M. in 'Are Mothers Necessary', *Listener*, 18 November 1976, p. 638.
87. Winter, S. (1969), 'Characteristics of Fantasy while Nursing', *J. Personal.* 37 (1), pp. 58–72.
88. Menzies, I., (1975), 'Thoughts on the Maternal Role in Contemporary Society', *Int. J. of Child Psychotherapy*, Vol. 4, No. 1.
89. Boston, M. (1975), 'Recent Research in Developmental Psychology', *Int. J. of Child Psychotherapy*, Vol. 4, No. 1.
90. *Our Bodies, Ourselves*, op. cit.

91. Steel, B.F. 'Parental Abuse of Infants and Small Children' in Benedek, E.J. and Anthony, T., *Parenthood, Its Psychology and Psychopathology*, Little Brown & Co., Boston, 1970.

92. Fromm Reichman, F. 'Notes on the Mother Role in the Family Group', paper read at a joint meeting of the Topeka Psychoanalytic Society and the Staff Seminar of the Menninger Club in Topeka, Kansas on 3 January, 1940.

93. *Spare Rib*, loc. cit.

94. Oakley, op. cit.

95. Rich, op. cit.

96. Oakley, op. cit.

97. Benedek, T. (1956), 'Toward the Biology of the Depressive Constellation', *J. of Am. Psychoanal. Assoc.* Vol. 4, pp. 389–427.

98. Landis, J.T. (1950), 'The effects of a first Pregnancy upon the Sex Adjustment of 212 Couples', *Am. Soc. Rev.* 15, p. 767.

99. Jessner, L., 'On Becoming a Mother', *Conditio Humana*, Baeyer and Griffith, 1966, pp. 102–15.

100. Winnicott, D.W. *The Family and Individual Development*. Tavistock Publications, 1965.

101. Breen, op. cit.

102. Kelly, M., *Postpartum Document*, ICA New Gallery, 1976.

103. Raphael, Leff, J., 'Psychotherapy with Pregnant Women', in *Pregnancy, Birth and Bonding*, ed. Blum, Human Sciences Press (in press).

104. Mahler, op. cit.

105. Winnicott, *The Child, The Family and the Outside World*, ed. cit.

106. Klein, M. 'On Observing the Behaviour of Young Infants', in *Developments in Psychoanalysis*, Klein, M., Heimann, P., Isaacs, S. and Riviere, J., Hogarth Press, 1952.

107. Beach et al., op. cit.

108. Freud, A. 'The Concept of the Rejecting Mother' in Benedek and Anthony, op. cit.

109. Harfouche, op. cit.